A SEASON IN PARADISE

A SEASON
IN PARADISE

BREYTEN
BREYTENBACH

Translated from the Afrikaans by
Rike Vaughan

PERSEA BOOKS
NEW YORK

CONTENTS

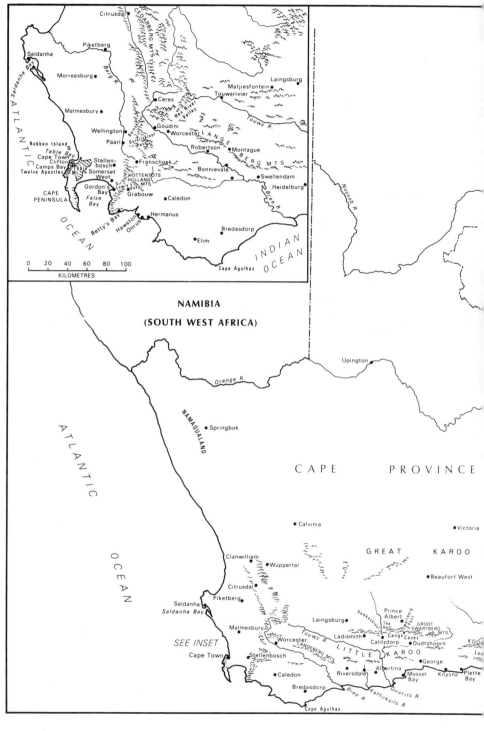

REPUBLIC OF

SOUTH AFRICA

INTRODUCTION

It is a wry comment on the literary world that it should require a nine-year prison sentence to bring to the attention of a larger public the work of the major Afrikaans poet Breyten Breytenbach. In 1977 a small non-commercial anthology of his poems was published by Oasis in Toronto under the title *Sinking Ship Blues;* and in 1978 a much more comprehensive selection, *And Death White As Words,* was brought out by Rex Collings in London. Breytenbach's collected works are at present being issued in Holland; an excellent French translation of an anthology of his poetry came out in Paris recently; and translations in a variety of other European languages are in preparation, prompted by a special award to Breytenbach by the jury of the International Publishers' Prize in 1978. *A Season in Paradise* is the poet's first prose work to be published outside South Africa, and through this publication one of Breytenbach's fondest wishes, often reiterated from jail, is being fulfilled.

1

Breaking off his studies in Fine Art at the University of Cape Town, Breyten Breytenbach left South Africa in 1959 at the age of twenty. After a colourful variety of experiences and odd jobs — including sailing on the Mediterranean and a stint in Norway — he landed in Paris and settled down seriously to become a painter. During the Sixties a series of successful exhibitions in Paris, Amsterdam, and elsewhere culminated in the showing of some of his work in a group exhibition in the Musée d'Art Moderne. In the meantime his marriage to the Vietnamese girl Hoang Lien (Yolande) Ngo — branded "Non-white" in terms of South African legislation — had turned his sojourn in Europe into permanent exile, accelerating the development of his political consciousness.

Breytenbach's increasing reputation as a painter, added to the wide international publicity that followed the refusal, by the South African government, of a visa to his wife to accompany her husband to Johannesburg where he had been awarded a major literary prize in

1964, turned the poet-painter into a rallying point for innumerable refugees and exiles in France and elsewhere. He had become a Name; and it could be used. From this recognition, and the growing burden of activities that sprang from it, Breytenbach drew a measure of consolation; at the same time he experienced an increasing sense of futility and agony at the thought of being a poet and a painter in a situation which seemed to demand so much more in terms of practical action. Commitment, he believed, was only meaningful if it could be translated into deeds. And the sense of being torn in different directions was enhanced when, in December 1972, the South African government finally relented and allowed him to return to the land of his birth with his wife for a visit of three months.

In August 1975 he returned to the country again, alone, in disguise, armed with a false passport, under the assumed name of Christian Galaska. It would seem that his aim was to contact some of the people he had met on his previous visit, in order to evaluate the situation and to devise a programme of future action. The exact nature of this action is still clouded in uncertainty as it seems that this could only follow, not precede, his reconnaissance.

Unknown to Breytenbach, the South African Security Police had tailed him every inch of the way (not that he'd done much to cover his tracks: on several occasions he'd arranged to meet some of his old friends in the foyers of large hotels and conversed quite openly in Afrikaans) and after a visit of three weeks, just as he was about to board his return plane, he was arrested. After more than two months in detention he was brought to court on eleven charges of what, in South Africa, passes for "terrorism." Many of the charges were patently ridiculous, and the fact that all the persons charged with Breytenbach were subsequently allowed to go scot-free seemed to corroborate this impression. However, Breytenbach's interrogators had succeeded, during his months of solitary confinement and constant interrogation, in convincing him that he might well qualify for the death sentence should he try to contest the charges in court. Consequently an arrangement was made whereby some of the more far-fetched charges were dropped, in return for a plea of guilty to all the others. The plea was accepted, with the result that a minimum of witnesses were called. The trial ended in scenes unprecedented in South African legal history, when both the public prosecutor and the

Security Policeman in charge of the investigation offered pleas in mitigation and asked for a minimum sentence. (In terms of South Africa's Terrorism Act a judge is not allowed discretion to impose a sentence of less than five years — with no remission allowed as in the case of ordinary criminal sentences.) It is easy to imagine the amazement of judicial experts and laymen alike when, after these extraordinary interventions, the judge imposed a sentence of nine years. Leave to appeal was refused; and it has subsequently been reported that all the documents of the case have miraculously disappeared.

About nine months later, in August 1976, a stranger turned up on my doorstep bearing a clandestine letter from Breytenbach. I found the individual highly suspect and rather naïve; but the tone of the letter was so desperate and the conditions of detention described in it so appalling that I wrote back, trying to offer a lifeline to the man who, since our first meeting in 1964, had become closer to me than any brother. At the same time I initiated what was soon to become an elaborate system of cryptic warnings, lest he allowed himself to be taken in by the young prison warder who acted as a go-between. The warnings, it turned out, were in vain, as every stage of Breyten's correspondence with me and with a variety of other people had been monitored by the Security Police from the start. And in June 1977 Breytenbach was brought to court again on a new series of incredible terrorism charges. (Among other and much more serious "offences" he was charged with having contravened the Riotous Assemblies Act by chatting to his warder.) It was alleged that he had planned a Russian submarine attack on the prison centre at Robben Island, and that, through the mysterious Okhela Organization he had allegedly founded prior to his first trial, he'd organised a vast plan of urban terrorism in the country, etc. But this time he had one of the best advocates in the country to defend him, and the judge proved to be a man capable of separating fact from poetic flights of fantasy. In fact, the judge found a total lack of evidence for the very existence of Okhela — which had been the main charge in the first trial — and in the end Breytenbach was found not guilty on all the serious charges. He was found guilty only on the technical counts of having smuggled out letters and poems — for which a nominal fine of some fifty dollars was imposed.

As a result of the inhuman prison conditions brought to light by the second trial, Breytenbach was transferred from the Central Prison in Pretoria to slightly more bearable circumstances in a Cape Town jail. But even now, more than three years after his original conviction, he is still allowed only a minimum of contact with other people. He may receive one no-contact visit a month, and write and receive one letter of 500 words a month. All facilities for studying in prison were withdrawn from political prisoners in 1978; and constant representations by a variety of influential bodies, including PEN International, have been turned down by Minister of Justice Jimmy Kruger — the same man who proclaimed that he was "left cold" by the death of Black Consciousness leader Steve Biko, and whose main comment on Biko's horrible death while in the hands of Security Police was, "Every man has the democratic right to die."

Breytenbach is allowed to continue writing in jail (but not painting); however, every page he fills has to be handed in to the prison authorities for "safe-keeping." The only prison poems available to date are those smuggled from jail prior to his second trial. No wonder that, from the scant information which trickles from jail, he lives mainly in a state of despondency, if not despair.

At the time of this writing (July 1979), a new Minister of Justice and a new Minister of Police and Prisons have just taken over, and there is some possibility that renewed representations by writers' and other organisations may, at last, bear some fruit.

2

Within a few years of his first arrival in Paris, Breytenbach's reputation as a poet was firmly established in South Africa. In 1964, coaxed by a writer/publisher friend who had been allowed to look through the large assortment of poems and short prose pieces the artist had been writing purely for his own pleasure, Breyten Breytenbach erupted on the Afrikaans literary scene with a volume of short stories, *Katastrofes (Catastrophes)* and a volume of poetry, *Die Ysterkoei Moet Sweet (The Iron Cow Must Sweat)*. These were jointly awarded a major South African literary prize. During the following decade six more collections of verse (the last of which was composed in detention before his trial and jail sentence), a short novel, and *A Season in Paradise* were published — most of them distinguished with important literary awards. (In fact, one of the paradoxes concerned with Breytenbach is that while he became one of the fiercest and most uncompromising critics of apartheid his work consistently enjoyed the highest recognition in Afrikaans literary circles.)

In all this work the most constant source of inspiration has been Zen Buddhism. As such, it is a dazzling marriage of the real, the ordered, the rigorously disciplined world of the senses on the one hand, and the mystical and imaginary on the other. Essentially, Breytenbach's is an imagination prodded and prompted by the visual — one is never allowed to forget that this is a painter at work — while, in its turn, the visual is infused and informed by fantasy, much in the same way as it occurs in the paintings of that astounding medieval modernist, Hieronymus Bosch, another pervading influence in the work of Breytenbach. In a more modern context, one may find exciting links between the poetry of Breytenbach and the work of the French Symbolists (notably Lautréamont and Rimbaud, the latter being a primary source of inspiration in *A Season in Paradise*), the New Realists of Spanish poetry (Lorca and the South Americans), or, occasionally, the cadences of Césaire and other negritude writers. And, for obvious reasons, there is an "internal" line that links Breytenbach's work with that of his predecessors in Afrikaans, notably the ecstatic lyricist Leipoldt, the more metaphysical and contemplative Van Wyk Louw, and the broad cosmopolitan tapestry of the Trieste-born poet Peter Blum.

Breytenbach offers, above all, a world of startling paradoxes, a comprehensive vision in which life is inconceivable without death, light without darkness, good without evil, love without hate, tenderness without violence, here without there, now without then, growth without decay, I without you. But it goes beyond the recognition of complements: one of the poles in each pair becomes, not only an attribute of the other, but proof of the existence of the other. Life *is* death, happiness proves sorrow, decay is a characteristic of growth, violence exists within tenderness . . . . And in Breytenbach's almost obsessive preoccupation with transience one discovers the very affirmation of eternity and infinity.

3

A Season in Paradise derives from Breytenbach's three-month return to

South Africa in December 1972, with his wife. He was quick to detect the hidden irony in the period the authorities allowed for their sojourn: in South Africa "ninety days" refers to the time a person may be detained without trial in terms of legislation passed during the Sixties (at present detention may continue indefinitely). So the "freedom" granted them also became, as it were, a term of imprisonment: and looking back on it now, one detects a stunning, prophetic note in much of Breytenbach's writing of the time, when seen in the light (or the darkness) of his own imprisonment a few years later.

Still the visit turned out to be a triumphal tour. The Breytenbachs' were overwhelmed with enthusiasm, praise, love, and homage. But there was a price to pay; the press followed them everywhere, and so a very private visit was transformed into a public spectacle. This accounts for much of the "hell" they experienced within the profound emotional experience of a "return to paradise."

In the centre of their sojourn there occurred an event which has acquired even greater significance since then: as part of the annual Summer School organised by the University of Cape Town, a week-long course was offered by the group of Afrikaans writers known as the "Sestigers" (Writers of the Sixties), who had been responsible for the total renewal of Afrikaans literature in the course of the previous decade. This had been an event of much more than literary importance, since it implied a challenge to all the icons of Afrikanerdom — in politics, in religion, in morals, in esthetics. It has become customary in South Africa to identify pro- and anti-Sestigers with political progressives and conservatives. And this was the first time all the members of the group, including Breytenbach who had been a nerve centre of the movement, met in public. It became a circus. It also became a decisive event in terms of the sociopolitics of Afrikaans literature.

Breytenbach was very reluctant to take part, but I managed to persuade him. And his paper at the Summer School — "A View from Outside," which is incorporated into *A Season in Paradise* — had practically the same resonance in South Africa as the famous "Winds of Change" speech in the South African parliament by British Prime Minister Harold MacMillan, in the wake of the Sharpeville massacre of 1960.

The Breytenbachs' visit ended on a sombre note when the poet's father suffered a heart attack, which cast a pall of death over the "season in paradise" and determined much of the nature of the writing that was to come out of it.

The book is much more than a travelogue, and the "facts" of the journey are no more than a point of departure for the real voyage undertaken through landscapes of the mind and memory and fantasy, and through virtuoso flights of fancy in the realms of linguistics and literary allusion.

The *Season in Paradise* embodied in the title is an obvious "reply" to Rimbaud's *Saison en Enfer* and it comes as no surprise to find a highly coloured account of Rimbaud's life and travels (both real and imaginary) in the very centre of the book. Rimbaud's "hell" is the dimension within which Breytenbach experiences his "paradise." Heaven is no longer the culminating point of a journey that leads through inferno and purgatory: heaven *is* hell, and hell *is* heaven. (This is demonstrated, even on the purely journalistic level, by Bretenbach's account of a visit to the paradisiac valley of Gamkas Kloof known as "Hell.")

On the most immediate level of communication, the "paradise" of the title is "the house of my Father which has many mansions"; it is the fatherland, South Africa, remembered through a romantic haze of the Baudelairean *vert paradis des amours enfantines,* and turned into hellish reality through the operations of racial discrimination, bigotry, and intransigence. And returning to this ambiguous land implies a process of reintegration with all the poet's previous selves — which explains why the book opens with an account of all his childhood "deaths."

There is nothing simplistic about this rediscovery of a remembered youth (and how apt that the village of his birth should also bear a name with paradisiac overtones, *Bonnievale!*): the poet's personal return also involves a return to the roots and sources of his community, to that collective past which he shares with those South Africans whom he both hates and loves. The paradise he is groping for coincides with the geography and the mysticism and the mythologies of Africa; that is why so many of his explorations lead back to an examination of the anomaly of being a white man in a black land.

But beyond all the geographical excursions there is always the

15

more profound journey through the inscapes of the self, be it in the form of political questioning, philosophising, fantasy, exuberant humour, or, in the final analysis, in the syntax and semantics of the language itself. Breytenbach's handling of Afrikaans is a pyrotechnical performance involving the use of metaphors and figurative constructions in a new literal sense, turning idioms inside out, forming stunning neologisms, compounds, composites, agglutinations, employing children's rhymes, Biblical sayings, and folk songs in radically new situations.

All the paradoxes created so profusely and so casually as he goes on, point towards the one final paradox of the multi-faceted narrative: Heaven and Hell, Life and Death are to be integrated. "To be integrated," he suggests, "is to be mortal; to be attached is to be pervaded with the sense of the transient" — which links up perfectly with a pronouncement in an earlier poem: "for this is our only unending paradise." The long and complex reverie becomes not only a contemplation but a celebration of death, since that is the surest way of exorcising life. And if a single metaphor may be singled out to summarise the book, I think it is to be found in the unforgettable episode of the musician spending the night on the mountain beside the body of his young dead wife and playing on his fiddle to keep away the predators.

4

Even before Breytenbach had completed A *Season in Paradise* he had made me promise to prepare an English translation. However, for a variety of reasons, it was not possible for me to do so myself. I had sufficient faith in Rike Vaughan to have the work entrusted to her — a faith which, I feel, has been amply justified by this sound and sensitive translation. It follows as closely as possible the directives issued by Breytenbach from jail: while, on the one hand, it incorporates those passages omitted, for political or other reasons, from the original Afrikaans edition, certain small, judicious cuts have been made, on the other hand, to eliminate cryptic references intelligible only to insiders, lines which would lose all flavour or sense in another language, etc. As far as the poems and the more lyrical or "experimental" passages are concerned, Breytenbach's wish was honoured in discarding literal precision in favour of new solutions in terms of the new language involved.

— André Brink
July 1979

TRANSLATOR'S PREFACE

A Season in Paradise presented special problems for the translator. It is true that *all* creative work bears its individual stamp or mark, and that to capture that mark, to interpret and convey the special "tone" or "mood" or "atmosphere" of a work, poses the greatest challenge the translator must accept — both the "agony" and the "ecstasy," so to speak, of his task.

But the complexity of this problem is compounded in the case of this work by several other factors.

Firstly, there is Breyten's "prose" itself — to say that he throws the "rules" overboard, to label his style "unconventional," to talk of "poetic license," occasionally bordering, even, on a seeming lack of grammatical know-how, is to say nothing at all about the extraordinary difficulties inherent in preventing the loss through translation of the infinite potential meanings, associations, and implications contained in each word or phrase or sentence. The rich imagery, the word-play, the unorthodox confusion of and interplay between fact and fantasy — these are the hallmark of the poet: if, then, the translator cannot be the final judge of whether or not he has made the world of that poet accessible, he may claim at least not to have made deliberate omissions, save in those instances (and they were negligible) where the intricate play on words in the original language would have become non-sense in English.

Secondly, there is the fact that so little is known abroad — even today — about South Africa, geographically, politically, historically — about its people, its languages, its problems, its beauty. So that where Breyten wrote about these, crediting his (Afrikaans) reader with a certain familiarity with things South African, no such assumption may be made on the part of the reader of the translation. I have, therefore, included the following:

1) a *map*, for which I wish to express my thanks to Mr. O. West of the Department of Geography at Rhodes University, Grahamstown, showing the principal geographical locations referred to in the text.

Those not shown (owing to the limits imposed by the size of the map) may easily be "placed" with the aid of details supplied in the text.

2) *Notes on Persons and Places.*

The *Persons* include all African "historical" persons, whether fully or partly named or "disguised," who would ordinarily be known to the South African reader, particularly where the information given about them will contribute to the understanding or will affect the interpretation of the work, and where such details would not normally be known to the overseas reader, or would be difficult to establish. I have, however, used my discretion with regard to II. *Persons named in part* etc., bearing in mind the Author's obvious intentions with regard to the deliberate "disguising" of certain relatives and friends, and have identified only those whose identities may be guessed quite easily by anyone with a little knowledge of the South African political and literary scenes. With regard to III. *Breyten Breytenbach's immediate family*, I have included this section to minimize the confusion arising out of Breyten's use of a multitude of nicknames, pseudonyms, pet-names, and other "disguises" in a work already teeming with unfamiliar "real" names, even though the South African reader too, is left largely to his own devices. I have excluded a) actual persons who are either unidentifiable, self-explanatory or whose identification would not contribute materially to a deeper insight into the work, b) fictitious persons and c) persons who may be regarded as "international" figures.

The *Places* include *brief* notes on geographical and political aspects of South Africa which may not be deduced either from the map or

3) A *Glossary* of South African terms, "foreign" to non-South Africans.

4) Explanatory *footnotes* within the text where necessary.

Cross-references refer in general to related concepts, words, or notes, and are aimed at broadening the reader's understanding of the specific term etc. which he is looking up.

Finally, making heard in one of the world's great languages the voice of a man who will soon have been silenced effectively for the better part of a decade, so that what he has said to the few becomes, in a practical sense, the property of millions, is a task which carries with it a truly daunting responsibility. I am, therefore, deeply indebted to André Brink who offered unselfishly to bear some of that burden, who gave unstintingly of his time, who shared with me his intimate knowledge of Breyten — the man, the poet, the philosopher — who recreated, as I could not have done, Breyten's poetry around the bare bones I provided, without whose constant encouragement and faith I should neither have attempted nor completed this venture, and to whom I dedicate my translation.

—Rike Vaughan
Grahamstown

For Hannes & Kitty & Yolande
with best love

A SEASON IN PARADISE

*(Journal, Nocturnal
Intrip, written with closed eyes)*

"So what . . ."

Scenes from a first death in the houses of the morning

My childhood years were one long waste. As an economic unit I wasn't worth much — I could hardly help myself, let alone others. When, for the first time, around the blessed age of three years and eight months, I had to poke holes in the ground as my contribution to the tomato planting effort, I was so worn out after twelve hours on the land that my father was obliged to lift me onto his shoulders, and it's no mean task to dig tomato holes from that height. There were no wars in which I could prove my mettle. The English had left the country and were engaged abroad somewhere in the suppression of fresh victims — the Germans. It was much too far to the nearest mountains where one might hope to encounter Prince Valiant, or Tom Mix, and the guerrilla war lay many years into the future. I succeeded nevertheless, in my humble way, in representing all these heroes personally in our village, which, regrettably, once again yielded no financial gain.

Also, I had the annoying habit of dropping dead now and then. This too was a squandering of money and precious energy: a fuss entailing coffins, holes in the ground, flowers and wreaths, Sunday school chums who were obliged to come and sing and help carry, the funeral parties afterward, and all the mourning paraphernalia for everyone. In actual fact we were much too poor to be able to afford deaths in the family. It took me a long time to be cured of death, and even today it still takes me by surprise sometimes. (Life is description of death.)

Later, when I was a smart thirteen years old, I was able to do my bit to help keep the pot boiling. It was then that I actually worked consecutively as a bricklayer, fencer, stoker on the trains like my uncle* Kowie without teeth, truck driver, shepherd initially and subsequently foreman on Uncle John Cloete's farm comprising several thousand morgen near Bredasdorp, night watchman in

---

*"Uncle" is a mode of address or reference to an older man, not necessarily a relative, or as a mode of reference signifying "man," "gentleman." The same applies to "aunt."

Paultjie Witaarde's father's shop, and, finally, as retailer selling Uncle Niek's sweet potatoes in the location. At that stage, at least, I had already become leader of the Catmen, this position bringing with it the responsibility for the treasury.

The trouble with dying is that one forgets so much from one death to another. I suppose that's not unusual, taking into account that one is reborn as a new being each time, that one has to be replaced biologically because one's matter and elements so seldom remain intact from one birth to the next, but why do babies have to smell so foul?

When I was small my folks looked different. My mother was round and pink with a floral apron, little round war spectacles and a thick braid wound around her head — resembling absolutely an Eastern European kulak woman. When she took off her glasses, her eyes became smaller. She was always going around with her hands under the apron, saying *kuru-kuru*. On one hand she wore two gold rings with large red stones which my father had brought her from the mines when he was still a smuggler. My father was much bigger then than now, with a hat, khaki clothes, suspenders, bow legs, and a pack of Cavalla cigarettes in the pocket of his shirt. He was a pumpkin farmer and his hair was sometimes black, sometimes brown, and occasionally blue. He never spoke much, as he had to irrigate, resting on his shovel with his eyes on the ranges where the brown scrub resisted the sun, while his red tongue spasmodically brushed the stubble beneath his nose. My eldest brother, B, was an enormous fellow with knobbly knees. He was in the habit of racing up and down our yard, brandishing a wooden sword and killing my mother's chickens in duels. Occasionally, getting carried away, he would pierce the windows as well, and very often he would beat me black and blue — in fact, I was his favorite sparring partner — during tea breaks at school or in the afternoons down by the river. The rest of the time he spent drawing pictures in books. Even today some of my nicest dreams smell of chalk and printing-warm paper. My second brother, B, escapes my memory altogether, perhaps because he was fair and not able to ride a bicycle, but he kept a lot of dogs and overturned hot soup onto you if you dared to call him "Stinkie." My youngest brother, B, was my real companion. He never stopped crying with clenched fists and shoe-sole lips, and he never grew any

28

taller. Old-Antjie-from-the-hills* caught and devoured him regularly. B, my little sister, was just a little baboon in the mountains then. We would be going out to catch and wash and shave and trim her later on, when my mother grew so fat that time and spent the whole day laughing, and when my grandma had already run away to Heaven. She was never acquainted with Bonnievale.

Bonnievale. That's where the big foul-up began. I was born and received in a thatched roof sharecropper's cottage, and was cut out for great things from the first wail. That's why I had barely turned six when they sent me to school! The village itself lies in a beautiful valley in the heart of the Boland and the Karoo. A river runs along it with the cheese factory on one bank and Uncle Red Daan's vineyards on the other. There's a station, and on the hill above the station where the road leaves the village for Swellendam, live Uncle Jors and Aunt Hanna. (Pretty poor, too.) At the other end is the graveyard and Grandpa and Grandma live just on the other side. I suppose Grandpa didn't want to have to walk so far. Then there was a lady who gave piano lessons close to Uncle Daan and Aunt Bettie Daan and a rich-in-earthly-goods Englishwoman in a huge house behind an avenue of bluegums who made us a present of a goose every Christmas. There is a road near the top dam where the dead horse lay rotting and where Pa hid from the water-bailiff. It also happened to be one of Antjie's hideouts. And nearby are a church and a vast rugby field where whistles can be heard blowing shrilly, and a vicarage and a church hall and the school where bells are continuously ringing and dusty kaffir plums trees along the street. Close by is our house with its verandah and its world. When I was leprous,† I was able to stare longingly in the mornings from the garden at my school friends as they walked, whooping-coughish from the frost, up to the koppies to search for kukumakrankas and to pick chinkerinchees. Then I would weep so bitterly that the tears would pour down my skin and burn the sores. In short, Bonnievale was an ordinary village with all the juicy white roots of evil well dug in.

*Actually, *Antjie Somers,* the name of a brown or black witchlike bogey figure, reputed to live "in the hills," who, traditionally, punished naughty children.
†Fact and fantasy are often indistinguishable in this book, and nowhere more so than in these reminiscences of early childhood. "Leprous" may refer here to a time of real physical illness (though not leprosy), as seen through the eyes of both the man and the child, obsessed with transience. In any case, its metaphoric meanings are intended.

Our home was a wonderful place where, among other things, miracles occurred. It had, as I have said before, a red verandah in front and a white one in the back. Also a kitchen, hallway, a bedroom for our parents, and a "den" for the boys with beds which provided cover when Ma was about to prod us with a cane or a broom handle, and where full piss-pots were kept as well. Between the bedroom and the "den" was a bathroomy type of chamber. Covered with goose-bumps we would occasionally hear Ma walking around barefooted here, her feet making sucking noises as though they were sticking to the cement floor. Or we would hear Pa sneezing and wheezing as steam bubbled out through the door, clinging in tiny wet traces to the hallway walls. Here we were grabbed and scrubbed without fear or favor until our heels, rough as those of a kitchen fowl, were rough no longer. It was always dark in the house.

One evening a frog played the organ for hours in one of the rooms. We hunted him by candlelight and heard him moving plop-plop through the house — thus: plop, plop-plop-plop, plop-plop. But the frog was so large that it didn't even bat an eyelid at Ma's scolding.

In front of the house was a garden. That was where Ma buried Pa's liquor bottles. They were both keen gardeners. Surrounding the garden and the house was a fence with a gate. Pa had us believe that he was a Springbok, and to demonstrate this he would regularly leap over the gate each evening. Because we remained skeptical — he was *our* pa, after all — he hopped over the gate one evening, braced himself slightly, took a few long strides and then sailed effortlessly over the church. Not over the steeple, admittedly, only over the roof. He was as strong as an ox and afraid of nothing. Sometimes he would take us along with him on the front of his bicycle when he went to work, both B and myself up front on the crossbar between his knees, and then he would make the bicycle sing at fifty, sixty miles an hour, and you could no longer distinguish the individual stones beneath the wheels.

Years later he bought a car, a new one every year actually, since, sucker that he was, he also speculated because he was continually being swindled. Everyone was driving Mercurys then. It was Mercury left, right, and center. Ours was a blue one, and where we drove, the dust was agitated. The older model had a rumble seat, and two or more of us always had to sit in the back with a traveling-rug around our legs, clutching our hats. In this car we traveled all over. I was always carsick, or thirsty, or I wanted to pee. It's hard to plead with your parents when you're sitting in the back in a rumble seat with your mouth full of dust. Sometimes we stopped the car so that I could be sick behind the bushes and suck an orange.

In the very same car we traveled one evening via Riviersonderend to Wakkerstroom where my second brother, B, was to play in the school band. He played the guitar and he was the youngest musician, the baby of the band. An hour ahead of schedule we were already seated, and every now and then he would poke his head around the curtain (this was still closed) from the bottom, to wave to us. When the curtains were drawn, he was sitting on the floor on a blanket. It was a heartrending performance and Hendrik Susan was present in person. There was even an Hawaiian guitar. As we rounded a bend on the way back that same evening, I tumbled out of my little seat just like a ball of dung released by a horse in full gallop, and broke my neck in two places. In the dark, no one had noticed my fall, and when they found me three days later, I was already dead and decaying and with baby Jesus. My mother was very sad.

At the back of our house were a see-saw, a couple of bricks used for barbecues, a cement patio, Dawid's small room, and a pear tree. Dawid, the brown man, was just as big and just as handsome as my father, but we were not as afraid of him. And under the pear tree I first discovered love. She was seventeen and an operator at the local exchange. In the evenings, around dusk, she would lift me onto her lap and hold me tightly, and I smelled the pear tree. There were other smells: the small fires beginning to crackle everywhere to cook supper, the lawns and flowers newly watered, the oil under Pa's Mercury, Dawid's working clothes, and my sweetheart's milkplump breasts. And sounds: the chirr-chirr of grasshoppers between lawn and hibiscus tree, dogs in the neighborhood barking at the smoke, the prayer meeting bell and the sexton's boots on the gravel path when he has emptied the bell of its peals, my mother puttering in the kitchen, the sucking and groaning as my father removes his Wellingtons, and my sweetheart's heart beneath my ears thud-thud thud-thud, just like the gurgling when my father secretly opens the sluiceways out of turn, or just like the plop-sounds of the frog. And

31

the sky is the color of mother-of-pearl like the palm of one's hand when one has spent a long time in the sea. That pear tree will never stop flowering again.

Uncle Niek and Aunt Joey's house was different from ours. They had a big orchard surrounding the house and a privy outside, painted red and with a seatboard opening shaped like a heart. Thus the heart is really nothing but a practical orifice. Next door stood the tall house owned by the professor with the hat. The professor had a sizeable fish pond filled with goldfish, red in color. When he wanted to feed them, he sat down on the edge of the pond and tapped two pebbles together, and the fish would come to the surface with mouths wide open, so that you could count their rotten teeth. They were clever, those fish: one afternoon when I went on my own to look at the fish, I leaned too far over and fell into the pond. The professor was within hearing distance, but he was so preoccupied — he collected butterflies as well — that I called out in vain. What with falling in and yelling, my teeth began to tap together like pebbles, and the fish were not going to allow themselves to be licked, they went for me and consumed me bit by bit. Nothing whatsoever remained of me, not even an eye or a sigh, and I was never found again. But for days the fish were too bloated to react to the professor's pebble-clicks. He was very worried about his little creatures, the poor old professor.

Grandma and Grandpa's house was something else again. Here everything was brown. The house was brown on the outside and blue and violet inside, the ridges along the upper part of the brown road running past the graveyard were brown, and for days on end Grandpa would sit on his brown chair on the back porch watching it all through and in his brown eyes. There were many fragrances in Grandma's house, all of them dark: cloves and biscuits kept in tins and Grandma's sad bed, because she was confined to it with the cancer, she had to keep the cancer warm. Grandpa Jan was strong and upright with broad spreading shoes and big hands. His hands were mostly fingers. I never heard him say a single word. He was already a hundred and fifty years old then, and a year or so before he had knocked a man out with one hand, though he had been out of practice for some time by that stage. Luckily, it was only a brown man. On Sunday mornings Pa would take Grandma to church, but Grandpa stayed behind on his brown chair to keep an eye on the graveyard. He was not taken in by the apparent peace. He was the best general in the Boer War and before that in the other wars along with Louw Wepener and Louis Trichardt and Majuba. He was a poor man, because he gave all his money to the needy and was not a bit interested in worldly wealth and opulence. (It's a family trait, this generosity.) His house in heaven will therefore be grand, with waterborne sewage and electricity.

One day, on our way home after having taken Grandma some soup, B and I came face to face with old Antjie. The horrible witch in her tattered clothes shuffled toward us with one hand extended, and B flung the soup bowl to one side, and we took to our heels back to Grandpa on the porch. He walked back with us, the whole ten miles, and before his bold and proud countenance old Antjie evaporated like snow in the sun. As far as I know, Grandpa Swartjan Dirk Breytenbach never wore socks; nowadays this fashion is referred to as "wearing Paul Krüger socks," I believe. He was, of course, a family friend of Paul Krüger's, but his beard was neater.

It stands to reason that our village was also visited from time to time by natural and unnatural upheavals, events, and manifestations. We had earthquakes and unfaithfulness, hurricanes and adultery and threshing machines, shearers, holidays at the sea, christening Sundays, frost, visits from kings, centenaries, circuses, and so forth. Uncle Red Daan who suffered from diabetes — both his legs have since been amputated; when the second was amputated he was too weak for the gas so that he was given only a local anaesthetic, but apparently he is coming along nicely now — and his wife, Aunt Bettie Daan, who could talk at sixty miles an hour, would always have themselves photographed: both puffed out with pride and cheese, and with Daan Jr., Pietertjie, Sanna of Aunt Bettie Daan, Burgert — who in the old days would bleat like a sheep and now snaps like a dog — Kaspaas and Eben-this-is-the-limit squeezed in too, they may be seen sitting in a rickshaw, boots and all. The man wearing the feathers and the horns was presumably posing there only for fun, I take it he wasn't expected to pull them! But I state without hesitation that my childhood years were extremely uneventful and perfectly ordinary on the whole; in our village, and in my family in particular, there was very little squabbling, strife or discord, and never any question of violence.

One distressing incident, however, springs to mind clearly even now. I had just started school and B simply had to come along too, though his position as an economic liability at that time entitled him to lie around at home for another year. And then I became infected with mumps and whooping cough. As a matter of fact, I have never quite got rid of those mumps, actually, and in later years I cultivated a beard to keep the growths in check. All the same, B goes to school by himself, and I am left standing in the front garden, clutching my mother's dress, and the children emerge from the school gate in a long line — as there are so many absentees owing to the epidemic, the remainder are going to the veld for the day. And as they walk, old B waves to me, and I can see his bald head gleaming in the sun, and his tears are reflected on his cheeks like fragments of glass, and I weep and wave back, because they are marching in a column like convicts in the direction of the veld where Antjie is undoubtedly lying in wait for them — as it is, she's especially fond of B — and who will I have left now to knock around today in my state of quarantine? (Or did this grief manifest itself only later? A friend sent me a yellowed postcard recently: little young Amsterdam orphans, all sporting identical gray tunics and shaven heads — Jewish hostages behind the fence of a concentration camp.)

Thus all good things come to an end. I took a drive one day with Uncle Koos Kok. He was in the habit of giving B and me threepence each whenever he saw us — to him we were Carnera and Boy Louw, because I was as thin as a beanpole and B as hefty as a scrumhalf. Uncle Koos Kok was virtually hairless and his face a mass of wrinkles from his crown to his dimple. I can't remember him ever having had teeth, which, of course, facilitated boozing. That day Uncle Koos was more than a little drunk so that he took a turn to the right, at a railroad crossing, and drove onto the tracks, thinking he was on the correct course. The roads in those days were not what they are today, and any man might have been forgiven for mistaking the quality and the nature of the roughness of the ride. I was fairly wet behind the ears then and did not wish to point his mistake out to the venerable Uncle Koos. But when a train suddenly loomed out of nowhere ahead of us, he was forced to face the truth, and he jerked the wheel over with an improper oath, and we careened headlong down the rail embankment. At that moment the passenger door of the car flew open, I rolled out like a hard ball from the rear end of a horse too impatient to squat and was sent sprawling down the slope into a field where a farmer was plowing. The farmer was not to blame. To tell the truth, at the sight of a car on the run with a wild bald-headed man at the wheel, pursued by the screaming train, the farmer probably released the plow handles and took to his heels himself. But the donkeys hitched to the plow had obviously heard nothing unusual because of their blinkers. First they trampled me and then the plowshares sliced me up all over the place on my body, but particularly through my neck, so that my head was just left lying there loose to one side. Thus my bloodsoaked little body was decapitated, lifeless.

Pa came to get me in the Mercury the same evening, my brothers B, B, and B bringing up the rear. Uncle Koos was demented with grief and self-reproach. Ma fainted several times and had to be brought around with smelling salts. At home they laid me out in my folks' bedroom (the beds in the "den" hadn't been made yet) after the doctor had attempted to piece my body more or less together again. The family decided to keep one of my hands, the left, with which I had been so dexterous, preserved in a bottle of alcohol as a souvenir. (In that way at least, their investment would prove not to have been entirely futile.) (But old Flash, our farm dog, later managed to get at the hand and to bury it in the garden among Pa's bottles.)

It was a stirringly beautiful funeral service. Uncle Koos insisted on being allowed to be one of the pallbearers, and Uncle Niek too, and in the end my Sunday school friends were unable to get a peek. First there was a service in the church. Grandpa was not present. Our church has always been gray, impressively nauseating and rotten to the core, as it were, and what with the dirges and the soft teeming organ music, this atmosphere was considerably enhanced. Out of the depths I call unto thee, O Lord! Lord, hear my cry . . . . There were heaps of wreaths and cards, some even from prominent members of our village, and also from a village councilor — possibly because my father had voted for him. Afterward I was carried outside in my coffin and wheeled up the hill on the little black cart until we reached the graveyard. Grandpa was standing on the porch, waving, with the wind blowing so capriciously in his gray beard. He was eating oranges and the small pieces of golden rind were strewn about his brown chair. It occurred to me to struggle into an upright position to wave back, but the lid had already been screwed down. Clouds floated lazily on the hilltops in the sun, like golden oranges in their rinds.

At the graveside the minister glanced at his watch and then named the final hymn, after Uncle Koos had thanked everyone graciously on behalf of the family, touching, because he finds it so difficult to speak in public without teeth. Afterward they lowered me into the ground and everyone filed past to sprinkle a few grains of lumpy earth onto my coffin. Someone may even have added a white chrysanthemum, but probably not — such gestures became fashionable only later when more folks could afford to go to the movies. At dusk it grew quieter, and the gravediggers arrived to cover up my handsome pine coffin while they discussed the latest tax hikes, resting all the while on the handles of their shovels. Fortunately it was summer and not at all cold.

My brother B is twenty-six now. He tells us that he bumped into Uncle Koos a few months ago, more than ever resembling an ostrich egg, and that Uncle Koos had given him threepence. In the light of the new monetary system and the astronomical cost of living, it's not the same thing anymore.

Two years later we said good-bye to beautiful Bonnievale for the last time and moved to Riversdale. I was a huge fellow of seven years and eight months, and my childhood years were only now about to be permitted to begin in earnest. Dawid moved with us too, and we went farming there in the shade of Sleeping Beauty. A year later he bit off the sergeant's thumb when the latter tried to drag him from the car which Agmat had stolen from my father. We spent three weeks traveling to our new home by ship, and B became horribly sea sick.

Christmas Eve 1972 (Preparation)

At the northernmost point where the earth is almost constantly barren and white, it is as cold as crystal there mostly, it was customary in old times to single out and celebrate the longest night and the shortest day, because that was the turning point, the depths of misery, and from that moment in time the days would grow longer, day by day, and brighter, toward spring. And then the tallest tree on every hill would be set alight so that the flames of joy might blaze against the sky and the snow around the trunks might glitter like blood and the crackling sparks might be fired into the dark. A tree, the flame of life, was sacrificed to the gods. The sparks as blossoms, but also proud like stars. Out of death comes a new devouring life.

(The Christmas tree decorated with lights, which we know today, is a poor imitation of that ancient rite.)

But this year everything seems at once beautiful and strange to me — because exactly one week from tonight I (we) will be home. "Home"? How long now have I been dragging my "home" around with me? How thick the crust on my back, the tortoise shell — a callous nail? It will be thirteen years, give or take a few weeks. But what will I find there? What late lamented "I" will I encounter there? This distance, this anticipation, the long winter are now the only things familiar, my home. And that which is there has become a subconscious, a wound which has healed, a memory, a past and a future, the blueprint of a dream, Paradise. *O, beloved unknown, o strange beloved . . . .*

It is not given to every mortal to find his Paradise. Paradise is the unknown, remembered. To me it was a land, a soil with people and mountains and seas and sounds at dusk: the end of the world, smoke, fruit, the familiar because unconscious way in which people walk and walk across a plain or among orange trees. I am in search of a simplicity, I want to rediscover an innocence, I want to absorb my own shadow and head for an infinity.

And it won't be like that. Perhaps I will be able thus to destroy the image and grow lucid? And the thirteen years then, what of them? Were they just a brief and delirious dream? A nightwatch between sunbreak and morning? How long it was, and yet, how quickly it sped by. And now I am only the sum of those thirteen years. I am a Frenchman and I am on my way to Africa, my cruel mother; I am a refugee and I am on a quest for that safety which was once mine before there was any need for me to recognize it.

We go to Mung Ngo's outside the gates of Paris for a meal. The world has stopped. Even the bombers have temporarily — for the sake of hypocrisy — ceased their devastation of Hanoi and Haiphong. The death sentence on a few hundred Vietnamese children has been suspended for two days. Praise the Lord! The capital of Nicaragua is wiped out by an earthquake, and the soldiers start shooting at bewildered looters. High up in the Andes the survivors of an air disaster are rescued after 70 days spent in the snow. They have cut the corpses of their fellow passengers (sturdy rugby giants) into strips and have eaten the cold biltong in order to survive. And by telephone we learn that the Southeaster is blowing in the Cape, the old Cape Doctor.*Africa!

We eat and laugh and watch television. I receive gifts: a bow tie from An Fon, and a calendar with a built-in thermometer from Chi Dieu. Here inside it is a cozy 20 degrees centigrade, but outside on the balcony where the white and deaf cat is sitting, the first snowsparks fly like the tracks of birds. The cat sits looking at the snow as though it — it is a neutered he — wonders what has become of the birds. Not far away an airplane roars up and away in the night. Africa!

In a moment we will drive back to our apartment within the city walls and the road will be smooth and black with hoar-frost. I will search for the pale stars because I'm unable to suppress my joy. Thou preparest the way for my feet: Thou makest my head fat and giddy with oil. My dream is a blazing tree.

*(The dawn is cold, and I afraid
— not for myself —
this rotting sack of burnished bones
— but for that which flows between us
and makes us
you and I
vulnerable unto
life and death)*

*The southeasterly wind from the sea so called at the Cape from early times, as it was believed that in suddenly cooling the air it dispersed or blew away disease and germs during the hot summer months.

December 30, 1972

Six-thirty. Another few hours, minutes virtually. The transition between winter and summer, life and death, Europe and Africa, being and alienation, castration which exile is and integration. Outside there is no sound, no bird, no wind or milk-cart or automobile. Nothing. Only a little bit of half-moon, at her post like a scabby cow made to mind her calf. Outside is death.

Now departure is imminent. He has not slept, and just as little the night of yesterday, and the night before that even less. One has to be dead first in order to rise again. And the excitement is contained by weariness. Weariness is injected into the veins to calm the heart. When morning comes he changes his clothes, looks at his naked body, at his ribs and knees. An aged monk seated upright, already in motionless meditation. If you want to become nothing, you have to make an early start. A meditation in which coming and going makes no difference. A silence. Neither winter nor summer. But between birth and death we have a little fun. Excuse me, Master, but it is an adventure into which you must plunge yourself with all your heart and kidneys and guts. You can't view it from a distance. An old "I" must be brought from down there so that he may finally lie down to rest.

All is in order; everything has been cleared up. At last he has even thrown the slippers he has been carting around with him for years as souvenirs of his country — fetishist! — into the trash can.

Gray the day will rise over the city, over the winter: it will make just enough light for one to see one's way out of this cold. And ahead waits the sun.

"Come, dearest, wake up! Get up! It's time to go!"

When you are very tired, it is as though you find yourself in the sea. (The sea is most likely the very tiredness surrounding you.) One moment you are as panicky as gooseflesh, convinced that you have left a vital something behind, that you are going to arrive late, etc. The next you relax again with complete equanimity, you allow everything to flow over and around you, as though these are not your affairs, as though your body is not involved.

On the eve of our departure we impressed our final instructions

39

and advice upon the thin American woman who would be taking care of the house during our absence. We had tried to take all possible precautions against civil war, the plague, labor riots and the deluge, and secretly hoped (at least, I did) that some stud would break in and enter while we were away to cure our lodger of her fierce chastity which gave rise to an unsightly rigor vitae. Our house is a house of love. We tried to keep our departure — and our destination in particular — a secret from all friends and acquaintances. Those who did guess vaguely what was in the offing, arrived to bid us farewell in the small hours of the last night, with gentle smiles and warm palms of hands, amused by our reckless excitement. A journalist, of the nosy newsy South African species who see their work as cartoons minus pictures, picked up our trail from London, and we could see his bristling whiskers darting about frantically in the slit between the front door and the floor tiles. Rat poison would not help much, because they sprinkle that on their cereal first thing in the morning along with the ashes from the accompanying compulsory cigarette. The only way out would be across the roof, suitcases suspended from ropes around our necks and shoes in coat pockets, like thieves in another man's night. Luckily whorenalusts are about as lazy as they are unprincipled. Whiskers from London evidently decided on the nearest pub as his ideal vantage point, and in due course the brown or red liquid there clouded his vision and dulled his hunting instinct. And speaking of shoes: Ashes was to accompany us on our pilgrimage. I mean, I want to include Ashes in this account right away. We persuaded him to come along, and a day or so ago he turned up from Rome, sporting brand new shoes — the next thing to small brown Volkswagens — with thick soles and thicker heels still. "Special snow tires," one might call them, or of the type worn throughout by Alan Ladd when he was acting in films opposite Ava Gardner and when they would stand her in a hole in the ground during the filming of love scenes so that they would be on the same mouth level.

We slept very little. In the street outside it was still pitch-dark. A taxi driver who, as providence would have it, lived on our own street, had just seated himself at the wheel, still half-asleep, to commence his day shift. We hailed him and he spread a portable red carpet and his jacket at our feet, because we were going on a journey to

40

the Great Great. His taxi, heavy with our junk, made its way through the gray suburbs to Le Bourget. En route we exchanged small mouthfuls of words. The city slumbered on and the realization that we were about to escape the gray day which was being born, away out of the winter, was wonderful, almost unbelievable. The driver spoke with a Midi accent. South!

We were allowed to choose our seats on board from a chart, taking into account who would plunge out how, in case the thing came to die on a mountain top. Then we had to wait for the announcement of our flight, for embarkation. Suddenly we were barely able to remain standing on our feet. You don't dare sit down anywhere either, for fear of falling straight down into the opening night of oblivion or in case you wet yourself out of speechless joy. Nothing to do then, but to have some strong coffee. Now you become quarrelsome, and tempers become frayed. Is everything and everyone here now? What about the hand luggage? I told you our stuff was overweight, didn't I? Who is carrying who's camera without an export permit? What the hell are they making such a fuss for then? Man and God be my witness: I have done all I could. But man is fallible. This time Ashes has wandered off somewhere. And suppose something goes wrong at the last minute? If everything were to fall through now? What if an earthquake were to rip up the runway, or a deaf sparrow were to nest in one of the jet engines, or the Soviets and the Amerimurderers decided to pick on this precise morning to settle their outstanding differences?

But at last. *"Les passagers pour Nice, Kinshasa, Johannesbourg sont invités ..."*

The scales tip, we enter the inevitable, we are poured from one reality into another. ... In a partitioned cubicle behind black curtains we are frisked by agents who clearly know their hands. Hold the camera aloft with the lens pointing upward and press the knob. Shutter-click. Presumably, in case it is a gun. And on board: air-conditioning, fastening of seat-belts; final psalm. I am aware of an itchiness in the scapular region where the wings will be growing. Day begins to break over Paris: gray buildings, gray smoke from gray chimneys taken up into the gray sky. Large and red and unreal hangs the sun just above the skyline of the city boundary, like a sun on a gray photograph.

When everyone's ears are well and truly blocked, the plane starts rolling forward, and suddenly we leap almost vertically into the air. The tiny houses and streets with the first of the early-morning ants fall away with terrifying swiftness beneath us, become unreal and grotesque.

About the flight itself there is nothing much to be said. Hypnotized people moving around in a trance with wide-open eyes like zombies probably share an experience similar to ours that day. You are predestined. And set like a bomb with a built-in mechanism aiming you at a target where you will explode at a given moment. You eat, you try to read, you gaze disinterestedly out of the porthole, you ponder, you sleep, you shut your eyes and see everything, it will never grow dark again, you wake up with a start only to realize that you were not asleep, you read, you eat, the sun is in your head, but it is an object the color of silver, very light, made of metal, devoid of any heat, the sun is a fish in the sky. Nice? An airport, shops, passengers wearing fur coats and carrying illustrated magazines, polished floors, customs officials with little caps. Not until you are over the Sahara are you seized again by the excitement. How grandiose and endless such a land is! We are flying higher than the cirrus clouds, but we see every ridge and rib and dune and petrified garden of what seem like rock formations and sand-eddies below us, the subtle nuances of color from yellow-ochre through gray to brick-red. Africa! Africa has an extra dimension. There is something about it which takes no account of man and his trivial futilities, something which is totally detached and unassailable. Europe is a submissive and somewhat feebleminded creature, like a cow with pimples or a cat with decayed teeth. But Africa is eternal. In Africa man is a wanderer, an occupier, a transitory phenomenon. The European has polluted his soil according to his needs: the African was forced to adapt himself to Africa. Not to take possession, but to be tolerated — or to be able to be part of. What does one lifetime matter in Africa? It's a long string of beads stretching from primeval parenthood to posterity, a string of beads clicking and clacking, easily broken and scattered, easily exploded on the sand and disappearing, and, anyhow the beads are but berries of the tree or manufactured out of clay. Man has always been in Africa. The African has no need to know his origin or his destination. He has no need to know because he has never labored under the misapprehension that he doesn't know. To know, to discover, to conquer and to tame and to rule — these are European illnesses. How can one speak, then, in the African context, of "progress"? It's the European who walks with legs apart because he has carved out two tracks in his mind — the good and the bad, the light and the darkness, the true and the false, the progress and the morality, the is and the isn't — and between his two legs the natural and the unquestioned and never-found-because-never-lost humanity falls away. For the African the dead stand just a little back in the shadow beyond the circle of fire, but remaining present, herding the cattle and rolling the clouds between the palms of their hands to make raindrops, and the descendants of the future are there already, are already building cities in the sand. Africa. Nor does the African, unlike the European, use his possessions as an antidote for death. Possessions belong to groups, to tribes, to the dead and to those to come. In Africa metamorphosis is the order of the day.

Transitory and phantomlike — a traveler in the desert, a dry skeleton temporarily wrapped in flesh. Yet not everywhere perhaps. What is true of northern and southern Africa does not necessarily hold good for the green and humid central belt. In Europe the land with everything on it grows smaller as you fly upward; in Africa the airplane is a fly.

We approach Kinshasa* around sunset. Awe-inspiring cloud formations stand around us in the sky as a fantastic architecture. Then we come in to land over tributaries of the Congo; vast, smooth as it looks, gleaming, alive, dominating, with the rays of the dying sun in bloody streaks in the water. Green expansions with gardens and plantations as far as the eye can see. Probably banana groves as well, and the leaves of these, surely like old-fashioned hats with slits to let the light through. When we land, it is already dark. When no one is watching, flashes of lightning beat the clouds with chains in the dark. The blessing of the Lord descends upon us — I mean, such is the humid heat suddenly engulfing you, that your knees want to buckle as you step down from the plane. It's as though you emerge

*Capital of Zaïre, in Central Africa.

43

from sleep to find a big naked dark woman rubbing all her love into you.

In the arrivals hall for passengers in transit each of us receives a glass of orange juice, offered on large trays by silent waiters. It's hot inside the hall and just as hot outside on the verandah looking out onto the night. We are carefully separated at one end, away from any contact with the Congolese. Here, in the blackness of Black Africa, our fellow passengers do not seem quite so at ease. Here beats a different rhythm. First brutal change in temperature; now this concrete building, this close night. Two of our traveling companions are black. Black and white. Already we are on our way to the Republic! On an adjacent balcony men and women are grouped around small tables. They are clearly neither traveling nor known to those arriving or departing. They are probably not even waiting the departure or arrival of a plane. They are evidently simply at the airport to enjoy a cold drink. Perhaps it is cooler here where the stairs to heaven start. We hear their relaxing conversations and study the gay dresses and head scarves of the elegant young ladies. Flashes of dreams. Henri Rousseau. (Who found his Africa and his Americas and his Asia in the Botanical Gardens of Paris!) Thighs, swaying hips, graceful arms with hand movements like limping insects, making you fluttery in the abdominal regions, round breaths — warm like mystery — giving sound to shape in saxophones, the rhythm of "high life." . . . (In my opinion there are only two "schools" of music able to compete with each other in Africa, and you hear the throb of the one or the lilt of the other all the way to the Sahara — the Congolese and the South African township.) Outside the lightning and the clouds have come to blows in deadly earnest. Isn't it Saturday evening? Millions of insects swarm around the lamplights of the building. Even when the rain begins to fall in extraordinarily large drops — there is something reminiscent of harvesting in this torrential downpour — the insects are not dispersed, but close in more densely still: they practically merge into the background, creating confusion between drops splashing upward and light-addicted insects.

The stars of heaven are a miraculous tree. Each one of us is the stem of that tree and we gaze at the stars as a tree might gaze at its own fruit, never to be allowed to consume it. Night is the true

reality. Day is made for people who imagine that there is a beginning and an end, and such people are under the misapprehension that the sky is blue and empty. The light hides the stars which are present. The light is a backdrop, is an illusion against which our thinking takes place. The night is boundless and reveals all. It is exactly the same with us. Our consciousness, that which we have learned and have filtered, that to which we have reduced and diminished ourselves so that we clutch it as we clutch a walking stick, while there is neither earth nor sky neither above nor below — our conscious gritting-our-teeth thinking is the day. And that which is suddenly there (always has been there), when we separate one moment from another, all those mountains and hollows which determine our being but of which we won't or can't take any notice (because our *sight* has become a form of ablepsy), where the words grow naturally as grass, when we have an overall view without realizing it, that other thinking — rich, manifold, knowing no bounds — when we see ourselves as a bee does the flowers — and we keep falling — or flying? — and aren't falling and flying one and the same, after all? *that* is the night. And in that night the stars were as a tree of joy with countless small flames upon each branch.
("dreaming is a way
of thinking further
in the dark")

Johannesburg. The closer we get to the end of our flight, the more the tension contracts in my stomach. My wife, Moes Sgaalp, doesn't look so hot either, but now, in front of those gentlemen, she won't give herself away. That's the way she is, how I know her. (What hell am I dragging her to? And how well she conceals her fear!) Ashes rummages in his luggage, transfers his belongings from one bag to another. Now and then we fly over tiny lights far below which are swallowed up again by the dark night. The plane starts its descent. Exposed, Johannesburg lies beneath us. Under our wings. The dark carcass of a dead animal, crawling with white maggots. The Golden City. iGoldie. Joni. Up to now Jan Smuts Airport was a piece in the puzzle of my imagination. The airplane touches down. Butterflies in my stomach.

Down on the ground it is much cooler than it was in Kinshasa a few hours ago. It is nearly midnight too, and the great glass building is practically deserted. We are escorted by a stewardess to the hall where the immigration officials await us, each in his individual glass cubicle. At intervals one may glimpse an official walking through the hall or down a corridor — short-sleeved shirt with epaulettes, short pants, socks reaching to kneecaps, and shoes, all this in white. Also porters, black, in ample overalls, same size for all the servants, programmed for a slow trot. Whatever explodes, blows out, happens now, come hell or high water, I am staying here. *I am here.* St. Peter, bearer of the key, is a friendly middle-aged man named Du Plessis who is slightly cross-eyed. He recognizes me at once from a distance, starts questioning me, calls some of his colleagues over: "Here he is, Boys." My wife hits a snag. There's something wrong with her papers. You have to fit the person to the rules. African the soil we are on, but English and correct the procedures. Starched navy officers in the heart of the interior. No, the realization that we, that these two trembling feet of mine are standing on native soil, has not fully dawned on me yet. Thirteen years. A lifetime. A waste. Then on to the customs hall. The world and the people around us fade. On the other side of the glass doors, in the huge arrivals hall, just a stone-with-a-little-spit-on-its-throw away stands Daniël Stoffelus Dingo Baas Daantjie proudly, almost upright, all by himself with his jacket over his arm. He has turned gray and has spread a little around the waist. He starts gesticulating that it's about time we got here now, dammit. And finally, after what feels like a century, we are free and the glass doors slide open. Hallo, Baas! Even if they wanted to, they couldn't catch me now. I would run, I would take off my shoes and socks and fly to the hills. I won't admit that we wept. Baas, here we are now. You didn't really believe it, did you?

Baas:
arrived from the North
from the cold
and rain still glistening on the wings

Africa is not green
but gray with heat
blood

46

a continent
that smudges the eye

the sun a flaming
sword
crystals of light bubbling on eyebrows
and moisture from sprinklers on blades of lawn grass
like butterflies in some paradise
our goggling eyes are all agog . . .

On the day prior to our departure — yesterday, a lifetime ago —
when Baas was already in Joh'burg waiting for us to arrive and when
he called Paris to inquire whether we were actually planning on
coming or what the fuck, I threatened him unambiguously on pain of
death if I found that there were others lying in wait for us too on
arrival; I threatened to catch the next flight back if there was the
faintest trace of a whorenalust in the vicinity. And Baas kept his
word. He was there by himself with his heartache-joy and his white
shirt covered with whiskey stains.

He has come to get us in his brother's huge cinemascope
Chevrolet. We pile in, boots, baggage and all. It's like an American
movie from the Fifties. The radio plays late-night music. Springbok
Radio. Saturday night. My God, it's Saturday Night, December
30th, and we are driving in a two-tone Chevrolet to the suburbs of
Johannesburg in South Africa! And we sing! I am the happiest man
alive. You wake up thus inside your own dream. This is the point I
have been dreaming toward, and this is what my compatriots who
find themselves in a similar predicament abroad, dream of:
Johannesburg, night, a car, music. The steering wheel is on the
right. The road signs look exactly like the ones in England. In the
white headlights of the car they loom up like hitchhikers: Benoni;
then an arrow pointing to Bedford View. Drive to wherever you like,
Baas; I couldn't give a stuff.

They lied to me, those birds of ill omen with their tidings of
death! Many years ago — the year before I left the Cape — when I was
still sharing an apartment at the bottom of Long Street — a real
flophouse it was, a "pad," a commune — with Leentje and Marius —
old Marius who has been in jail for so many years now — we also had a

resident ghost. Kees Humfer was his name, a Dutch seaman who had died a couple of centuries earlier on that specific farm (during a fight between two drinking buddies, someone must have stabbed him with a knife) but he wouldn't allow his spirit to take a breather. Marius and Kees couldn't stand one another. "Dutch trash," Marius was always calling him. (And we probably didn't realize the spirit was a security man.) All the same, during one of our many séances I sounded Kees out about what the Future held in the hollow of her hand for me. He hummed and he ha'd — and most of that has come true — and then predicted that I would leave the country. This was still within the bounds of probability, it was normal that a young painter should want to go to Paris; but then he claimed (out of spite, pure and simple?) that I would remain in those foreign parts until I died, never to return! I believed him. One believes a ghost, doesn't one, for what would be the point of his deception? Kees, if you ever lay eyes on these words — and I hope with all my heart that your soul has given up the ghost by now, because, true to our promise at that time, we did engage a priest to get you to lie down, remember?—but if this bleeding and driveling on a page is completed, and if it is then wrapped in a little book, smuggled past the censor, and if you should read it somewhere, someday while the wind romps in the pages before it is fed to the Boer goats in time of drought, then I want to say only: so there, you old liar!

And hardly a month ago, in November actually, a Yugoslav fortune-teller, plump with reputation, came to my studio in Paris to take a look at my fortune. I spread the cards out, and he scribbled on a scrap of paper and decided, regretfully, that I would only be allowed back into my country in three years' time and that it would be too late by then anyway, that I would never see my father alive again. Ivanovic, you damned scoundrel! *En voilà pour ta gueule!* "Soothsayer," ugh!

We spent the first night, the wedding night, in the house of Baas Daantjie's brother, Neels. Actually, we had not completed our journey yet, but like warriors on a crusade the promised land had already come into view on the height, already we were in the shadow of the city walls, and we could lay down our arms and remove our armor for vigorous polishing and rinse our throats with local wine. It

48

was a spacious house with big lawns stretching down to the street. Somewhere behind the house, we were assured, was a swimming pool, and surrounding the house were flowers and indigenous shrubs, proud and silent in the African night. Plants standing guard in the night, on the lookout and listening for the morning with fire. A great flea-bag of a dog — I think his name was Karools — came to greet us with a ceremonial tail. There was food in the house. Biltong and litchis and fruit. And wine by the bottle from the cellars of the Boland. Our conversation rambled. How do you say such joy? If I could I would enlist the aid of Li Po and Omar Khayyam. All I can say, is: even though a joy such as this may be unique, even though you know in advance it can't last, even if I had to die immediately afterward, even then I would wish for nothing deeper or greater. (Or wait, wait . . . unless it be the liberation of our land. But that day . . . . Come, kill me now if you must! If the houses were to collapse and the troops to lay barbed wire barricades across the roads, even then I would go to the house of my father.

Sgapal was deadbeat. (By this time my face too was already white with exhaustion like a white man's.) Every now and then she would give my hand a very tight little squeeze. That means: It's real! We deposited her upstairs in the bridal chamber on a huge white bed. Ashes went in search of, but didn't find, the swimming pool outside where the stars were beginning to fade and a first fever-light light was beginning to touch the horizon. Back inside the house he almost drowned in the tub in the bathroom. At five-minute intervals, I had a pee on the lawn. We went to lie down. I shut my eyes and dreamed that I was sleeping. Behind my eyes the sun was a fixed and humming presence. Two hours later we got up. In the kitchen an enormous breakfast of hot *putu* cereal and eggs and fruit was already waiting. It was the morning of the 31st.

And when we woke up, we were still in heaven.

December 31, 1972

Back to the airport. The Chevy is left in the parking lot where Baas' brother will find it. Already the airport looks different from last night. Evidently many people are making a trip on this last day of the year. The land of South Africa is full of South Africans. No black passengers. Are they too permitted on domestic flights? It's Sunday today. We buy that Sunday cramp, *Rapport*. It is reputed to be the Sunday cramp with the largest sexulation, the widest percolation. It is therefore a kind of Afrikaans equivalent or version of the *Someday Times* and is printed simultaneously in Cop Town, Bloomerfountain and Handyburg. We appear on the front page, looking like escaped convicts. (Well, Baas has many friends . . . And Baas' world . . . And he is like a sieve without sieve wire . . . .) Visa obtained! Followed by an account of our *case* and an eye-witness description of my wife, Gapsel, who, may the Lord be praised, dear anxious readers of ours, for the walls of Jerusalem are still standing firm, is not too conspicuously or provocatively *non-European*. From now on we are newspaper property, okayed, breakfast titillation.

(And allow me to get something off my chest right away: the whites are so dense, so patronizing, so "friendly" that they don't realize that we — just as all the other browns and blacks in the country, I'm sure — wipe our asses calmly and deliberately on their "acceptance" or their lack of it equally.)

Amazement. Why have we returned at this specific point in time? Exactly what was in the minds of the authorities when they granted our visa applications, I cannot even guess. (But I am grateful.) From our side, however, dear reader, I am obliged to let the real cat out of the bag: in a month's time it will be thirteen years since I tucked this country away in my heart, too unaware of it then to take it with me. And thirteen, as we all know, is an unlucky number. You must examine the heavens, you must be able to read the dust and to taste the wind, you must decipher the writing of the ant and be able to interpret the morse-code of the grasshopper's flight. Therefore we must act swiftly, ready on our marks, get set, and go, or else dive underground for a whole year. In addition one has to take into account that we are still in the year of our Lord 72, albeit in the nick of time. Add it up yourself then: seven plus two makes a total of nine, the most sacred number. In a few days' time it would have been too late. We simply cannot allow such an opportunity to slip past.

Today it is as if all action takes place in slow motion, and sounds, though they do still exist, approach one on a different wavelength, do not invade the silence. Airplanes depart from here to all corners of Gondwanaland. Our flight is announced. Two stewardesses welcome us aboard. We sit in front on the righthand side, within the realm of decomposed fear; I mean, we are sitting right next to the shithouse and during the flight we will be accompanied non-stop across the land by shit. It's warm outside, but overcast.

My skull wants to split and my mouth gapes in a permanent idiotic smile. Our bodies — Baas', Ashes', and my own — are enveloped in the sweat of last night's celebration. Don't think. I have a yellow flower in my buttonhole. Where does the flower come from? Ashes is still sitting behind us. My better half, Maspel Thi Mymsol, moves this way and that to take photographs through various portholes of heaven flowing past slowly beneath our wings. O, wide and bitter land. We leave the breakfast tray untouched. The stewardess announces announcements with an aspirin accent. There are holes in the ground all around Kimberley. In every hole lives a gigantic and totally transparent spider. There are buildings around the holes. Green scrub, yellow earth. Things will go on decaying. (The course of my thinking licks like a flame at the endless water of the course of time. Suddenly I am reminded again of the graybeard, well into his forties, lying in a Paris hospital, suffering from cancer of the face. Out of pity they covered his face with a veil in the terminal stages and kept all mirrors out of his reach. Until a compassionate doctor helped him out of the world with an injection.) O, wide and bitter land. The plane lands. My wife suddenly catches sight of the name of the airport.* Her heart misses a beat. My sweetheart. (Don't be afraid, we won't get out to tease the dragon.) The doors of the plane are wide-open. A warm tongue comes across the desert which can't be that far away. The heat comes from all sides, not really from the sun. The earth is a mouth.

Our flight is resumed. Fewer farms below us. Veld. A road, like a taut blue wire along which a vehicle would glide like a drop of dew in the morning. The captain's voice comes over the ether. Informs us where what dam and which village or sight is situated. Baas, Ashes

*Probably H.F. Verwoerd Airport in Port Elizabeth, en route to Cape Town. All major South African airports are named after South African Prime Ministers. Verwoerd was the chief architect of "apartheid," as we know it today.

and I show my wife our land. But it's not our land, it's mine, mine, mine alone. I look at Ashes. We look through the portholes. Then I have to pinch myself. Is there, anywhere on our dying old planet-orb, more of this breathtaking beauty? Villages are dotted about at intervals, defenseless and vulnerable. The land turns gray, the mountains black and scorched by wind and sun. Thirst. A couple of rows to the rear sits a familiar, an archfamiliar figure. He is wearing a little green hat with a speckled feather tucked into the hatband, and he watches us from behind his smile and his newspaper. His teeth gleam like small polished microphones. Mr. Huntingdon! Of course! What a coincidence that he should find himself traveling on the same machine as us. His smile tugs at his mustache with little jerks. He has much patience. And he has orientation. Baas is engaged in a whispered conversation with the stewardess who speaks such a precise and pill-healthy Afrikaans. Baas' breath sneaks up her tunic via tiny fair hairs. Beneath us the world tumbles around and around. I won't say anything. The stewardess has tiny fair hairs on her tanned forearms. My wife is invited to take pictures through the large window of the cockpit and from various other angles. The heart is a scallop. No, the heart is a horn of plenty. It doesn't matter what the heart is. It doesn't matter that death rides with us, dressed in a gray suit and a little green hat. I don't want to know what orders he carries in his briefcase. I don't want to know his troubles. Please don't tell me about your troubles. A flying machine bears me back, across all the years. Pain written on that sand passing through the hourglass. Under our feet there is land now upon which my feet have already stood. That is where I sat behind a bush. Over there is where I hung bits of myself on a tree, and washed other bits in a rapid stream until the cuts turned white. The plane tilts. The captain's voice. A turn. Wellington. A steeple. A rugby field. A wonderful gesture by the pilot to enable my wife to take a better picture. The Adam's apple is made of fossilized tears. Nothing matters. Table Mountain suddenly, Apostles* huddles together, and other mountains. A gray fogginess, pollution so soon, low over the city. Above the sky is blue. It is still early. But we have been traveling for years. Ocean. Airplane veers. Gradually we come down out of the blue. We have been

*Properly, Twelve Apostles: mountains on the western Atlantic side of the Cape Peninsula.

52

descending for some time. Panic — for Mymlons is not strapped into her seat yet as she should be. She must not arrive bruised or pulverized. Not now. Houses more clearly visible suddenly. Houses on a sandy plain. All at once the earth starts moving out from under us at an alarming speed. An eternity. One tries to land. Then a muffled shock and flapping of wings, of vanes, attempting to stop the device. Then we are on our legs and trying to collect all our luggage together. Then my legs are shaking. (O Lord.) Then the doors are opened and along a gangway the astronauts climb to the bottom. Then we go down the gangway. Then it is hot outside. Then we walk along the tarmac toward the large building with the glass walls. Then it takes a very long time. Then I feel as small as a cockroach climbing a wall. Then there are people standing behind the glass. (And waving.) Then it takes a very long time. Then my wife is laughing and my legs are shaky from shaking so much. Then my mother is waving to us on the other side of the glass wall. Then there is a tepid breeze over the airport, the breath of a friendly and tranquil animal. Then there are more people behind the wall of glass.

And we are inside.

Hands, faces, teeth, jackets, lips, flowers, light, sandals, brothers, shade, a pipe, hands, smiles, shyness, my father, children, a floor, luggage, my mother, eyeglasses wet with tears, shirts, Basjan, strange women, Cloete, children, small hands, nephews and nieces? Andries, wrist watches, embraces, words without sounds, family and friends, sounds but wordless, Daantjie's offspring, my father, Basjan's socks reach to just below his knees, handshakes, air-conditioning, glass, hands, angels,

Never again *then*.
Never again *then*.
Never again,

(chicken)

mummy
    I thought
I would never come home again,
neither on the iron horse at dusk

53

through lotus-lakes and fires,
nor via embassies past sentries with blacklists
staring across drums of coal
into the night where halt and who-goes-there rub sides —

and then
    I was here:
        out of the blue:
with a rooster in my breast and sweet wine in my veins,
and there you come
dressed in white age but cheeks still peaches and cream
and beyond the tears stands pa
so squarely delighted
and even a leftover brother with beer and beard —
how'sit!

after all
    I am here, am I not?
as large as my life
in the catchment area of the airport,
remember, ma — where all the breathing is —
somewhat dilapidated from the distant journey,
a sobhat on my crown
flower and lungs all lumped together in the jacket,
new Italian shoes for the occasion
my head filled with tongue and my heart all scab —

but mummy you know it's me, don't you?
and behind me my wonderbird,
my airplume,
as befits a refugee from abroad,
my wife and my love —
my musicians the gunbearers and etceteras
are bound to come on a later flight of fancy —

and oh
the mountain wears a dress-shirt,
the clouds fade and flap fluid into the air,

every palm tree has a fluttering gizzard —

I am here all spitspickerish
as a coon band at New Year
and tonight we will light a fire on top of the table:
I hang my heart in the childhood cradle
of the front-door wind
and raise my song and my here and my wife:
all those years of eating my fretful heart out
were a too long-winded heartbreak waltz!

After a while, and one way or another, we rolled to the city in various
cars along broad avenues through suburbs. Occasionally we saw palm
trees beside the road. One can have faith in a country with palm trees.
On all sides of the route running from the airport of Dar-es-Salaam to
the city itself, grow the same high and graceful palm trees. Only
many more of them. Some of my people left the airport and headed in
different directions for their own destinations — our companion,
Baas, André, Mr. Huntingdon. In the city we stopped off at the
house of one of my brothers. Here Ashes said good-bye to find his
own way in his little brown Volkswagen shoes and with his
cumbersome luggage. We sat down inside and tried to create images
of joy out of words. Then we ate some of the specialities and delicacies
of the Cape. My brother, my unwilling brother, in evidence of his
prosperity, lives in a restored house on the slope of the Mountain. He
has two children in his house: Anna with the eyes, and Koos who eats
ants for breakfast and is going to take after his uncle Basjan, poor
thing. Many years ago when we called at the Cape for a handful of
hours en route to Lisbon, we also had something to eat with him and
his wife. Then it was a farewell meal and in an apartment. Now it is
an appetizer. We get into Pa's car and drive to Onrus. Basjan is at the
wheel and we take the wrong road. Every fiber opens up, every feeler,
all senses try to take you in. You move successively through the various
layers of your own being when, without the ability to place them, you
recognize things, surroundings, panoramas, and are taken on tour by

your own memories. And what is a person after all, but a collection of memories?

Sir Lowry's Pass runs up the Hottentots-Holland Mountains: white vertebrae. Along the road are houses placed a little way back from it in the shade of trees. Oubaas relates how he learned that we might come. At the top, from the narrow ridge of the mountain pass one looks back onto False Bay with all the reflections of the sun, the sun has scattered its coins over the sea, and the Strand at the sea, and Gordon's Bay. Bread has washed up on the white sand. It's a different dimension, it has other colors, underneath the shady spots there are colors, it's good to drive more slowly through a landscape seen from an airplane only moments ago, a century ago. We follow the road through apple orchards and pine forests, past Grabouw, and then gradually back again to the sea, and the apple orchards smell of apples while the pine forests smell of sunlight. It's the Caledon road, but we take the turn-off to the right in the direction of Hermanus and the Klein River Mountains. Just before reaching Onrus itself, one passes Hawston, a fishing village for brown people which, from the road, looks fairly respectable and not too shabby. A signpost points to Vermont and then we are right at the turn-off to Onrus. Rachel is waiting for us at the bungalow, dear Baby Puddle Pinkydoll, and her as yet rigid husband, Cockadoodle, Mietjie and Aunt Susan and Basjan's better half, Bobby.

We get out, we laugh, we unpack, we eat. Behind the milkwoods and the Port Jacksons* lies the sea, making a noise. You stand on the verandah, hands akimbo in the small of the back, and you laugh while you gaze out over the tree tops toward the sea which you hear making a noise but do not see. We eat tomatoes and sweet melon and grapes fresh from the vineyards of the Boland. We throw ourselves onto the bed in the room prepared so sweetly for us by Ounooi and Mietjie. While we are almost asleep — I say almost, because the room is filled with deliciousness and the roar of the waters, and outside the voices of my people, of our people, hum, they cherish us in their voices — while we are almost asleep, two Papparazzi from *The Bugger*† march into the yard and try to force their

---

*Port Jackson willow/wattle: *Acacia cyanophylla* and *A. longifolia:* originally a native of Australia, introduced about 1857, now a plant pest in many parts.
† Word-play. *Die Burger* (Citizen); leading Afrikaans Cape newspaper.

way into the house without any sense of shame whatsoever and without the slightest hint of respect for that meager first bit of family intimacy for which one has yearned so long and so bitterly. Presumably, they want to inspect and handle the exhibits.

After supper we take a walk in the dark to Biltong and Joors' house nearby. Moths around the light of the only lamppost. Bats, probably hairy, in the gutters of the dark houses on empty lots. Above us the Southern Cross hovers on its two hands. An enormous growling monster, a dog by the name of Skylos, comes at us. Biltong and his family are sitting around a fire in the back yard. We are just in time for wine and coffee. Jan Biltong is a spring-loaded and intense little sihouette in the glow of the flames. He regards the return of the prodigal son with head cocked and a sardonic smile in the beard. Out of the dark, from the wings projected onto the wall of the cave to the left, two more shadowy figures emerge, Jack and Richard, like characters from André Brink's *Looking on Darkness.* The flames lick at them, faded images from a distant past. Jack has become gnarled and gray — beaky like a house bird which has lost some of its feathers and has only hair left; Richard is fat and garrulous — both sad and smooth at the same time like an old farmer who really enjoys a following at holiday time only. We can smell the sea and the smoke of the fire. Milkwood here, the Milky Way there. When it is nearly midnight, we all walk under the dark trees down to the beach where a bonfire is lit every New Year's Eve to welcome the new year. Uys joins us, too. He hasn't aged at all, no matter how hard he tries. "If only a phrase were given me . . ." he complains in imitation of Mallarmé. Like a polyglot tame duck he leads us to the beach. On the white sand at the edge of the restless sea the tree is ablaze already and, sizzling, the sparks fly high into the air and vanish among the stars. Other sparks splutter onto the sand like berries being spat out. In the circle of light around the bonfire I see the beloved faces of my nearest and dearest. It's midnight. First moments of the new existence. The new is announced by the expiation of the old. A tree, which is life, is sacrificed to the gods and the spirits watching over our fate. The water burns. The flames are wet. The two will survive together. In Europe the snow lies white like this sand beneath my bare feet. We kiss each other. We are contented. We are happy. We are safe.

January days, 1973

Subsequent days pass like dreams bathed in oil in which you fall from one situation into the next with a progressively reduced jolt. Resistance is lessened. It's not necessary to pursue events at a walking pace, to understand standing. It's not a matter of take it or leave it either; you are part of. (And the less of an outsider you are, the less the need to write down. Writing down is a surrogate and a substitute. Writing down is both the symptom of illness and the illness itself. The difference between participating and writing down is the same as between knowing and having knowledge of.) The days are clear and without pain. The quality of *light* is entirely different from in Europe. Perhaps that's because I look back with this light into that which is unconsciously, and therefore totally, a part of me. *Now* and *then* confused, are being confused. Maybe to me this light is therefore timeless. I was dead and now I am alive again, just as the impossible has come true this time, too. And added to that: I am always here, I am always lying around here anyway — for now I find myself again — even without my knowing or realizing it. There is no need for one to know it either. But the sun burns harder and more mercilessly too. All the same, the climate, though temperate in the South compared to harsher extremes in the interior, is not what Europeans would call "civilized." The wind blows fiercer and across greater distances. The sea is a dense ocean. (The world's great winds originate in Africa — the mistral, the sirocco, the simoom; the Cape southeaster . . . .)

horizon
equals:
ho! rising sun!

You wake up with the noise of the sea in your ear. The sea fills the house. The house is an ear. You yourself are sound breaking and flowing, to swell again. I pulled up beauty like a blanket over my lap. At my feet lie the orchards of memories. The trees are heavy with oranges. A cool and golden sun hangs in every tree. Don't stray in the orchard. Don't check to see whether they still exist. Memories have a right to existence. The smell of the sea pervades the house. The tree shakes its branches. Even when flying the birds don't stop calling. There are hundreds of birds. There are just as many birds as there are letters in a book. I had no idea that so many kinds of birds still exist. There is the common Cape plover which shrieks tiny sword pricks on moonlit nights, and then the tame swallow and the peasant swallow and the cliff swallow, the rag swallow and the little wagtail, the red-chested cuckoo, sometimes, and all kinds of louries and woodpeckers, the monkey-bird, the bronze cuckoo and the hoopoe, and then the shy reed hen and the equally shy thick-kneed plover, the clapper lark and the capped wheatear, the butcherbird, the Cape tit, the thrush and the batis, the familiar chat old bacon fat and the bush warbler, the grass warbler and the reed warbler, the flycatcher and the Cape robin, the honey-eater and the white-eye, the swee and the waxbill. The Cape barn owl dwells in old buildings, the dabchick perches on rocks, and the African moor hen scurries among the reeds. And Cape sparrows by the bunch. In Europe I know only city pigeons, tough and crippled, and cocky sparrows and from time to time a blackbird and in the night an owl like the cry of a blind man in an unfamiliar maze and sometimes, very rarely, a stray raven driven across the city from the interior by the wind. There are birds here with red breasts, birds with green cheeks and black gills, birds with yellow waistcoats like wedding guests, birds arrayed in glistening gray, birds who are discreet counselors to the king, birds with hoods, birds with bubbling voices, birds singing with the sound of cool berries. This too shall all perish. When you lie down to die, they will have to dig a grave as large as the world to contain all the memories. Memories shouldn't lie rotting on the surface of the soil. Memories are fertilization. A thousand knives flicker in the sun. I squatted against the wall and felt the room surge.

I would that a silence came into my verse
I would that my verse live on silence
a silence like sails above a boat:

to write a poem
setting that weight afloat
is like blowing into the sails

We walk at the edge of Africa. You hear the whole world from here. The ether has a voice. We hear chatter on the radio. We hear the signals and the codes, the wheezing and the whistling. Africa is a continent filled with voices. A wound filled with birds. An orchard with many suns. With the blood-red of flamboyants. Hibiscus flowers are broken pulses with ants already among the hairs.

I split a pomegranate. The exuberant mouth of a whore. Even the teeth are stained with lipstick. We are in Africa and yearn for Africa.

Monday, our first day. Our friends pay us a visit. Baas Daantjie Thunder and his wife Nici. Andreas who is full of knowledge, and Alta and Danie and Biltong and Joors and Biltong's brother, At, who builds dams against the drought. We sit on the porch in the sun. We are still bloated from the New Year. Baas smells like an all-night binge. When he has a hangover, he shows an interest in literature. He sits with a book on his lap to keep his knees in line. Below the house, which my father bought from a karakul farmer, lies a camp site. We see a naked man with a briefcase taking cover behind a Port Jackson willow. It's a gorilla on holiday — Colonel Huntingdon or one of his sidekicks. He's accompanied by a stoutish colleague, also in the service, and similarly disguised, but sporting a prim official mustache, one Master Basie. Between the camp site and the house runs a gravel road. Now and then a vehicle passes by in billowing dust. A clergyman with throttling collar and opaque eyes on a pastoral visit. Fishermen in an open jeep with red necks and long fishing rods beaming out like rays against the sky. An angel on a motorbike. The skin has been stripped off his wings by sunburn and looks as though it might be sore. Dogs bound into the yard and dig in the brushwood. The house next door is unoccupied and boarded up. The garden is neglected and somber, a hall for snakes. A mouse scrambles across the cracked stoop.

The sun draws closer to the earth. We grill meat in the back near the kitchen door where Cocky and Raggy have built a special barbecue area; one built the bottom and the other the top section and both are dissatisfied with half the job. Cockadoodle (also known as Clucks or Ostrich-ass) talks talks talks, and when he runs out of breath he turns his eyes toward heaven, sighs like an old man and says aye . . . and God heeds him and new words surge up once more from the depths. The meat is delicious. It tastes like the meat of animals.

The wine is as good as any French wine. At last you feel free of your armor. Home from the pointless crusade. Around you people are speaking Afrikaans. Already it sounds quite normal. So obvious. Gamtok, my wife, is serene and happy. Mietjie has gone for a walk. She has a lover in the woods, says Pa. "A good for nothing, if you ask me." Aunt Susan laughs with the nasal laugh peculiar to the Cloetes. When we go to bed, the sea is still making a noise.

In the mornings, early, we went swimming. The sandy beach is higher up at the spot where the bonfire was, close to Uys' house with the broad back verandah where he can drink his brandy-and-ginger-ale like an old writer, complaining of his stomach and gazing out across the reeds and the bulrushes surrounding the freshwater lagoon which is virtually dry now and devoid of birds. For us, the nearest bathing-place is a pool protected by sharp rocks. A little lower down there are more gullies between the rock ledges, but these are sometimes choked with bamboo. The water is as cold as electricity. Oubaas removes his glasses before wading into the water: that way he can't see how cold it is. Ounooi lies down flat and utters little rosy giggles from the cold. Cockadoodle talks talks talks the water warm. I swim in and out so fast that I emerge again bone-dry a hundred feet away.

We took drives along the sea. Hermanus — an impossible English coastal resort for retired mandarins and bowls-players. Die Kelders. With difficulty you climb down stone steps to a spot where the caves have been hollowed out of the rocks for centuries by the sea. Sour figs and ghuna figs grow on the slopes. We pick some and strip the succulent leaves off to eat the small sticky fruit. Their tartness makes your gills draw water. Sun-and-sea-white shells are strewn in front of the cave, and where you walk there is a crunching sound. In days gone by, a thousand years ago when man was not yet so foolish as to think that he is clever, these caves served as dwelling-places and shelters for the Strandlopers, the early Khoi people. We are living in their world without actually being aware of it. Their words, customs, habits, and even a little of their knowledge is widely dispersed in this region. We took over their cattle, the cattle with the humps and the spreading horns, and their dogs, the golden ridgebacks. In places where they discovered a natural passage through the mountains, we eventually built a road. Gentle and lithe people they must have been,

61

and their world was a paradise. Until the arrival of the barbarians with their countenances like masks of death and the rods of destruction in their hands. (The rods which, one day, in the hands of descendants, shall be rods of liberation . . . .) But those old people, the people-of-people of the land of nowhere look at us still from the shadows. At the entrance to the cave stands a brown caretaker, a lackey who has to sell tickets to those who wish to enter the secret chambers of his forefathers where the cool waters drip. But that's ancient history. And the blood of my race now flows in the veins of the caretaker, too. And my race has turned him into half a man. A "brown-man," a deviation from the norm, a thing which is only able to weep and to become a whole human being again once he has removed me from the scene, and in so doing he will either cleanse or annihilate himself. His past, so we have taught him, is a disgrace — a failure, at any rate, if he looks now at his pitiful and contemptible present—and what does the future hold for him? ("Don't worry," our white bosses tell him, "our children and grandchildren are sure to sort your problems out. But at the moment we have more pressing headaches: our own survival, that power which belongs to us alone and which threatens to slip from our grasp every now and then in the dark, how to pay off the second car, the term of study abroad, the game farm . . .") Mietjie is not allowed to enter with us. Mietjie is also brown. Lest their breaths pollute our air. There is a time for white people and a time (early in the morning or late at night?) for brown people. Question of hygiene. Of kind belonging with kind. For their own good. For the preservation of our indigenous cultures. When we emerge again, Mietjie is standing far away on a rock, gazing idly at the sea and the sky. Just as well she has a squint.

We drive to Uilkraalsmond. This is where the farmers from the wheatgrowing regions of the interior would usually camp, would spend the summer months. Trucks carrying tents, wardrobes, chairs, beds, a couple of sheep, chickens in their coops, and servants. They probably still do the same today. And then there would be dancing and dust would be kicked up to the rhythm of the concertina and to the rockbeat of the heart. Go away heartache! Come here, gorgeous! Scram! Cotillion and polka. Step-to-the-side and hop-dance.

Against a dune above the sweeping white beach and the brilliant blue sea we lie down, build a fire, and eat. Elbows clasped around our knees, we sit and gaze out to sea, as the people of old would have done, more than likely. We watch the sea as if it were a film show. You realize, almost with a shock — if this had been Europe, or even America — such a lovely sea filled with words, such an exquisite strip of beach — it would long since have become infested with hotels, houses, service stations, ice cream stands, cafés, and what have you. And you would be forced to pay through your ass. And gradually the plants would turn gray and the sea would fill up with cans and chicken bones and toilet paper. Thus man soils the environment. Man is pollution. Western industrialized money-rot — man pollutes not only physically, but also morally. He is a culture-murderer. He is a sad case. (ZAP! ONE TIME!)

Ounooi is wearing her old green soft-brimmed hat. Oubaas dozes with his skullcap covering his nose; Tokkiemym is looking for shells; Cockadoodle talks against the wind, talks a little round hole in the wind; Rachel is sleeping. This is not a sea for galleys. The untamed sea advances upon the land like wild horses eager to take a look, but remaining warily and proudly just out of reach. It's a sea for wrecking ships.

We drive to Elim. When I was a child, I allowed myself to be gulled into believing that every man gets a house in heaven after death, that one's good deeds on earth build that house brick by brick. Some houses are small, because some people-on-earth are mean and sly and fierce; the poor, on the other hand, and the meek and the humble receive palaces. That's how I imagined those houses. Pink and blue and white and yellow. On earth, unfortunately, the tables are turned. What perseverance the poor must possess, how farsighted they are, how greedy, even, to suffer so stoically for those fancy villas of death-side (lapasite). But he who laughs last, laughs best. That's why you can't sleep in heaven, because of all the laughter. An old man rides down the street, perched on top of his donkey-cart like an owl. In front of the house, on both sides of the main street, grow the Adam's figs. "Now this is Elim," my mother says. We are not far from Bredasdorp. My mother's people are from Bredasdorp. "My late father," she recounts, "worked for the Divisional Council. And his helper, the late Manie Hans, used to live here in Elim long ago. Such a hardworking man he was. Never complained. Never a day's illness.

Ayah Dorie, too." Ayah Dorie was the midwife who helped all Grandma's children into the world.

A lovely old rooster, of the true stiff-winged, fan-tailed, bossy variety struts across the road like the only constable of a small village. We pay a visit to the water mill. Below the mill, behind the village, are the orchards and the vegetable gardens of the people. It is cool and shady there and furrows run criss-cross so that everything may be watered. The tomatoes are small but ripe. A warm fertile smell rises from the moist earth. The mill stands in the shadow of tall, venerable oaks. In a row we kneel next to the trough to drink some of the refreshing water. We drink the water and smell the earth and feel the coolness. A sense of wholeness. The church has been whitewashed completely inside, the cracks too are white. The church ought to be the focal point of the activities of the village. There is something melancholy about a small village and a church such as these. A small community which has isolated itself here, pioneers in an uncompromising environment. Trees do not grow by themselves. The light shimmers across the hills, then across the mountains in the distance. Going to church must be an acquiescence and sometimes an almost unbearable ebullience of fresh hope, like a thing growing in your throat. One senses the childlike faith here, the simplicity, the lack of show. To them God is alive, is their common denominator. Ma tells how the graveyard, "the acre," is decorated with flowers every Easter, how the village women, clad in black, spend the entire night there, singing. But not sad songs, no, songs of gladness and joy — of "hop-dance," I'm tempted to say.

We buy cold drinks in a small shop diagonally opposite the church. There is mesh screening in front of the windows. It is a typical general store where groceries are still sold. From afar we see a procession of mourners approaching the church. The bell tolls and tolls — such a desolate sound in this vast landscape. Bells toll the air to shreds. There can hardly have been a more human and a more despairing sound down the ages than this very tolling of a bell. The procession appears small and defenseless. Small black people under a blue dome; reverberations like sound from a bell. As eternal as people. They approach very slowly. The pallbearers, carrying the coffin on their shoulders, go in front. Closely following them, the next of kin in black with bowed heads and veils hiding their faces. An unhurried almost fatalistic pace. Morning dress and a Bible. Hymnals. Old men holding hats in their gnarled hands. Women with taut faces and hands clasped on their stomachs. Also younger girls wearing brighter dresses and broadbrimmed hats. (For them there is not yet the abyss between Saturday night and Sunday morning.) A colorless breeze ruffling the girls' hair and making you aware of the curves of the young bodies underneath the dresses. From life to death. It must be lovely to be buried thus. Like blue smoke the voices waft up to heaven. The church is filled with sound. The deceased holds his breath in order to listen more carefully to these sweet and high-pitched sounds — for the coffin is well and truly soundproof — and in heaven above, in the poorer and in the wealthier quarter alike, the retired lean forward on the verandahs, cupping their ears.

We drive back with the sun. Elim with its shabby little houses lies to our rear as such villages lie the world over, as in the sertão in Brazil, for instance. A day will come when a leader will step forth from a cave in the hills, with stuttering flames in his mouth and a light in his eyes, and for a while God will become a dance, an intoxication, a Power able to rectify injustice. But then pink people in brown dress, with loud voices and shiny weapons and dogs will arrive to restore order, to take away the "agitators." You have the right to live apart, to be poor — you are free to be poor, absolutely free — provided you do not wish to be tarnished by the possibility of *free choice,* provided you don't live so far apart that your poverty no longer implies the wealth of another.

Neatly dressed, we're on our way to pay a visit to prominent people — Lord Diffuse and his wife from The Bolt. Behind us the Mountain draws its blanket up to cover itself. The south-easter raises a cap in protest . . . . The Cape is eternal. (It was a rush to get this far. Earlier this afternoon, probably flushed with excitement and conviction, I was still in the throws of a heated circus up at the

Ruiniversity*; there can be few sights as pathetic, surely, as a group of writery types suddenly exposed—perwhorations, consistently skirting slippery Truth, partly provocative and more than wholly calculated for effect, so that, on the one hand, one is worshipped, or so one imagines, in the course of such a Lenten week, and one loves it, while increasingly sinking, on the other, into a deepening frustration and depression. On previous occasions in the Netherlands and Belgium where culture-audiences are even more spaniel-like in their lapping up of such scattered gems than here, I have participated in similar word-guzzling affairs, and there would seem to me to be a logical pattern: during the opening days while the ego is a balloon and probably laboring under delusions regarding personal abilities, to put it mildly, I am extremely randy; then follows such a deep exhaustion and disillusionment, and finally, toward the end, an overwhelming self-pity.) With the sweat of the fray still on my brow we raced home to dress for this evening. Jobba in a pretty black skirt with tiny white flowers and a black top. I in my all-purpose black suit and polka-dot bow tie, my brother in his drip-dry-plastic-trousers-and-jacket.

In front of the house next to the verandah we are met by a couple of thoroughbred tail-wagging dogs. Then the master emerges to receive us. Lord Diffuse is an imposing man, dignified and friendly and considerably more handsome than the cartoonists would have one believe. He has fine teeth and eyes and large Buddha-ears — an indication, according to Eastern tradition, that he will reach a ripe old age.

In the spacious old drawing-room of the homestead — its dimensions, as well as the servants who are to enter later, are reminiscent of a somewhat old-fashioned hotel or rest home in the off-season, only Somerset Maugham is missing — we are introduced to his charming wife. In his appearance and his conduct there is something of both Boer and Briton, which is to be expected from a seasoned ex-officer in the South African army. One cannot help noticing, therefore, the photograph of him as a young man in uniform, and references to that time — the time of the war — crop up

*Word-play. Refers to the University of Cape Town where the "heated circus," i.e., the U.C.T. Summer School, during which the author delivered his controversial address, A View from Outside (see page 151), was held.

frequently in his conversation — possibly because we have come from Europe? Mrs. Diffuse is more typically a lady. In a few years' time, it seems to me, she will be playing bowls in the afternoons in the sloping sun, wearing a white straw hat. (One sacrifices a greal deal for accessibility, one struggles to obtain a human image.) She is the one who actually gets the conversation going, and in the course of the evening it would seem that she is more "left," more critically disposed than her husband. He may simply be more practical, but as is the case with so many Saffrican white folk, he equates "realpolitik" with conservatism.

During the meal, where Ybo notices he takes longer over saying grace than Oubaas does at home, there is his secretary too, a partisan political lady, and a pretty young woman from the Afrikaans Department at Stellenbosch. We eat, and we drink good Boland wine. The conversation turns to prize cattle and the unjust (and basically dishonest) stand of the English Press — the purple Press — a topic for which my brother will always climb onto his chair.

The impending student crisis is discussed too. Recently I enjoyed a meal with some of the NUSAS* representatives and mentioned at the time that I would be meeting Lord Diffuse. I wanted to know if I could put in a good word. But they were convinced in advance that they would be sold around a bend a little further down the river by the so-called Opposition, that it would therefore be futile, and possibly even dangerous. I express my pessimism. Anticipate the introduction of new legislation to curb the above-named organization. But our host does not share my fears. It's not necessary, he says. "Paul Pretorius is just a fly on the wall." Existing laws will suffice to clip the wings of this "small and unrepresentative and self-perpetuating clique." The patriarchal streak, so much a feature of Saffrican bullytics, is clearly much in evidence here too. They're young rascals, children who must be

*National Union of South African Students, a student organization for whites. Usually written N.U.S.A.S. The "impending" crisis refers to the growing dissatisfaction among students at English-speaking universities, black and white, with government policy toward and interference with these universities and the protesting student organizations. N.U.S.A.S. identified with the demands of the black student organization to end white control of black universities. Widespread demonstrations, protests, and "sit-ins" in 1972 were broken up by the police, and sixteen black and white student leaders were served with banning orders in 1973.

reprimanded. Taught a lesson. I hint at something to the effect that liberties shouldn't be tampered with. But these are cleared away with the dishes and replaced by custard and jelly and canned fruit.

My brother and our host proceed to wet the moon on the lawn; I find my way for the third time to the unfamiliar large old toilet. Over coffee we return to affairs of state. It is suggested that close contact exists with the "non-white" spokesmen. That a policy such as the one entailing federation* has not simply been picked at random. It is also deplored that some brown leaders, in the cultural field too, have become so embittered, so hostile. And then Lord Diffuse repeats his conviction that change can be brought about by the ballot box only, and therefore by the white voters alone. Yes, he replies, he thinks there is still enough time. When I mention urgency, he refers to the solid defense force — which obviously does not cover the same area of discussion or notion of priorities. Though he is aware of General Hiemstra's recent controversial address in Potchefstroom, about how thin the shield is. And he was already acquainted with the general's views, as they were frequently obliged to join the same line during state functions to be allowed to touch the venerated hand. Adversity may be warded off if only we would stand united. Our writers too!

He questions me about the forthcoming French election. It is clear that relations with France are a cornerstone of our foreign policy. I argue that the socio-communistic alliance will not be able to win the election though they may nevertheless be able to canvass the majority of the votes. And that this may then possibly herald a period of more intense social unrest.

The secretary/adviser suddenly asks me why capitalism should be regarded as worse (as a system?) than socialism. (And I ask for more brandy.) And, she says, if only people would first become actively involved with their immediate environment and society. (Ah, I was going to say!) People live in ivory towers.

We also talk about the tragic cases of "European" people who

---

* A policy debated from time to time by various Opposition parties as an alternative to the policy of separate development (see *Glossary*). Lord Diffuse, or Sir de Villiers Graaff (his real name), refers here to that brand of federation policy adopted by the predominantly right-wing United Party, of which he was the leader for many years. As U.P. policy favored a federation of the present "white" provinces of South Africa (i.e., nine-tenths of the land) and the "homelands" (black), thus entrenching the policy of apartheid and the status quo, it was rejected by blacks and white liberals.

have been "demoted" to "non-Europeanhood." We learn how many of these were rescued by the personal intervention and intercession of Lord Diffuse. I'm sure he's the kind of person who helps where he can.

It has grown late. We say good-night and make our way back by the white lamps of my brother's car. I take off the tie which has been throttling me all evening. Lord Diffuse is a good farmer and a good man. "Too good for politics."

"Returnwaterdeadreturnwaterdeadreturnwaterdeadreturnwaterdead

"And then, then I was in the train in my land with Jolie-Yolie, and together we stood in the corridor linking the compartments, with our noses pressed against the window while the train gnawed through the gorges, glided over the ridges, meandered along the slopes as slowly and as methodically as a caterpillar and the panormas opened up ahead of us, vistas were unfolded to be replaced again just as suddenly by a rock cliff or a peak or a precipice in khaki in pale green in grays in rose so beautiful my God! my love! so beautiful that you could smell the haziness, could know how deep the sun's life and color has eaten into this pre-world and all the time I was telling J-Y this is my land just look over there now (and small fires were licking here and there like half-tamed creatures in the darkest shadows) and here so-and-so's battle was fought and there whatsisname hid his wagons or his elephants in caves in winter and look my God! my love! how those withered shrubs sparkle and the hazy shimmer surrounding that peak over there how majestic how intimate how incredible my land for sometimes it was close to my eyes and warmer than a hand and I knew that my throat was about to burst like an over-ripe flower and I stood there beside J-Y and warm tears completely blinded me for it was indescribably moving exactly as in a dream.

"Returnwaterdeadreturnwaterdeadreturnwaterdeadreturnwat-

"And at the sidetrack, high up in the hills there we passengers pushed each other out of the way to get hot water for our tea or coffee flasks from the stationmaster in his ticket office and when eventually

69

it was my turn too the engine was already whistling a melancholy note of warning and there were a few more people in the line behind me and the stationmaster was spiteful and ignorant but he didn't understand me in spite of the hot water flask in my hands until at last in my distress I worded the Afrikaans language in my mouth and urgently asked for the necessary

"erdeadreturnwaterdeadreturnwaterdeadreturnwaterdeadret-

"And how his eyes turned narrow-blue and vindictive and how the onlookers recoiled with a hostile buzzing and squatted down baring yellow fangs in a hypnotic hissing and how I then discovered realized to my horror that I was standing there *naked* as the dead and how the train pulled out slowly (like a caterpillar) and the smell of the smoke and the soot and then the circle of the curious detached around me and on the platform the policemen with the hairy knees approaching unhurriedly

"urnwaterdeadreturnwaterdeadreturnwaterdeadreturnwaterd-

(that light/that silver thing haunting the vineyards/
the sea upon which both fishermen/and lovedrunk can wander/
home is where the mango trees grow in the snow/
the eyes two vast locomotives/iron birds/
the sky their nest/anxiously traveling/traveling in their blindness/
they translate their flights in hieroglyphics/
and what a pity)

January 3

Inevitably some of my notes are going to be sketchy, just touching on this and that and getting only a light grip on things. Also, some of the references will most likely be too private for the probable reader. But I am writing now first and foremost to try to remember for myself. You have been warned — it's a notebook. If you have the flesh, I provide the bones.

Today Ears and I traveled in his kombi around the mountain to Somerset West. The route takes us around Kleinmond and Betty's Bay to Gordon's Bay. Breathtakingly beautiful — the sky so clear that distances are deceptive. Table Mountain in the distance. Winding road and rough sea. Halfway there we pick up two young hitchhikers, two small brown children, a boy and a girl. Although there is plenty of seating at the back of the kombi, their instinctive reaction is to squat on the floor. God knows who taught them that brown men do not sit on white men's seats, and God knows from where they're running away and where they're going.

In Gordon's Bay we call on André's parents-in-law. The village is full of palm trees. "You can have faith in a country with palm trees." From here we all drive over to Dingo's house, in SW. A spacious house with a wide lawn and a great variety of flowers and vines. Paintings on the walls and books on the shelves — a complete set of Tarzan and Tom Mix and Roy Rogers, for Dingo is in the literature business. Sandra, his small daughter, is as pretty as an edible doll and his son, Hangball, is lying with legs apart, laughing with a toothless mouth. Mullet are being grilled in the garden at the back over a small open fire, and the wine is waiting. We decide to start off with champagne. There is one other guest, a friendly doctor named Beinart, an athlete as far as the bottle is concerned. When the team emerges from the dressing-rooms, the crowd roars as though they have gone mad, thereby starting all the dogs in the neighborhood barking. Dingo takes up position close to the scrum. Clearly a man for the attack. With a little corkscrew-run Gertjie Beinart advances down the touch-line and when he is tackled he stops short, pops the cork like a man who has his timing worked out to the last detail, and ... drops for goal! *And it's over, ladies and gentlemen!* White and blissful is the froth. And there goes Dingo once more with the glass, and he's done it again! into the corner . . . . But first a little more refreshment.

The cultural mess reflected by the labels on the wine bottles is an abomination. It's a hodge-podge of French and what-have-you. Spanish wines and things. What is depicted picture-wise is no different. What the hell is wrong then with our own designations —

71

are we afraid that the world will think we have no *cultyure?* This nouveau riche brassassedness may also be observed in the way in which all old wine-flies have suddenly blossomed into wine experts (present company excluded). Lips are smacked, the liquid is swilled around in the mouth, cheeks bulging, some guys swallow their tongues. Then heads are held to one side and meaningless moaning sounds are exchanged. Luckily, like all affectations, it doesn't run too deeply, and by the third bottle wine is wine once more and the world is right side up again. With my hand on the carboy, I am obliged to admit that the local wine takes its place among the deepest and most delicious with which I have had the good fortune of becoming acquainted.

As is fitting and proper, the men form a group away from the others and tell dirty jokes among themselves. We also discuss the little piece A. wrote in today's paper. It sounds fairly unbalanced, a kind of "Tokenism," jaw resistance and incitement. But these are sins of which I too have often been guilty. What's it like, I wonder, to be a brown man in this country?

At sundown we drive back through the mountain pass, home. Home! Home! Come, make yourself at home, dusk! Come, make everything sweet and fragrant.

Ma's sister, Aunt Anna, formerly, when Uncle Piet was still alive, of Stompneus Bay where the fish factory is, Pierre and Hentie's mother, is now visiting in Onrus too. With her is Piggy, Pierre's small daughter. Piggy plays with her jump-rope under the tree next to the fence and Aunt Anna makes music. Ma's was a large family — around 18 children — and all very musical. At one time they even played together as an orchestra. Of all the Cloetes only a handful of sisters remain now and although they don't often make music anymore, they still laugh a great deal when they are together, and it sounds like the playing of all kinds of instruments.

In the dark we listen to the radio, to all the sounds of Africa. South Africa is attached to Africa. On the wireless then there is talk of "terrorists." (Those so-called terrorists who will come to power in a few years' time and will then be fêted as politicians.)

(I want to write a poem about the Southern Cross.)

January 5

The days start assuming the normal length of days. We begin to let go. Just a few more unexpounded notes, topics for later perhaps: 1. The unsavoriness of newspapers here. The filthy, low level. Readers are truly treated like sheep. The fuss made about our visit. If you cross an ass with a shark, you get a journalist. Obstinate and thick-skinned — and ready to guzzle anything showing a trace of blood. (But I must take into account that we are upset because we are personally involved. Was I being too naïve in expecting to be left alone? Aren't all papers in all countries the same? Even so, viewed *objectively,* as the swindler would say, even so, the Saffrican newspapers take the cake. And not in regard to our "newsworthiness" alone. They are full of sensational trivialities, there is no depth or distance. In addition they are unbelievably biased. This may be because the market is dominated by cheap newspapers whose only concern is a rapid sale. One misses the — deceptive? — solidity of *Le Monde* or the *Guardian.* Or do I miss only the sophistication? Consider also the fact that the Saffrican newspapers are without exception party political mouthpieces. Would I hold a similar opinion if they were controlled by a party with which I was basically able to identify? It's common knowledge that reporting, like any communication medium or history, is invariably selective. But what goes against the grain is that the presentation here, while insolent, has no dimension. It's a superficial agitation.) 2. Onrus — *restlessness, unrest,* beautiful descriptive name — that my parents should have decided to buy here, little realizing that it had become a kind of artist colony; the entire Clifton Mafia* has been transferred to this resort, it seems — Uys, Jack, the Rabies, and what-have-you. Also Gregoire Boonzaaier and, I think, Cecil Higgs, and a house is under construction for Elsa Joubert, too. It's not a good thing for borderline cases to cohabit in this way. Soon it could turn into a ghetto, and our country has too many of those already. (Surely the only country on earth where there are more ghettos than normal residential areas. And where there's a ghetto, a pogrom isn't far away.) I maintain that writers and artists should go and live in Soweto and Langa and in that new monstrosity,

*Playful reference to a group of artist friends, formerly living on a steep cliff overlooking Clifton beach, one of the most beautiful and popular on the Cape Peninsula.

Bonteheuwel.* Judging by conversations, it appears that "Afrikaners"—the writers, at any rate—are getting up on their hind legs over censorship; new bills, etc. Must admit that I gloat somewhat. What's the use of getting alarmed now, when the Afrikaner writer lost his soul long ago? (In all fairness—there were exceptions, in differing degrees of intensity, too. Jan Rabie, Uys, André, for example.) But those who now, long past midnight, suddenly wake up to the "censorship" bogey, for them, surely, it is a matter not of principle, but of self-preservation only. And what then of Can Themba who is dead, what of Nat Nakasa who is dead, what of Zeke who is embittered, what of Lewis who has become alienated, and what of and what of and what of? A bit late in the day, Boys. The weeds have long since choked the garden, but did we not gloss over the danger at the time, actively jawing or with resounding silence? How did it go again? State Security or some such, or, yes, but *we* are dependent on our own small nation while *they* have a world market. What has that to do with the price of freedom? We have still not realized that our freedom depends on others, that it is inseparable. The Afrikaner is no "exceptional case." For his isolation, his mongoose-hood in modern times, he has only himself to blame.
3. The heat. The hike to Twisgat with Jan and André and Simon and some of their friends. Into the water there, bare-assed. Float on your back in this glorious sea, this glorious clean sea which smells of sea, and look up at the mountains. Time doesn't count. On the seaward side of the rocks sea-ears are taken out, pried loose with an old screw driver or a knife from the rocks to which they cling closely in turbulent waters. Biltong knows the difference between male and female. To me every sea-ear out of the water on its scaly back with the smooth suckerlips opening and closing, gray and slimy mostly, is like a caricature of a grossly exaggerated female sex. You are allowed to remove only those which are the size of a broad hand, and then only five per person. Some of the big old chaps are said to reach an age of thirteen years, and during that venerable timespan they move but a

*Soweto, Langa, and Bonteheuwel are townships for non-whites. Soweto, acronym for Southwestern Townships, is located on the outskirts of Johannesburg; the population of what has become South Africa's largest black "city" numbers well over one million. Langa is one of the largest black townships on the Cape Peninsula. Bonteheuwel is a new "colored" township developed to accommodate brown people who were moved from District Six, which was changed by law to an area for whites (see *footnote,* page 83).

few feet. The Japanese are very fond of our sea-ears. There is a canning factory somewhere in the area too. The equipment used by the men who do the taking-out is pretty primitive. They arrive in a light van and someone dives overboard holding a snorkel in his mouth and weighted down to hold him under, and then he searches the seabed. Scrubbed clean and beaten to a pulp on the rocks, finely chopped and grilled with a variety of herbs — as only Joors knows how — or stewed with onions and tomatoes, it's a dish fit for kings! On our way over a gentle dune to another cove we discover a half-buried and semi-decomposed seal, stinking to high heaven. Gnats and flies in evidence as usual, whirling around their meal. The thing, strangely female, gutted, lying there on its back like a putrefied cross. How did it get there, so far away from the waterline? Southern extremity of a continent. Implanted crosses of Portuguese. An animal wishing to die in seclusion? Dying there close to the eternal sea. What was the last the eyes saw? Do seals have yearnings? We cover the decay with additional sand. Furious flies. Stench of putrefaction is always the longest to cling to one. 4. Say hello to Uys. He keeps watch. He keeps a watchful eye on death, like an old lame bird in its cage with alert beady little eyes. I would love to be an old man soon, like Uys — even though he is so young! — but with fewer complaints all the same. We sit on his comfortable back verandah. Uys who has absorbed the culture of the Latin world. Also the only South African poet I know of who is really well-known abroad. Whenever and wherever I mention in literary circles that I am from South Africa, the reaction is frequently — "Oh, Uys Krige!" He is still interested in everything, is inquisitive, nibbles at everything. Everything disintegrates. Time kills. *Il est mort de sa belle mort.* That wonderful knowledge existing between us — that which binds us beyond all inconsistency or the present is transience. "What stands out is how quickly it passes." Uys is, as we are always saying too glibly, a great poet. And with the passing of time he will become greater still. A poet swimming against the current, but away, thank God, from the State-university-Germanic poets. A *human* poet. It's not possible to speak of a civilization, rather of a putrefaction. (Above thoughts are not connected, of course.) Poets — the blessed, the dammed. When he was visiting us, he got on well with Ma and Pa. Ma calls him Uysie, though she is probably younger than he is. He regales Pa with

75

yarns, one after another, of his youth and his travels. While at the university they would see who could fart the furthest; burning matches held to the backside and then phhhhhht, the long blue flames measured — and he indicates proudly the distance between extended thumb and middle finger*. Naturally you had to charge yourself with beans beforehand. 5. Receive by telephone and via Biltong invitation to participate in summer school. Seminar or something. Cannot afford to say no, for should I be so afraid? But I *am* afraid. (And Captain Crow is even more afraid, but she hides it so well. And she is afraid not only of what might happen to us, but afraid especially that Ounooi and Oubaas may get hurt.) I think we fascinate the people here a little. It reminds me of the monkey I saw in the zoo at Vincennes, how, entirely engrossed in his game, he was playing with a duckling, stroking it for a long time, until he had throttled it in play, and then turned his attention to something else. A VIEW FROM THE OUTSIDE AND AHEAD: we are few but we have a great responsibility. Afr. writer is establishment. Part of problem or part of solution? Whom and what do we write for? We are but one subsection of South African culture. Land of the Southern Cross. Poets do not make revolutions, revolutions make poets. (Sometimes.) And later that afternoon we drive back across the mountains — first time for us — to Wellington.

Lazarus in Grevilleas

(For O. and O.)

then that year in a twilight-fire
on a Friday of the first month
I came home,
back from the dead
back into the home of my father

all is always all so strange
every drawer is drawerful of remembered delights

*Author's footnote: An apt word my father uses—according to him it is traditional—for "to fart" is "cutting fingers."

an old house and a high wooden ceiling
daubed with security

in the room a gardenia glows white
as the folds and stopping-places
of a heart
my travels have no points of repose anymore
and I have forgotten all

I can walk!
a sun sinks in all colors of putrefaction:
the clouds are released
flowing like mountains through the rose
of heaven

outside in the dark ants dart across the yard
and the crickets start screeching of stars
for here every star is a sun —

what used to be boundaries
fall away
fear and festivity are alliterative flashes of the fire
you know that this body is a companion
that all the information will remain unchanged
while the companion mutters senselessly and dies
but here I shall never die
o life is sweet and sore
o death is exquisite
but here I shall never die
here is the home of my father:

January 6

Yesterday evening we reached the haven of safety. We drove through
the back gate into the yard. So little has changed here. The outside

rooms of before have become a little grander and are now divided up into separate little apartments. In one of these lives an old lady, Mrs. Knox, an artist, crippled and close to the ground, with some cats. Then there are garages put together with corrugated iron for the cars of the boarders. The garden, which used to be there before, no longer exists. But luckily the main building is still exactly the same from the outside. Inside a few changes have been made. There is a living room now where the huge dining hall used to be, and, sealed off by a wall, the room where we are to sleep. To the rear of the kitchen a small bathroom and a toilet have been added. The enormous old rooms under the attic are cool; the back door is still where it always was and beyond the back door is a verandah, partially closed off by wire mesh against the insects. It's a raster of new impressions super-imposed on the blueprint of a dream. And everywhere there are portraits, and souvenirs placed on the shelves or behind glass doors — things the memory of which I had thought forgotten. A glass bowl, for instance, won with a raffle ticket at a show while still at school. On the book shelves there are still some of my school books. But other family friends of Oubaas and Ounooi, Uncle Okkie and his family, are now living where the Presbyterian minister used to live in bygone days — and where the incredibly tall date palm stands admon-ishingly in the garden. My wife, Honeybox, is enchanted at once by this fantastic old house. We eat at the kitchen table. Ounooi is going to see to it that we grow plump again. In the evening Baas and Nici call on us, along with Ampie and his rather shy wife, Stella. They enter the house by the dark hallway with a cardboard box containing some of the choicest wines. I had already become acquainted with Ampie by correspondence, but I had a different picture of him in my mind; thought, in fact, that he was bound to be a staunch Transvaler because he teaches Afrikaans. It's a pleasant surprise, therefore, to meet an unprudish and easygoing young man with very white teeth and long black hair. Oubaas starts talking — something he doesn't often do — and boasting, too, about what a good farmer he was and of his successes in the mines.

Today, before noon, we went to the Cape to watch the black minstrel troupes. The road to Paarl is just the same as always, downhill with the graveyard on the right, through Newtown (further to the right one sees the wisps of smoke rising from shanty towns) and past

Daljosafat and Huguenot. On Saturday mornings the streets of Huguenot are black with farmhands coming to the canteen and the liquor store. We drive through the Paarl farmlands until we reach the main route running across Dutoitskloof Pass from the North. From here the freeway takes us right into Cape Town. Klapmuts is still recognizable, but where there had been just a few cottages previously at Kraaifontein, extensive residential areas have sprung up on both sides of the road. Man is devouring nature, occupying the land with his ugly and pitiful expansions. New villages mushrooming like these must be a phenomenon characteristic only of countries where the displacement of population groups is an accepted facet of life.

In the Cape we have a meal at the harbor café. We are evidently recognized by one of the waiters working there, an elderly Indian, and he greets us warmly and expresses the New Year wish that all of us, people of all races, may learn to live together with mutual respect in this one and the same land. We eat lobster and crab and other Cape seafood. The choicest delicacies of the Cape. Outside boats and ships of all sizes and from almost every part of the world lie rocking in the oil-dark water of the harbor. Farther still, of course, but from here we cannot see it, far out in the Bay is the island for political lepers*. Our mark of shame. We don't need to see it to be reminded of it. I dream about it sometimes. Then there is first the blowing of a wind and afterward the calm voice of a wise man across the waters. And he speaks more or less thus: "To overthrow oppression, to that mankind gives its approval, and that is the highest pursuit of every free human being . . . . You see that there is no easy way to freedom anywhere, and more than one of us will have to walk through the valley of the shadow of death, again and again, before reaching the mountain peaks of our longings . . . . At your side I will fight this Regime, inch by inch and mile after mile until we have conquered. What will you do? Will you be with us or working with the Regime in its attempts to suppress the just aspirations and desires of your own people? Or will you keep silent, silent and neutral in a matter of life and death for my people, for our nation? As for myself, I have made my choice. I shall not abandon South Africa; I shall not surrender . . . . Only by

*Table Bay. The "island for political lepers" refers to Robben Island in Table Bay, which has been variously a penal colony, leper colony, mental asylum, and is now a place of detention for political prisoners.

suffering, by sacrifice and militant action may freedom be won. The struggle is my life. I shall go on fighting for freedom until the end of my days . . . ." Then the voice is silent, but its echo travels far across the land. In my restless dreams that island of shame appears in the early morning mist as a quivering, like a dead moon floating on the surface of the waters. But you don't have to see the island to be always conscious of its presence. It is where the lawful leaders of the land are isolated. Like a gleaming spear they shall remain stuck into the side of the bull. The wound shall become inflamed. The bull in bewilderment shall grow weaker and weaker, shall be forced upon its knees. In only a few years' time those island dwellers will set foot ashore at the Cape once more. Will they be able to forgive and forget then all these destructive and destroyed years? They are the leaders. Their shadow, the injustice done them, eats deeper into the land. They shall never be forgotten. Old, as old even as mankind itself, are the attempts of reactionary regimes everywhere to cast the spokesmen of the people out into the outer darkness, to exile on islands — and it hasn't worked yet, it won't ever work either, not in Greece or South America or Viet Nam, not in Portugal, not in South Africa.

The Cape is dead and gray and ugly. On the way, and here too, the scars left by the drought were conspicuous. Or is it because my eye is not accustomed yet? On other occasions when we have landed in Africa with a huge bound from Europe — water-soft Europe — I have noticed that it takes some days before you grow used to the spectrum of colors in this differing environment. In the beginning it's almost as though everything is gray and dry. But after a while your look goes deeper. And when at last you are transported back to Europe again, it is like being put down in a bowl of ice cream which is excessively sweet. And yet, though there are many people about, and small troupes of coon bands everywhere too, it's not the same spontaneous, exuberant atmosphere of merrymaking which I remember from before. We have a beer on the verandah of the Carlton Hotel above. A little lower down in Long Street, right in front of the bar above which I once shared an apartment with friends, stand a couple of tipsy dancers, clearly in a kind of stupor, an *état de grâce*. Later we watch the troupes passing by. A pathetic sight.

There are fewer of them, they straggle along in dribs and drabs. And a considerable number of police vans carrying dogs behind strong wire fencing in the back. I know it is customary in some other countries too, but can there ever be anything lower, anything more abhorrent than setting dogs upon people? How insensitive we must be to allow it!

On our return to Wellington we receive a visit from a local minstrel band. The men are dressed up in blazers, and they *sing!* "It's our South Africa/Land of our *(of* my *brother, sings the captain's voice, clearly audible above those of the others)* birth/When I get up in the morning the sun shines from the sky/from the blue sky/all over the blue mountains/over the blue sea . . . . "You try to hide the mistiness in your eyes by fixing your gaze grimly on an undefined point in the distance. We get onto a friendly footing with a few of the singers. One is called Dawid Moses. Another, a young man, has long curly hair and his name tattooed on his forehead: Lucifer ("and I don't take no for an answer!"). He tells us that his lover, his cherry, has just left for Greece. Everyone wants to go away, but they sing about South Africa. What a torn country!

The difference in the ways people react to our presence is striking. The white people — family and friends excepted, of course — are curious, but view us with a measure of suspicion, as though not too sure what to make of us, as though we're nothing but strange phenomena after all; the black people have an open and direct and welcoming approach, there is almost a warm kind of feeling of conspiracy.

I'm dreamin . . .

What is less well-known, among older persons too, strangely, for they might be expected to remember more clearly, or perhaps the opposite holds true and elderly people remember less, maybe their memories are empty houses where the wind now makes breeding-places-for-the-wind, shame has corroded the insides of the houses; what is less well-known, is that the stars we see are the beaks of dark birds. Dark birds which can never die. They peck, they peck. They guzzle, they guzzle until they have pecked each other's eyes out, because they do not want to see their eternity until they have devoured one another, and all the blackness disappears. But in the evenings they shit each other out again, blotchily, and their black feathers cover heaven and a twitter of beaks start to peck, peck, guzzle, guzzle. Aim at death which is shit and foul! Guzzle fear out into the open!

In history, on page 2000, there was a country with the name of Africa. Between the feet of that country, on the ground, like an unmentionable thing which befalls one in one's fearfast years when certain cloaca muscles fail to hold their own, there was a region named Shit Africa in the naming language of the mouths of the namegivers. And shittier even than that, like an aborted fetus, there was an island surrounded by water and the name of this was: The Island of the Robbed. The Island of the Robbed — the Height of Misery — was the dwelling-place of many chosen ones, for they never saw the stars. (Now who would want to see the stars when you can stare at the lights on a jailer's boots?)

In the hollow secondless hours of the nights during which the Robbed never saw the stars because huge lights on tall light-poles kept all darkness at bay, they — *viz.,* the Robbed — became aware of visions. When you are forced to look into yourself, camped off by gray walls, then you turn diviner, then you see. And they saw: how Holey G—, by the intercession of his Spirit, went in to Meraai, Yusuf's cherry, to have intercourse with her, and how she begat a child of Spirit and Blood. And the child's name was Going Home, Hope, Themba, his name was All-mightiness, Amandla! for all the outcasts and living dismembered, his name was Bread and Sufferjam, his name was Koesôlo-Clockclock, Pretty-name and Muntu-sosa, Gatiep and Ramun, Dubula the Dove, his name was Jessie Em Jesus. And he was as black as a wonderful open dream of wings in front of the window, as black as an eternal bird. All the sirens screamed and the whistles whispered and a star which was covered in blood indicated the place where the break-away seed had become embedded. And in the townships around Joni the people started an uproar and behind the brushwood barricades of the kraals upon the arid earth shadowy shapes loomed up with mouths full of fresh earth and with bobbing plumed headbands and clattering cowhide shields and through the streets of the Upper Cape poured the nylon-and-silk-arrayed glittering ghosts from Ghostville — that part which used to be called District Six*. O! O!

But the sea's white foam washes up onto the island, endlessly and saltily locked like blood inside the body. And the black captives hear the loudspeakers saying it is Christmas morning, hear Bing Crosby's voice coming across the ether just as a motorboat would growl across the waters: "I'm dreamin' of a white Christmas . . . ."

January 8-12

We are going to drive all over the place. First little lance has been broken. Deeper layers will be unearthed. Softened images. Falling apart. The stroke of an etching-needle here. Bruises there. Emphasis on man. Bluesnow. My thinking was a comfortable place my thinking should be a steep incline a dangerpoint a signal. Open your legs: let me thrust my killer into you. Forehead itches — where the horn wants to grow? Panus is also around here somewhere. "The flaming elephant." Everyday life in Wellington. Jan works on the blinding iron roof in the midday sun. Uncle Sankie falls over when he becomes unconscious. Uncle Okkie has a soft job, he plays at constable. Missus Knox is too old to ride the broomstick. I trim the lawn with sheep sheers. Barbecue to make the evening blue. Dawid, Mietjie's wild son, is just as cross-eyed as his mother. The frangipani is all fragrance of love. Tall and broken grows the Pride of India. There is a funeral. All the laborers and servants hold a funeral. Some of the Pride of India is picked to be placed inside the coffin. The coffin is filled with flowers. While it is covered up a blind old man comes to the edge of the grave, comes to chant-chat with the deceased companion. "And give my regards to September and to Joel and to Paulus, and don't forget to tell Violet not to worry about me, I'll be joining her one of these days." Where silence dictates. At the wine

*District Six, a traditional Cape "Colored" quarter, was recently taken over under the Group Areas zoning to be an area for whites, forcing the "Colored" population to move to townships on the outskirts of the city. There was a general outcry when District Six was proclaimed white, but all efforts to reverse the decision proved futile.

83

show a drunken stranger who is an envoy accosts me and says into my ear: "Then do what you have to, but do it at least with love and mercy." Africa, afflicted by acne. Some of the spots are ugly. Not everything is fine. Just as well that God, in His kindness, decided to make it dark when people are asleep. In Paris there is often wind because there are so many small balconies. I am an African. What is left after a hundred years? System suckers. Assholes wrapped in rotten meat. Open sores. Not the nakedness of Adam, but clothes of paradise.

On the day of the eighth I called on my publisher in the Cape. It was a eunuch, one Ts'ai Lun, who invented paper in the year 105 A.D. It was he who processed finely chewed strips of plants into money, clothes, and toilet paper. Since then progress has been upon us. Paper gave rise to literature (among other things — for there were also telephone directories and paper bags) and literature to writers. Another branch of development led from paper via printers to publishers. (The men of letters have nothing to do with paper. They use their hands or their shirt-tails.) Today the meeting-ground of these two branches is the publication of a book. Publisher publishes a book and gets writer to fill it with writing.

My publisher's offices occupy one floor of a large and central Cape building. Having wiped my feet on the doormat in front of the door, I knock on the door. I have to go on knocking for a long time because the clattering of typewriters and the barking of orders at clerks and typists by supervisors are such as to wake the dead. The people are occupied in an intensive business. The healthy sunlight, filtered by venetian blinds, barely penetrates from outside. I do not even dare look at the secretaries' shapely legs. Some of the peoples' foreheads gleam with concentration. I attempt to find my way and my man. Try to explain that I have an appointment. I am sent from one office to another. Some of the people are engaged in research, others again measure the books with rulers and then make mysterious little marks in large files. Telephones ring shrilly and now and then exhortations, unintelligible to me, come over the intercom which is present everywhere. There are two security men sitting in one of the waiting rooms already. One is rather greasy and it looks as if he has just recently been mauled severely by the sun — maybe he was on a secret mission somewhere in an African state, because he has been burned to a kind of liberalist-pink; the other person, elderly and wearing the rank of colonel, is quivering his service-mustache. "What is your orientation?" asks the officer, but I shut the door again quickly. In an office at the rear, among mounds of books and invoices, I find a messenger and a girl on the floor, half underneath a desk, and both as naked as it pleased the Lord to create them. Although they are now lying next to each other, his fully paid-up member is still agog with motions, and it's obvious that they have just unanimously passed a resolution. No, they don't know where the man is whom I have to see, and they are pretty exhausted since they have had to practice and exercise to determine whether some of the more acrobatic scenes as described in a forthcoming book by one of the writers in the business could indeed be based upon an approximation to reality, yes, a thankless task but that's the way it is. Buren* cannot afford to push unfounded allegations onto the market. It reminds me irresistibly of a description in *The Golden Lotus,* as translated by Chin P'ing Mei — *Hsi-mên set the woman on the edge of the bed, pulled down her trousers, mentulam manu cepit, florem in postico temptavit. Sursum deorsum plus centies magno sonitu se urgebat. From their rapid breathing and their behavior it looked as though they wished to break the bed into pieces.*

At last I do actually bump into the big boss himself — Mr. Abe Brown. He has no time, unfortunately, to see me now, but if I would be so kind as to go and wait downstairs in the Café Royal where one of their reps may be able to give me a hearing. . . . There is no need for me to be concerned about anything, however, because everything is running smoozly. On the way out I nearly got lost again. Just to the right of the draft-room I hear the bleating of the Namakwaland goats which are kept in the office of one of the directors — the one in charge of distribution — to get rid of the surplus copies.

The corridor outside is crowded once more with prospective directors, goatherds looking for work, lecturers and critics who are only hanging about for a sniff at the books please, security men whose sole aim is to distrust the peace, and in addition, a sprinkling of

*Buren Publishers, Daantjie Saayman's publishing firm and the publisher of several of Breytenbach's books as well as others which were subsequently placed under embargo or banned.

writers, bloated with inspiration. Below in the forward command post, otherwise known as the nerve-center — the Café Royal — I am granted a brief interview by Mr. Snaayman. He has earphones fixed to his head of the type one expects to see in telephone-exchanges, and on his lap he holds a walkie-talkie gadget. The man is near dead due to overwork and is a nervous wreck, judging by the state of his fingernails which have been chewed to the quick. Now and again he takes a large swig from the double shot of water in the glass in front of him. "So what," he says to me before I even open my mouth. Thereafter he offers me a water and soda, on the house, and points upward with a blood-stained finger.

All through the blue vineyards on the way back to Wellington I resolve always to stick to my writing.

Cape to Rio

a great and bitter and barren land ...
a land where the earth shudders and jolts
and volcanoes have newly become cold ...

Table Mountain the bow bracing itself against the foam of oceans
sending the white sails fluttering across the peak

for the wind rises
the wind causes the rigging to sing
and as butterflies from an Oriental poem —
but the surf is much higher here
and wilderness and desert much closer
to the body

there is little refinement
no kings mourning dead civilizations
and the only make-up is the white blind
                              of death —
and yet, as butterflies from an airy poem

86

the yachts dart from the Bay toward joy:
the *Old Glory, Jakaranda, Concorde,*
Albatros, Rangoon Lady, Westwind,
Outburst, Impala, Buccaneer, Zwerver,
L'Orgueil, Golden City, Silver Streak
and *Dabulamanzi* — "he-who-cleaves-the-water"

ships and wings and flags sails birds
                        to Rio

past Robben Island:

where prisoners surely can hear the sails
flapping against the sun
where eyes search against the sun
so often and so far
that like water they may pursue
the specks of freedom to the horizon
where it is dreamt that someone anyone
will reclaim the water
so that the people may walk dry-shod across False Bay
to the great and promised land,
where one dreams of the run
from Robben Island to the Cape ...

tanned youths adjust the sails
and topple the waves
                        it trembles and throbs
like the rhythms of a poem
                        and past Robben Island past past
sweep *Old Glory, Jakaranda, Concorde* ...
ashen patriarchs stoop
                        to count and arrange the grains of salt:

January 13

We reach Somerset West quite early. The big dog is running inanely around the garden. Baas Linus, fresh as early morning Springbok Radio music, all clamminess and aftershave, carefully loads the cardboard boxes of precious wine into the trunk. Man must make provision, and prevention is better than cure. But in the mornings, despite his clean-underpants-and-brushed-teeth look, one hardly gets a word out of him. He stammers and stutters. Teeth clicking terribly, like the wings of a flight of herons all arriving at the same time, looking for a place to sleep in a tree which is too small. The shivers and shakes.

Say hello to Nici and Sandra, and then up the mountain in the Opel. Highway. When one takes to the road like this, it is always to infinity. A fairly modern Chinese poet — Wo Shi Hong — wrote in the classical style (about a dawn viewed from a train between Chambery and Aix-les-Bains in the French Alps):
wind thrusts eddies of cloud down
      low across the lake,
in small boats fishermen search for fish
below the dark water —
the cigarette has vanished: there is still smoke,
the mouth is shut: the breath is seeking refuge;
high against the peaks
the first golden light —
clear pools of sound after a silence —
combing the trees:
man is naked

A wind has bent over the grasses and shrubs on the slopes and flattened them in places so that the mountain gleams silvery. A shiver for the nakedness of seeing. And behind us the silver sea so early in the morning. For a fleeting moment only, the dizzy realization of the eternity of all life. The detachment, the no sympathy of it. No room for my small need or comfort. *It was here before I was. It will still be here when I gave gone. My being here is of no consequence. The present "I" nothing but a passing point of departure, a dotted line, that's all really.*

The Caledon road runs uphill and downhill. In a dip where the main road crosses a farm road, lies Boontjieskloof. The namebearers of the family who farmed there have been dying in a violent manner for generations now — drowned, run over, falling into threshing machines, etc. The explanation, I believe, is that there is a curse upon them, spoken by pilgrims in a horsecart who, in days of yore, got themselves into some sort of difficulty in that neighborhood, begged in vain for assistance from the people of Boontjieskloof, and came to a bitter end there. After a little while the Langeberg Mountains loom to the left. For hundreds of miles they will hang like a petrified waterfall, a blue curtain all along our route — with folds and pleats of sunlight and ravine. (Throughout the Boland one is aware of the blue and golden mountains. Let me assure the reader that I am by no means planning to describe it.) Baas Linus sings. There is heartache and joy in our land. Baas Linus tells the story of the peacock which landed among the guinea-fowl and how the old shepherd, never having set eyes on such a feathered creature before, arrived breathlessly at the back door the following morning, exclaiming anxiously: "Folks, come and see! The guinea-fowl have gotten a king!" And of the futile attempt, too, to catch the bird which succeeded in taking off just in time: "I was about to grab him, but he had already brushed his coat, and was off." Baas Linus tells us of the men whose schooling isn't up to much, who come from the country to work in the city and then try to show off their English. And how one day, when he had expressed his surprise at the fluency of So-and-so, a young lad, he was told: "Well, Sir, his speaking isn't all that marvelous. He picks the words before they're quite ripe."

We fill up again at Heidelberg. The ground sparkles like a new suit of clothes. Past Riversdale. Via Kafferkuilsriver. (At the end of this short section, I want to tell you what Riversdale was like in prehistoric times.) In winter, in my childhood, when the river was flooding and the little ford near the farm was impassable, we were obliged to use the train bridge on this side if we wanted to get to school. This is where the aloes start growing. In my time there were mysterious "lone wolves" in the veld along the ridges who dug holes, placed a bucket at the bottom, and arranged the lopped-off aloe leaves around the hole, like a crown, with the cut sides protruding over the edge and over the bucket. That was done to catch the sluggish bitter juice. Medicine was then made from the juice. For the stomach, probably. Medicine so acrid that one's stomach would bolt and forget all about being queasy. There were baboons in the area then, too, but they spoke a distorted Afrikaans, and jackals — now and then an entire commando on horseback was obliged to go hunting to keep those chicken- and sheep-eaters in check — and golden eagles with wings half spread, shamelessly taking up positions close to the dying sheep, making the dragging sound of a fine metal fan. There were mountain antelopes too, and impalas and rock rabbits, and at night the scrub hares were ruthlessly caught in the sharp glare of searchlights — bewildered, blinded, and *pshuiiii!* between chewing and swallowing, life and lead are gone together. It must be good to die like that, immediately, like a blinding conversion. Our whole lives we struggle to get into the right position for death. (Then I think of Mr. Huntingdon and his gorillas, his torture-experts, the men with the gray calluses and the clammy little hairs around the pulses . . . .) And there were farmers in black hooded carts, with lace-up shoes and chewing-tobacco held in their cheeks. Perhaps it is all the same even now.

We drive across a high bridge over the Gourits River. No acrophobia or balancing-rod. Baas' foot steps on the accelerator as though the latter were trying to get up. The countryside grows more arid. Mossel Bay. Now we see the sea again. Good morning, sea. Then George. Between George and Knysna the road is caught suddenly in sharp turns and twists, and on either side seemingly impenetrable vegetation towers above us, casting a greenish twilight over everything. We turn off a little further on to take a look at "the world's tallest tree." The occasion is celebrated with a bottle of first-rate wine. Wine is excellent for hunger and removes the acid taste from the mouth. Here Tarzan approaches us shyly, after a while, to greet us. Jane is also in tow. Her one naked tit is black and blue with bruises from the way in which Tarzan is always beating her on the breast with the back of his hand, just to be able to boast again for the record: "Me Tarzan, you Jane."

In the village of Knysna, Bearman the Boxer and his wife join us again. They had gone on ahead earlier in the morning by kombi. We almost east at the local hotel, but all proceed instead to Plettenberg Bay where we intend to spend the night. We are warmly received by Siegfried Siegie Stander and his wife. Their house, which is situated more or less on a slope, has a magnificent view of the bay, the bay where the incoming surf crochets an edge to the sea, the miles of white beach, and on the right, in the haze, one sees an unsightly new building which is attempting to muck up the view. And with remarkable success. It's a hotel trying hard to be a copy of its swanky Las Vegas-type counterpart. The muck, just for the hell of it. Mercifully, the sun is about to disappear behind the low hills behind us. We walk into the foaming cool sea up to our hips.

I am forced to draw a veil over what happened later that evening. Not that it was all that wicked, of course, but the case of wine accompanied us into the guest house — one doesn't want to take the chance of something like that turning acid overnight in the car. What I do remember is that there was fierce arguing about trivialities. Siegie is a solid man, but his faith prevents him from imbibing any alcohol, and out of a deep sympathy with the nuisance of his principles, Linus and yours truly and Boxer allowed one bottle after another to vanish, so that Siegie might not be led into temptation.

I remember the Bear, on all fours, engaging at one stage in a conversation with the carpet and Linus becoming embroiled in an altercation with a rose bush outside. The rose bush evidently convinced him because the next morning we had to turn the hose onto him right there. A bee had just started buzzing his ear again. After a healthy breakfast of scrambled eggs and champagne we all went out to sea in Siegie's boat.

It was late afternoon before we were able to say good-bye to our host and his wife — by this time there was such a degree of confusion of personalities that I left as "Stander" — and also to Bobby and Bearbox, who would be continuing their journey up the coast to Durban. Linus pointed the nose of the car in the direction of the Kouga Mountains and the gravel road took us higher and higher, until there were no more farms or cultivated fields, only tinted clouds and inaccesible mountain chains, ridge upon ridge, primordial dragons now fossilized, and space, and then gradually, total vast night with her immeasurable cloak full of holes. The small swish-sounds of the mountains in the night. Also dust lingering on in the dark. God's hiding-place.

91

On the evening of the 14th we arrived at the cottage owned by Uncle Martin, the philosopher, the Taoist. The moon hung above the valley.

(for Uncle Martin)

on the way to Upper Kouga through narrow passes across landscapes
trembling in the dying light of the sun
where darkness takes the world peak by peak
we came over a rise
and turned off to where a house tugged the moon
as pale and secure as a word
in one's own language familiar to the mouth
and there was light in the house:
it was good,
we were glad

the people of the house came to meet us
in the fireplace the embers were still red
wherever fires are lit there is profound conversation
we ate the fresh bread
with jam of mulberry and apricot
and we partook of the wine
and later, outside, sniffed the oven
for it was still warm with the smell of something
        from afar coming alive
and thus it was good
thus it was all by itself
thus it should be
for there was no guest or host anymore
and we were glad

we drank of the water seeping
        from the mountains
we gazed at the old and somber mountains
how they stood guard around the basin
and at the stars above the mountains:

the cross above the gorge
and the others
  like fires on a black scorched veld
we noticed the wisp of smoke in the moonlight
and heard the frogs masticating time
on a single tooth
and the cicadas still singing the praise
  of the sun of yesterday-and-tomorrow,
and we were glad

we do not know the petnames of the stars
the trees are lovely but unimaginable
in the dark one does not see the vistas
in the dark
we learned that farms around there
  were named after the yearnings of the heart
  so heavy and so cool:
Begrudged, Depths-of-Despair, Inopportune,
all the way to the top of *Damnation Gorge*
but what was as it might be,
and thus it was good,
and we were glad
to be with you

may there always be a light burning in your house
may the frogs remember you
may your apples grow sweeter every year
and your grapevine greener
may your friends bring wine when they visit you
may the house you have built remain pervaded
  with the fragrance of cedarwood and geranium leaves
may the walls of your furrows not cave in too soon
  and crumble into ruins
so that the water may flow even more limpidly in them
may the stars and the mountains and the silence
watch over you and your family
now and tomorrow and on all mornings and evenings
and in the night of each one of those days

By day, one is able to see. There is always wind in the poplar grove. The poplars are yellowing. Uncle Tao had them sprayed, wants them to die off gradually, for they obstruct the flight of the eye to the hills. Here and there ghuna figs and stretches of prickly pear. The aloes lie in ambush. Against the slopes the aloes grow like figures who stand listening all day to someone praying in the plain below. This is an earthy region. And the eye's eyes are opened. And draw the pain out.

Uncle Tao walks in front, knapsack over one shoulder, small khaki hat on, pipe in the toothless mouth, ugly as love itself, gun under the elbow in the hope that an animal will stand up to be shot now that hunting season is over. Or, if there is no other way, then perhaps a rock rabbit or a guinea-fowl or a couple of wood pigeons or a donkey or even old Moses or his hut. We walk together to cover the four corners of the farm, even Lambkin has fallen into line. *Firedog*, the dog actually belonging to the neighbors, but having promised himself, body and soul, to Uncle Tao, named thus because he is able to lie and sleep almost right on top of the fire until his skin glistens and flickers as a result of the tiny leaping sparks — Firedog joins us with equal enthusiasm on our quest for game. At a cottage belonging to one of the farmhands, we allow ourselves a rest in the shade first, tobacco is shared and pipes are filled. Then we squat, feet wide apart, elbows between the knees, blowing out smoke and gazing far into the world as though there were something to see, and there is nothing. The wife of the old farmhand brings her young infant for Little Missie to see. Then we resume our hike, give the dam a wide berth, pick a finch nest, and reach the farmstead by going through a bluegum wood.

The wine, which had been intended for Uncle Tao too, received an irredeemable blow that night at Siegie's and now there are broad hints, repeated and loud smacking of lips, and spitting, heads are shaken, and sighs are heaved from the deep place of yearning. In addition, Uncle Tao says hardly a word, only keeps humming the whole time, a tuneless tune, and casually passes farts, with obvious pleasure. Some philosophers speak with silence; Uncle Tao chooses to bring his deep thoughts to the surface in a different manner.

One of the friends of Uncle Tao's son is lying in the dark room with a swollen face. It seems that he was bitten by a spider a few days ago when they spent the night in a cave in the mountains. On the

94

same afternoon we walk along the riverbed for a couple of miles to a deepish pool, undress and swim. Uncle Tao's son asks us to bear testimony to this historic event — his father doing battle with the water — for apparently it is as rare as a moon-landing. We do not come across leopards, and the baboons are over the hill at a gathering or a rally.

That evening, we sing with great determination outside around the fire to forget the dreadful lack of wine, but Uncle Tao's note is not there at all, and the night is immense above us. Firedog lies closer to the fire, the aloes are black on the inside and on the outside.

January 16

Preparations for our departure have been going on since early morning. The sun is seated in glowing contentment up in heaven: it is going to be hot again today, the sun is going to set shrubs and aloes and trees alight, and smoothly burned stones and fiery red earth will reflect the radiance of flames.

Very clearly, departure rests like a heavy burden on the shoulders of the owner of the farm. Uncle Tao makes a last few rounds. In spite of the languishing heat he is wearing a velvet suit, a shirt buttoned all the way up, and a string tie — the kind worn by cowboys having a Saturday night out on the town — held in place below the collar button at the top by a ring into which a stone has been set. In short, a kind of anachronistic elegance. I would say it's as if Uncle Tao has been invited to a gathering of all the characters from Franz Kafka's works, and now he has dressed up (to be on the safe side) to suit the occasion. The gun, wrapped in flannel, is placed lovingly in the back of the trunk; this has to go to the Cape as well, in case the elephants start running amuck again in the forests of Wynberg.*

*A suburb of Cape Town; the forests referred to, which were there once, have long since disappeared.

95

The dust-trail pushes our car forward up the rise. Zig-zagging, the road climbs up and up until the farmhouse far below and the protective trees in front of the house — not quite tall enough to offer shade yet, except for one plum tree a little further on where Linus and I played quoits while all around our feet lay the rotten plums which had dropped from the tree, and there were many bees which had come to sing around the mushy flesh of the fruit, and later both of us hobbled to the verandah with bee-stings like sword-stabs in our toes ("you shall dance on the tip of my sword," he said to her) — until the farmhouse in the little hollow and the protective trees trying to thrust the shadows toward the house as a dog bays at the moon become small and grotesque and until we are about to go down across a last narrow little ridge of the hill, now out of sight of the farm. Up to this point Uncle Taos has been sitting more or less twisted around in front next to Linus, holding the farm below and the surrounding fortress-koppies in both his eyes. At last he sighs pitifully before adjusting his position, and from here on in he hardly says a word or shows the slightest interest in the landscape racing by.

Singing, singing the car's rubber tires speed along the asphalt down a long valley — where many apples are grown — between tall mountain ranges on both sides: the Kouga Mountains, the Kamanassie Mountain in the distance (small tokens of esteem in these names, messages left by the people of the older civilization, our ancestors who were here before us), and further still the Groot-swartberg Mountains, and again later on the Langeberg Range. The windows of the car are halfway down: a hellish hot wind, arid, strains to enter. Uncle Tao does little talking from the top, merely farts at regular intervals. An inverted punctuation to what flies through the eye? Comment upon a dead landscape? Anguish at the thought of returning to the city? Distress signals? Joy in the farmfare he himself cooked these past few days? The reasons and causes for man's do's and don't's are secret and a mystery. As Paracelcus said: "Anyone who imagines that all fruit ripens at the same time as the strawberries know nothing about grapes."

The landscape quakes under the onslaught of the sun. Little Karoo. The lush fuck-all grows waist-high here too. Dead landscape. The route takes us into the void. *Le gout du vide.* (Almost observed with shiver of local pleasure.) Farm tracks turn off for no rhyme or

96

reason, two white trails, each time, heading for the iron-koppies. Hop! Behind the koppies lies the moon like a stranded whale. The creature is slaughtered and the fillets and hunks are stuffed into the hard ground — not on account of their fertility, but as mattresses for the dead to lie on so that they may perspire less. Is the earth not ripe in summer? The boulders, the fragments of rock are scattered over the earth like pared fruit.

The mountains dance. Shake the thoughts loose. Make a blood-shake of the thoughts which keep flowing drowsily where the land is lowest. Just let the thoughts dance, then, let them become scrub. There are no sheep here to eat the dancers anyway. *"Je n'ai que ma vie et je la risque aussitôt, chaque fois qu'une difficulté se présente. Danser alors est facile, car la pensée de la mort est une agile danseuse, ma danseuse, toute personne est trop lourde à mon gré; c'est pourquoi,* per deos obsecro: *que personne ne m'invite, je ne danse pas."* (How's that!)

The fact that we have to keep trying to search for communication in this way — trying to make contact — is it only for the connection, then, the kick?! The negative aspect of communication is that it is an impediment, an arbitrary representation of what should (could) be said, and of which the very means of communication forms in itself so great and qualifying a component already. The giving of form implies the killing of other potential forms (formulae? formations?). The louder you speak, the more broken the silences. Writing is pollution — for the writer certainly, even though he may not be touching his almighty ambition by means of writing (ambition, I am trying to say, is a genital organ in the intellect, a bone in the mind, and of even less use than a reed in the bog) — but also for the language, pollution also for the reader. And yet, we are sitting on the seesaw of history; we can't go on merely continuing to write like this about the lack of values, the inefficacy of writing itself. Writing is also *points of transition.* Should also *take a stand:* and give a *name* to the stand and *standing* to the name. And also, a poem for instance is a passage of the voice, of the breath (but I digress).

I need not mention your names
you need not be witnesses any more
grandpa Jan grandma Annie grandpa Hendrik grandma Rachel

and before you
            the gray line of ancestors
who now in a net of bones hold captive
                        the earth's crust
and before you
            o sacred
                black and yellow
heirs of Africa:
this land asking for water is given blood
this land which bears the fire within it

what remains?
the broken motion of an arm
describing lost riches
and now building gray buildings
and the tread of a foot
slashes open the proud rumbling of warriors
                                    dancing
around the bonfire high against star and wind
and the sudden still instinctive
                shake and stare!
of the blue and black eye
recalls a space sees far plumbs deeply
dream open remember
                and then vanishes again
behind the union of hate and fear

this land of memory
this land beyond history
this land of the dead
my land your land our land
this land asking for water is given blood
this land which bears the fire within it

But I must not digress too much. (I digress). And not insist so
stubbornly on trying to grasp and, worse still, interpret everything.
Trying too hard to understand. Trying to understand too much leads
to a standstill. All right then, it's hot. And so what?

Singing, singing on the tarred road, the Opel of Baas Dan. Oudtshoorn, Calitzdorp . . . . On the other side of Calitzdorp we stop in a ravine between red facades and walls of rock which trap and store the heat, and under drab picnic-trees we share the provisions purchased in the village. Uncle Tao has a jackknife, the only eating utensil we have between us for that matter, which contains a complete set of opening and cutting devices. Calitzdorp, Ladismith. In the front seat Uncle Tao talks little farts ten to the dozen. The people of this land — or more precisely, some of the people of this land — know how to build houses against the climate of extremes. They are seldom tall, but nearly always deep and then surrounded by a broad verandah, and a little further on, trees too with long branches full of shade. In these strongholds they entrench themselves against the destruction of the veld. That's why it is all the more striking that these people, understanding so intensely the need for shade, dared to house their farmworkers in small square dwellings without porches. Real ovens. If you were to ask them about it now, convinced of their charitableness, they would probably impress upon you that these tenants don't pay rent, that the dwellings have been painted, etc. For the ruling class, the white men from the dark ages, are convinced that they have good hearts, that they are just, that they offer protection, that they brought civilization. He who detects a smell of something rotten in the present system is either unrealistic (the soft little dreamer) or a communist — and the communists, as we all know, are nothing but jealous of our good life, they're after our diamond fields and our gold mines. It's not even a case of racism anymore. It's an ethnocentrism. It was decided long ago how and what the "other" is; we "understand" him, we "live" with him; he is "sin." We wear the glasses of a brutal oversimplification, a white-black division, a perverse puritanism, a willful stupidity. "Africa is tough," we say. And by "tough" we mean "simple to understand and easy enough to handle if you're man enough for the job."

And what is too ugly to make room for, I mean really make room for in the consideration of events, can always be laughed off in mutual understanding. Mr. A.S.K. Pitman inquired (during a court hearing? A judicial inquiry?): "I suppose shock treatment would make him talk faster?" And Captain G.N. Erasmus replied: "It will help his rheumatism." (And I imagine that the court hooted with laughter; even the quaking guy in the dock would have been hopping up and down until the tears poured down his cheeks.)

Ladismith, Montagu . . . . Don't look for trouble now, brother. Dance, let the associations roll; dance for your own death and that of your compatriots. These things in your country — such as Western civilization, isn't it? Such is progress. Uncle Martin, I came across a reference recently — I don't know in what context it was used, perhaps it was really poking fun — where Francois Mauriac had written: "*St. Augustin ce bougnoule.*" ("Augustine, that nigger.")

When we enter Montagu through the last gateway we are all babbling like lunatics about ice-cold white wine and water and shade. At Wellington we drop off Boesman. The hot wind in the back of the car prevented her from breathing. Her throat was dry.

We drive on to the Cape with Uncle Martin and take him home. And that's where the delicious wine is waiting. The Lord provides. Thereafter Baas and I drive to his house in Somerset West so that I can pick up the car he has offered us for the duration of our stay. We stop in the Strand. There's not a soul to be seen on the vast stretch of white sand. We change and run into the sea as if the fire of the Little Karoo is still fluttering on our shoulders. These are the moments making all disintegration bearable. The breakers come down on us, thick with water. Beyond the surf from the bottle-green depths someone suddenly surfaces in front of us. He is elderly and determined and dutiful and the tiny drops of seawater glisten in the little mustache meant to make him look like a man: "What is your orientation?" he asks me furiously, but I have already wheeled around and swum ashore faster than Johnny Weismuller and do not stop running until I reach Baas' house in Somerset West and jump into the car, sopping wet, and drive home, via Stellenbosch and Paarl, and the evening shadows grow longer and longer, like patches of scorched earth.

first prayer to the mantis

they say, little creator-insect, the old men say
that the star-fields and the worlds and all

100

that revolves and grows and sighs and perishes
were created by you, and that you planted an ostrich feather
in the dark and behold! there was the moon!
o primeval being,
        you who fired with love
consumes your lover, why then did you
abandon
their descendants — all mankind —
do you remember? those you called forth from the mud?
there are fires in the sky, mother, and the moon
is cold as shoe, and a black lament like smoke
mingled with dust — for your black people, peoplemaker, labor
like fertilizer in the earth so that money elsewhere
for others
may accumulate —
yolkyellow little praying priestess
        hear our smoke and our dust —
punish those who have reduced your people to slaves!

Yessir! I grew up in heaven surrounded by angels in dusty working clothes or floral aprons. That was near Riversdale. On a farm four miles from the village. Kafferkuilsrivier.

When our little trek arrived there that evening, it was already dark with a big round moon and Flash, the farm dog, to welcome us. Around Riversdale the moon is big and round. To tell the truth too, the moon lived in the cypress tree in front of the house. Deserted was the farmstead in the moonshine, and Flash barked. We stood in the yard and looked at the moon — it lay like frost over the yard — and sang.

There were seven of us in our family. Pa who became Oubaas, Ma before she was Ounooi, Jan, already Blikkies then, and Cloete Stinkie, Basjan who would later be De Beertjie, and me, and Dawid. Dawid was Dawid. He had been working for my father forever. (But before his time my father had another man working for him, long ago — Hansie. Hansie was a bachelor and he boarded with us, in a side-room. The maidservant also occupied one of the side-rooms at that time. This Hansie was terribly jealous, his bachelorhood notwithstanding. Couldn't bear some of the other men courting her on weekends. And consequently simply prevented them from coming into the yard, "for my baas doesn't like strangers wandering in and out of here." Threatened to beat them up. Then one evening when it was almost dark, Pa, in a mischievous mood and out to goad Hansie a little, hung his jacket on the gatepost and placed his hat on top so that it would look like a human being. And Hansie, as usual, came to take a look from time to time to keep a watchful eye; and it was a weekend and on weekends Hansie's eyes were not all they should be — weary from the week's work. And he looked . . . and looked again and then stormed the gate and laid into it with his fists, sending the hat reeling!)

This same Hansie was very handy with chickens. So Ma gave him two chicks, a hen and a rooster. These two stayed in a small coop in his room with him at first, and later, as they grew bigger, they would spend the night perched on the old-fashioned posts of his bed. Early in the mornings, at nightbreak even before the day had been able to free itself, the little rooster would crow high and wide.)

(But Hansie got TB . . . .)

(And climbed the Mountain, out into the wide world . . . .)

And Dawid came to Kafferkuilsrivier with us. He sang a lot and he cried a lot.

When Pa went back to Bonnievale in the Plymouth for two or three days every now and again. Dawid insisted on going too; wasn't he also from Bonnievale? Him and his family? And on the return journey Dawid was invariably drunk. Sozzled. Before long he would be singing lustily in the back of the car.

"Dawid!" my father would yell, "you bloody so-and-so, you damned miserable no-good washout, will you shurrup?!" If that didn't help, he would slam on the brakes, climb into the back, and punch. Dawid would be as quiet as a mouse. For another mile or so. Then it would be the same thing all over again. . . . Singing and punching, they would arrive home.

The baby did show up in the end. My sister, Rachel. Baby. Pinkydoll. Puddles. When the time came and the hour dawned, for when a child is born time breaks like the breaking of the day, and it was in the night, Pa tried to wake old Doctor Vansyl. The phone rang and rang. But the old bugger, he is also dead now, was already as deaf as death then. At his wits' end Pa decided to go and get him. He couldn't take the Plymouth because at night this was parked in the barn where the huge rats peed on it so much that you couldn't start it up. He was forced to use the truck which was always parked under the trees. It was a misty night. Pa had to crank the handle for an eternity before the engine fired.

Old Doc Vansyl came out to the farm just as he was, in his pajamas. And during the waiting for the time to come, they made coffee. Talked about all the old and new villages which should never have existed really, small and mission-stationish as they were then. Maliestyn, Prinsalbert, Vermaaklikheid. . . . Lone-church-hall villages.

My mother recounts that we refused to go to school the next morning without inspecting the newcomer first. What you haven't seen, you don't believe, and the eyes must take possession. Only then would she exist. (And we were curious; wanted to try to grasp events. All we knew was that Ma had become so fat and so jolly. It was at that time that she laughed like a finch.) The morning was misty, white, and cold, I remember it well. A trembling, something very tender and pale and dark at the same time, like a secret. The secretiveness of birth, a new little person in the house. And what is more, they said it was a girlchild! Four small boys standing outside, noses and foreheads and cheeks white with being pressed against the pane just, please, to be able to catch a glimpse of the newcomer. Until the old grumble-doctor called us in to take a peek. And we were allowed to tiptoe to the crib. (And it must have been wonderful, the birth, as wonderful as when a ewe in the yard or a cow in the shed gave birth, I would always watch that in fascination, the lamb or calf being pushed out, wrapped in a bag of mucus, how the ewe or the cow would clean it with her tongue, and its first awkward attempt at getting onto its feet.)

Three days later Basjan ran away from school, ran those four miles home, as Sub A small as he was then, and as far as he went he picked flowers for Pinkydoll. Sorrel!

That road was ours. Morning after morning we had to drive to school along it in a small horse-cart. We had to get out of bed long before dawn. Ma would dress me by candlelight while the others harnessed the horse. Pa would load a bag of alfalfa onto the back of the cart, and when I was wedged tightly between my two ungodly brothers — this was even before Basjan started school — on the bench, Cloete would crack the whip and start the wheels crunching on the frost which lay across the yard like moonlight morning after morning.

On the way there Cloete held the reins. In the afternoons it was Jan's turn, and to provoke Cloete he would lay into the horse with the whip. And frequently Charlie, our beloved Charlie, bolted. Sometimes because Jan was whipping him, other times because either the worn girth or one of the reins snapped, and occasionally it was a matter of cussedness, plain and simple. Always it was perilous, and we were miles off course before one of them was sufficiently brave to crawl along the shaft to curb old Charlie at the bit and force him to a halt. (In later years we were picked up at the farm gate by the delivery van transporting other children and milk cans to the village too. While we were waiting one morning, I happened to want to relieve my bladder urgently, but my brothers had to help me, clumsy as I was, to undo the buttons. My little me was barely beaming away in the cold frosty air, when they yelled: "There's the van!" and with malice aforethought they proceeded to put me back into my trousers, back to front.)

In the village we always unhitched at the first shop, just across the bridge. Uncle Martiens de Jager has stables for the farmers' horses in his backyard. Cloete loved animals; on the farm he and his feet were constantly surrounded by other dogs besides Flash. The fact that Charlie only had alfalfa to eat, stuck in his throat. One evening he complained bitterly to Pa how the other horses were given oats and how old Charlie peered longingly over his alfalfa at the fodder in the other troughs, until the tears eventually started trickling down Charlie's cheeks and clung in dampish tufts to his mane. (And then? Now that same Cloete is embittered against man *and* beast.)

I was barely-big-small at the time, and just in love with my first sweetheart — Annette, the headmaster's daughter. My brothers had to spend time than me at school every day, because they weren't as smart, and I had to wait for them in Uncle Martien's store. At the back of the store where it was dark, underneath harnesses and buckets hanging from the ceiling, where more grains of corn than one could think of filled brown hessian bags with gaping mouths, the type of bags tied up with an ear on both sides when full, waiting to be

104

scooped out and weighed, rustling and full of sunpebbles, where the smells were somber and cool and the heat in the street outside was only a distant singing, that's where I slept while the sun was setting, and that's where they would find me, curled up on the counter. Then we would go and pick out Charlie's great salty hindquarters among the other horses', the harness smelled white and insipid, and we would hitch him to the cart and start back long the koppies where the aloes grow pitch-black.

There was a shallow ford — a small bridge, really, but more of a ford than a bridge — just before you reach the last rise and the house. When the river was in flood, the bridge was impassable. On this very bridge Pa once hit a donkey-cart wham! head on. I don't know what became of the donkeys, but the driver plunged out of his nap right over the top of the bridge and into the river, nearly drowning among the reeds, and the shaft of the donkey-cart went straight through the dashboard and was sticking up between us.

It was the resulting damage to the car which led, not long after, to an expedition to the village. Jan and Dawid set out for the dairy with Charlie and the Trap full of milk cans. Just before reaching the village the road runs across a long bridge and then veers sharply to the left, passing under the trees and onto the tar. Charlie, presumably owing to the castigation of Jan's whip — he was a fascist even then — took the bridge at a crazy pace and couldn't make the turn at the other end. With a terrific din Trap and milk cans and horse hurtled to their destruction down into a ditch beside the road and up and out again, in among turnips and cabbages. An old lady living nearby got such a scare that her imagination caused the occupants to land in the mountain-brown whirlpool water of the Kafferkuils River. (O, how sweet that water was!) Distress signals were flashed across the telephone wires. Pa was on the land with his tractor. Lena, the woman who worked for Ma in the house, ran to the fields, hollering, with her apron over her head to signify the tidings of death to Pa. Uncle Frans Matthee was just drinking a cup of tea through his breathscraper-mustache with Ma, and he and she left forthwith in Uncle Frans' soft-top-Chevy. Cloete in hot pursuit on his cycle. Halfway to the village they met up with Jan and Dawid making their way back, unhurt. And when the procession turned around, they saw the cloud of dust raised by Pa heading flat out for the village on his tractor. At least the plow was not hitched on, if I remember correctly.

I also recall that fatal day when Charlie was to die. The sun could not have been shining that day, but there was light, for the scene is engraved on my memory like the grooves made by a slate pencil. He was probably suffering from horse-distemper and was in considerable pain. We were helpless. In the end he could no longer stand up straight, but kept milling round and round on his side, desperate, dying, with enormous poker-stiff wild eyes and frothing foam on his lips. Cloete or Jan, I don't remember which one, tried to soothe and comfort him for hours, tried for hours on end to lift the head, contorted in agony, onto his lap, and his shorts and his thighs were smeared with sticky foam. To us, at any rate, who stood crying at a distance, it felt like hours. (And now, many years later, Charlie is still dying.) Until Pa had mercy on the creature with his gun.

The remains were dragged away with a tractor and buried a short distance from the house. Maybe the grave was not deep enough or maybe the ground itself was rotting: in any case, the stench was unbearable a few days long and later. Our love grew fetid, our hearts rotten. There were gnats and blue-bottles like mourners at a rich man's funeral.

But Pa had another horse, De Wet, a thoroughbred chestnut that would prance around the yard with arched neck and snorting, at a brisk trot or a cocky canter. My father bought that horse on the other side of the mountain, and on its back he was a Field Marshall! Jan was the only son granted the privilege of riding De Wet each Friday evening. (Then again, Cloete was the truck driver although he was too short to reach the pedals and still see where he was going, so that the truck half overturned once, while crossing a ditch with an enormous load of hay, which slid down, burying the two farmhands who had been riding on top, fork and all.) Jan had to go to the veld with Dawid once a week to herd the wool-mob to the pen near the house so that the sheep could have their backsides sheared to keep the blue-bottles and the maggots at bay. On Friday evenings, therefore, even before the dust had settled, a sheep would be slaughtered. There was anxious bleating and scuffling and blood in the yard and the cantankerous old rooster which could kick you (or me!) so painfully just when you absolutely *had* to go to the privy out there in his territory, this old rooster stepping high in the evening light, with

106

much flapping of wings — very overwrought with bloodthirsty excitement.

On such evenings the sun would sink behind the reeds in the marsh along the river and it would be time for us to be scrubbed clean mercilessly in the iron tub on the kitchen table, and the stinging would be dreadful because our legs were continually covered with scratches received when playing on top of haystacks or while treading wool in the balers during the shearing season. (Shearing time . . . . The dour brown shearers outside in a row along the wall of the barn; the shears which are fragments of the sun; the sheep a grayish yellow like the ground and trapped in the ring, caught with forked sticks; and the tiny mouths of blood all over the snow-white naked skins . . . .) And it was time for the fig tree to scrape its branches eerily against the kitchen window; it was time for bean soup with boiled corn and bacon; and the evening prayers, the family prayers, the on-the-knees under the table peeking at each other or sometimes the awe and astonishment at the dark words coming so deeply from within Pa, the mysterious words — not just quasi-Dutch formulae anymore — which made him a stranger to us, a link, binding him to the generations whose blood is mingled in his veins, the words which are like biers for little-known relatives. In his prayers Pa talked to us, told us of his inner-talk. And when it came to question time after the reading, the whole day's living and hurt was often just one big lamp above the table, a lamp singeing the moths, and sleep would overtake me open-eyed.

Outside Flash watched the night, from the pens down past the coriander lands which shoot by shoot resembled dahlias at flowering time (so that Vannermerwe, the policeman, stopped on the farm road one day — it was a policeman's duty to keep an eye on all the goings-on in his district, wasn't it? — and said to his sidekick in the side-car: "Well, I'll be damned, if you'll look at those fields of flowers! You can take my word for it, that farmer's a madman!") and when it was ripe, it was threshed blow by blow by Mai and Pai — two Hottentots and one a straw-cutter, both older than Yore, older even than the Old Testament—to the bottom of the fruit orchard where the tallest walnut tree in human memory grew, as shiny as brand-new Buicks, and golden sourcheek quinces, and pomegranates, and prickly pears — and I'm not even counting the aloes since they were just aloes.

There was honey, though it had to be smoked out of hives and though the bees covered us with welts. There was milk which was milked warm and foaming from cows with a good many whoa's and easy-now's, though you were obliged to move your stool all the time to keep up with the udder. There was an earthen dam which was a sea for a zinc bath (Zinc Bath the Sailor), even though the thing irrevocably sprang a leak well-nigh midway between America and the Coast of Death. There were duck-soldiers in the reeds and red-straw plovers right there on the bank. There were caves in the veld and robbers in the poplar grove. There was a loft where only apples could be eaten. And there was going to the village. To go and see Tarzan that evening when we were almost trampled to death by the hordes. Or going to the village all spruced up and in our Sunday best to see King Djords and his wife White Train* and when we got there even the taillight of the train had already disappeared and then there was nothing to do but to try and beg one of those medals with the safety pins from the other children. Or (going to the village) simply to sit outside the hotel in the car, waiting. Until Pa, turning into the yard one afternoon, missed the road and the bridge and we were obliged to climb in an upward direction to get out through the doors.

For already there was wine in the land then. Dawid received his two bottles on Saturdays, and occasionally Lena, too. One Christmas Uncle Koot and his wife were paying us a visit, and on the day before we all had a picnic down by the river. (The river was the boundary between Uncle Gert Muller's farm and ours. In the river was an islet. We boys — that is to say including Gert and Gys of Uncle Gert and Aunt Mattie, and Johan — held our deliberations there. Flash was so strong he could pull you through the river while swimming if you held onto his tail. Then we would dig some of the lovely saffron-yellow and red clay out of the riverbanks to make clay-oxen, or ammunition for our clay-sticks. That's where we kicked the puff-balls to pieces to see the dust fuming up. And sometimes we would round up the white horse belonging to Uncle Gert's ancient deaf

*King George VI and his family who paid a visit to the Union of South Africa, still a member of the British Commonwealth then, in 1947; the White Train was the special train in which the Royal family toured the country.

108

squatters in the corn field on the opposite bank and ride him without saddle or bridle. That's where Absalom was left hanging in the tree. And that's where my sweetheart-in-the-mulberry-tree sang a love song to me.) The roast for the following day was already in the oven, however, and Lena, whose task it was to keep an eye on the kitchen, had already received her Christmas present: a bottle of red wine, not to be outdone by Dawid. When we came home late that afternoon, Lena was lying under the table, snoring, and Dawid was seated next to the fireplace, singing. And all that remained of the roast was the aroma. Ma got at Lena's ribs with her foot. When she realized what was happening she flung her skirts over her head right there. And when the enormity of his misdemeanor caused Dawid's glassy cross-eyed gaze to widen too, he let forth one roar and then bolted right across the wide yard and headlong into the marsh, sending the reeds snapping and the sun flying off again, dripping wet. Luckily it was not the last time we laid eye on him, because Dawid was fond of my father and Pa was fond of Dawid. They were a twosome. (Dawid, for that matter, was broody and grumpy when other workers were brought in to help with the shearing and the tomato-planting. Ostensibly he would have nothing to do with "trash" and always worked on his own away from the others. Then he would draw himself up on the slightest pretext in all his dignity as "foreman" and snap at them: "Hey! Do you know what this farm is called? 'Do Or Die'!") But unfortunately this was not the last of his sins either.

Pa hired a Malay to drive the tractor, a sharp fellow who knew his onions, and robust. He was newly in Pa's service — and Pa had just bought him a new khaki shirt, khaki pants, and shoes — when it was decided that we should spend a weekend at the beach. At Stilbaai. Ma did some baking and bustled about. Pa filled up the Plymouth. He also had a sharecropper working for him on the farm, who went by the name of Klasie Otto — a washout of a fellow. Otto and the farmhands were to see to it that the tomatoes were watered. Underneath the oak tree there was a hefty sow, allegedly thoroughbred, and very expensive, which was scheduled to produce young that very weekend. Orders were that she too was to be kept wet.

When it came to pulling the car out of the garage so that we could load up, it didn't take Pa long to discover that there wouldn't be enough room for all our junk, since Ma never takes to the road without a past and a sturdy future. Nothing to do then, but to load up the truck instead. We departed with bedsteads and tents and provisions for an army of Khakis. We had hardly cleared the first hill, needless to say, before Otto took the blue Plymouth into the village. Spent some time in the hotel, since it was warm, and drove into the damwall on the way back. Not much of a driver. And when he reached the farm, the Malay said: "Now it's our turn. Hand over the keys." "Not on your life," protested Otto lamely, but when the Malay threatened to ventilate him with a knife, he decided it would be more expedient to let the baas' Plymouth take its own course.

Not counting Abdul who took the wheel, four more men climbed into the car. And among them, in the back, was Dawid, drunk as a lord. Because this was his master's car, and where the car goes Dawid goes, all the way to Bonnievale.

Supposedly, the idea was to go to the Cape. Unfortunately some people don't feel that they are truly driving if they can't also stop at a gas station. Even though the tank is full. And in the village the garage owner smelled the rat and called Vannermerwe. The Plymouth was cornered right there. Abdul was arrested after biting Vannermerwe's sidekick's little finger right off. Dawid too, in his state of inebriation. The others ran. When matters were investigated on the farm, they found Otto at the organ in the living room. It was a fine harmonium and Otto was fond of music.

When we returned on Sunday, Dawid and Abdul were behind bars, Otto was still playing the organ, and the sow was bone-dry and burned-to-a-frazzle by the sun, the unborn piglets probably dead in her belly. The case was heard on Monday. Pa had to testify. About halfway through the proceedings the court adjourned to give the magistrate and the public prosecutor the opportunity to go and check that all was still well at the hotel. The accused, next to Vanner-merwe, meanwhile, simply waited in court. Pa, too. Thinking: such an expensive sow, and on top of that the new clothes, and my crooked car with the fender buckled by crashing into that damwall — and the next thing he knew he was standing in front of Abdul and punching. One blow only. Abdul crumpling. (*Sock it to 'im, Pa!*) Vannermerwe just about wetting his pants. "No Lordie, Uncle Breytenbach! What's Uncle doing now?"

"You must excuse me," Pa said, and he brought his brown hand to his eyes, "I was blind."

Abdul was given three months. Dawid twenty days or a one pound ten fine. Because of his drunkenness.

"Baas," Dawid wanted to know, "will Baas bail me out?"

"Yes, Dawid."

And the two of them went back to the farm and Dawid bent down over a full bag of corn and Pa took a strap and gave Dawid a sound thrashing.

Yessir! When it grows dark, I hear the wind coming through the trees. The branches groan as though corpses are hanging from them. To paralyze Lena, we would hang some of the corpses from our imagination from those branches on moonlit nights, and she would end up shivering under the table with her dress over her head. And sometimes, when the sun flashes across a stone, I smell the woolly warm smell of sheep. And when I shut my eyes tightly and curl up into a little ball on the floor, I hear the beating of my heart, and then I listen carefully, for beyond those beats of a heart attached beat by beat to the heart of long ago, lie orchards, people, worlds, I. Then all that still exists. Almost. Then heaven is round. Nearly.

Dawid is dead. Pa told me that this evening. And he's not a young man anymore either. While he gazes, down the hall, out across the verandah, into the village street, into the night, back again. He sat talking to himself. "Dear old Dawid," he mumbled.

When we had to leave the farm because Pa had gone bust, and after we had tried once already to give Flash away to a guy called De Jager, and Flash who had a mind of his own had come back again dreadfully thin, his orange-golden skin devoid of the old gloss, and after he had been given away a second time — after all that, Dawid, who was to have stayed behind on the farm, who would not be coming to the village with us, squatted against the wall and wept as though his heart was mute, and without a drop of wine in his body.

"But what are you crying for, Dawid?" Pa asked, "wasn't I always beating you?"

"Yes, Baas. But it was all out of love."

It was love's all.

Please don't cry, Dawid.

(When I was little, an unkempt and elderly fellow was always setting up his easel right in front of Pa's service station — that's the service station in the hollow of the road leaving Riversdale, just where it makes a turn and picks its way, as it were, and starts running more deliberately like a road which knows where it's going; and I could never work out why the man came there to paint, for what was there to be seen but the dark pine forest across the way: a somber waterfall full of pigeons bouncing up and down like springboks? At the bottom of his paintings, which he always signed before applying paint, I saw his name: *Winsent van Gog*. All day and every day he stood there, even in the hottest heat of the water-eyed-noon. Always dressed in the same clothes: a very wide and very short and very grubby pair of linen trousers, a black shirt topped (by day) by a wide-brimmed straw hat with stunted little candles fastened all around and onto the rim of the hat. His calves and feet were rough and chapped, his hair and beard wild and red, redder even than the pointed flames of the candles. There he would stand, painting with abrupt and threatening gestures swiftly: a few seconds of fixed staring in front and a little to the right; then sweep-swap swipple-swopple dotted onto the palette with a brush and from there on hurry-hurry diligent-little-hairs on the canvas as if his brushes were fingers and the colors coals. And the scene was invariably the same — and not once did it correspond to anything which could be seen in the environs of Riversdale. For our service station was but a drab place, covered with the dust kicked up by the sheep farmers' trucks which came to fill up there: The painting then: always a kind of wheat field in which, or from which, a red sun was attempting to hide or escape—and Riversdale, Albertinia, and thereabouts wasn't even wheat-growing country. In the evenings when the service station had already closed down for the night and the dog had been chained to the gas pump to stop the workpeople from siphoning fuel, he would still be standing there; and always, just before it grew completely dark, he would blow out the candles and very savagley draw a big cross through the fresh paint [as in raw flesh]; then he would wait until the moon rose and the sun on the canvas began to glow like an ember, before starting to scream most horribly — like an animal — and curse and try to drive away the vehicles which had long since stopped going by, evidently on account of the dust; and Pa would never allow me to put milk outside for him in that little blue enamel scoop-bucket of ours. Was it the black land of the pine forest — such a treacherous nest for the moon — which upset him so? I don't know. Years later, when the service station was sold, *Winsent van Gog* was included in the sale price as being a living advertisement and curiosity. But much later still, a wheat field actually did take the place of the dark forest. It seems that *WvG* forgot to snuff out the candles one evening and rushed into the forest, flaming and moaning, as bright as a sun from space to space, so the story goes, and set forest and night ablaze. The forest was burned down to such a stump that the farmers could start growing wheat there — and his charred corpse is probably lying there too somewhere under the sod like a burned-out meteorite quenched by the rain, embalmed by the sun, and absorbed in the rustling golden stalks sweeping across the blue canvas with sturdy little brush-strokes. That's why bread sometimes leaves an aftertaste of thinners in the mouth.)

("Confidence is: going home at night — after a visit to Uncle Gert and Aunt Mattie and Gys and Minnie which ended late — the whole family one after the other along the footpath down to the river, across the little bridge and then up the hill to our house, squarely white in the moonlight "like the bark of a yard-dog"; for there is moonlight and there are large living pulsating stars in the immeasurable space of the night; and the peaceful sounds of people walking along a footpath, and the dark, like the first people, like people of all time; the dark is friendly, the river-spirits will bear us no malice though the mistiness may lie like early breath upon the water, and words are exchanged and passed along the row, and occasionally little laughs or sighs too; and I am already more or less beyond myself in the infinite love of untroubled sleep, so that Pa has to lift me onto his shoulders and I smell the brown protection of his arms: we belong to the earth and we can walk over the entire earth.")

Only the sun survives

January nineteenth, 1973. On the way to the Karoo, across the Du Toitskloof Pass, passing along the Hex River Valley and then Touws-rivier, Matjiesfontein, and from there on the world seems without end, without variation. It's hot. If you don't make an early start today, you're going to discover you've been found out. Even so you must walk in the veld in two's because, as a friend put it, if the sun found you alone today, it would stab you to death on the spot.

The sky is as opaque and as blue as a human eye; focus, there certainly is: when you step out of the car, it is definitely you who are the focal point of the sun. Yet, that eye doesn't spot you; you are just one more ant on this merciless plain. The eye is a magnifying glass.

In a book entitled *A Separate Reality,* Carlos Castaneda describes how he is initiated by the elderly Don Juan into shamanism. At one point, under the influence of a ritual aid, he must endeavor to obtain admission to the Otherworld. But that Otherworld has a "keeper" who must be defeated first. Castaneda gives an account of his confrontation and combat with this hideous, polywinged, armored monster and when he comes to his senses again later, he is lying on his side next to a perfectly ordinary gnat on a blade of grass in front of his nose.

Just as formidable and equally ubiquitous are the cicadas, the keepers of the local Otherworld. You don't see them, but you're constantly aware of their presence. The noise they make is as piercing as the sound of an electric saw or the whining of a drill, only shinier — the characteristic sound of the insect, something having life, but that life is inhuman with its own peculiar rhythm and intelligence, and because it is incomprehensible, it is menacing. After a while the metallic whirring of the cicadas and the heat of the sun are confused so that one might say: the sun hums, the sun sings.

First you become aware of the heat — not so much that of the sun, since the entire universe above and below is sun — and then, of the apparent absence of color. As the blue of mountains and the green of trees also fade in the inner eye, however, there is a growing consciousness of the colors characteristic of the Karoo — the black and gray scrub, the red and yellow of the earth, all the boulders in their many shades.

114

Yolande sits bolt upright in the front of the kombi. She doesn't want to wear dark glasses because, according to her, it would take all the colors away. To her this primeval world must be almost Biblical, something until now existing only on the pages of geography books.

And no matter where you look, how you search, there is no sign of life, and no hint or rumor or promise of rain. The only farming done hereabouts is with sun and stones, and the stones are thriving!

It's our intention to learn, if possible, how the people live in this land of drought; how they adapt themselves to the climate and the circumstances, if indeed they do; what, if any, their prospects are.

We stop at Laingsburg and call on two helpful Agricultural Extension Officers* to try to obtain some kind of general view of the problems of the district. These people sympathize with the way the farmers feel, but at the same time they have to try to remain objective. The impressions we receive of the farmers, by way of these two, are confirmed later in personal contacts — an incantation of hardship, an acquiesence, a dogged perseverance: man clinging to the earth, but the earth turning to dust.

With the exception of a few scattered showers, the last time it rained in this region was in August 1971 — time and again we would be struck by the water-clear memories of the people; everyone knows, down to the exact day, when it last rained, and the last rain before that one, and before that, and ... Actually the present drought is not exceptional. Statistics covering the past 41 years show that it was partially dry for 49% of that period, and for 21% of that time dry altogether, and altogether means the proclamation of emergency grazing camps.

Drought, in fact, is not a deviation, it is the norm. And it would seem, too, that conditions are gradually deteriorating even further. It is difficult to determine the average rainfall, but it is not more than four to five inches per annum at the most.

Then what exactly is a state of emergency? According to one of the spokesmen, it is when the life of a man or beast is endangered, then it is an emergency.

The air-conditioning in this pleasant office ensures a delicious

*Officials of the Department of Agriculture who are stationed all over the country to assist and advise farmers on agricultural matters.

coolness. It is here that farmers with calloused hands come and try to account for the terrible reality on the veld outside where the countryside trembles under the onslaught of the sun. It is arid, dusty. Against a hill behind the village, white boulders spell the legend: WEAR WOOL LAINGSBURG. "But the wool has gone to the dogs, the meat market has gone to the dogs . . . ."

Wear Wool. Over the hill a new village—a "scheme"*—has been established for brown people. Now they themselves say: "We live in Wearwool."

We ask whether many sheep have already died and whether the farmers have to feed all of them. (To me the distinguishing feature of drought is the grimacing skulls of sheep.)

"No, I can't really say that the sheep are dying yet. But almost all of the farmers are stock-feeding. Some farmers are too proud of course to apply for the subsidies. They're afraid that folks will say they are bad farmers. There are some who are still holding out. There will always be those who'll even sell a dung-cake, won't there, and then its shadow too.

"Heck, if only the donkeys and the ostriches hadn't cleaned out the soil so . . . ."

And Laingsburg isn't even worst off. They say it's really bad around Prins Albert. Is there no end to it then?

"There's nowhere to flee to in the Republic. It's dry everywhere. And what's the use of selling the ground now? You're lucky if you get six rand a morgen at today's prices. It was eight not so long ago."

But statistics teach you nothing except figures. We must try to meet the farmers themselves. We stop at the gas station and an excited little girl asks Yolande whether this is the circus at last!

We drive back across the Buffalo River. River? What river? When was the last time people here saw water in the river? One may as well put up a signpost to a river anywhere along the dry road; the veld could lay equal claim to that designation.

Just like you, the other travelers through this god-forsaken countryside are tied to the heat-belt running across the hazy hills. Only that which is made of metal, only that which is seasoned and headstrong, can exist here. The vehicles drone on of their own

*Properly "development scheme," i.e., a new township.

116

volition; the drivers are turned to stone, clutch the steering wheels as though these are their lives. Even the cars can't bear it in the long run: we passed several car-cemeteries, full of wrecks and carcusses, the color of rust like the stones.

Occasionally one sees a farmhand on the road, on foot, gaunt in his or her ragged clothes, seemingly without a where-from and without a where-to-then.

Leaving the tarmac for the gravel road, one moves across the desert in a tower of dust. At the first farm, given the hope-lost name of Fish-water-hole, we stop. Mr. Alwyn Nel's farm, but he is away. An iron-roofed house entrenched behind windmills and small patches of corresponding greenery give the whole the look of an oasis. It's a humble dwelling and yet the occupants are regarded as some of the district's more well-to-do residents.

In the Karoo man and beast are branded by the sun. An old billy-goat in the yard stumbles out of the way of our kombi. A lame dog, decayed and stinking from the eternal sun's standing, comes bounding at us.

Mrs. Ralie Nel tells us about the water holes which are drying up, except for one windmill, and that one is brackish. And the rain, she says, has never stayed away so widely before.

"All the people, all the districts are having an equally hard time," she says with a wave of her arm over the nothing," it's all becoming desert . . . .

"Some of the womenfolk were obliged to find jobs in the village. Not for much of a salary either. Some farmers spend the week there too and drive out to the farm on weekends to keep an eye. Well, what else can you do?"

They've been farming here since 1939, but the last 15 years or so have become more and more of a struggle. "We're back where we started from."

Two of her sons have left home. One works as a mechanic. It's as though life on the farm doesn't agree with them. Except, that is, for the second one, Koot. "He gets on with the job."

Below, where the river used to be in the old days, a handful of peacocks and guinea-fowl scatter as we approach. Yolande is fascinated by the enormous spike-thorns of a tree which has toppled over or been dragged along by the floodwaters. I tell her about clay

117

oxen and she picks some of the spike-thorns for Paris. The sun sits in the trail of the windmill and it glitter-flashes and creaks. From somewhere comes the stench of a dead sheep.

It's feeding time for the sheep. The soil is inhospitable. A cork-old farmhand and his grandson, Dawid, shake the alfalfa out onto the hard earth. The old man also has difficuly walking. Sheep huddle together against the fence and bleat and beg just like hungry people. Drought has tamed them. Even to the lay eye they seem sun-lean, stunted.

The sun is just beginning to set as we head back for the village. I don't think one ever dares look the sun in the eye here. By evening the koppies grow black and beautiful with a terrible melancholy beauty. There are more windmills in the village than there are television aerials on the roofs of some small Italian towns.

Paintings of water scenes cover the dining room walls in the Grand Hotel where we stay overnight — dams, seawater, even a wall hanging depicting a Dutch village with its canals and water mills. Everyone talks about water, remembers — to the last detail! — about water, dreams about water. The same would be true for the hotel in Prins Albert the next day. Here there was even a painting of a fat dam in the middle of the gray Karoo and, standing on the bank among the reeds, an ephemeral young woman in Victorian dress, gazing her eyes out at the water.

We are served at table by a middle-aged brown woman whose legs are giving her a good deal of trouble. Her total toothlessness gives her a permanent tongue-in-cheek look. How do the brown people, at least the ones working at the hotel, feel about the drought? "Well, the Lord looks after us. Laingsburg is dry, but it has enough water. We get our water from below, as you know. Yes, the farmers complain, of course. You see, they want the water from above."

In the twilight outside one looks for a purpose to this reality. Surely the people can't just live their lives away in this sweltering heat? But the vicious circle is inevitable: it doesn't rain and the clumps of grass and shrubs die and when the rain finally does come, there's nothing to hold it, the stones don't help, do they? and the soil is washed away and what is left is dry so that there's nothing for the scrub to grow on.

And the village, like the country, runs dry. At the last census there were 3 112 people in Laingsburg — some 800 white people; the Asians had to go, but there are still 15 of them left, of the elderly; the rest are brown people. The village still has a high school, but this should really have been scaled down to a secondary school by now. The number of pupils is declining.

The drought is driving some of the farmers to town and dispersing the young people to other regions. It's the end of the week. We chat with some of the farmers who own townhouses. Mrs. Salomi Conradie, Mr. Tom Conradie's wife, now lives in town permanently. She had to go out to work, even though some of her children are still small and at school. For all intents and purposes she and her husband are now living apart. A young Mr. Nel — tough and brown from the sun, with bleached hair — and his wife, Daphne, are visiting the Conradies. More farmers are finding themselves in a similar precarious position. "I mean, we are *dry* now, aren't we?" Mr. Conradie says, and they are waiting here in town for the veld to come alive again.

"It's not that I like the work, Sir," Mrs. Conradie says, and Mrs. Nel nods in agreement. "And the work isn't difficult either. But I'm counting the days. We don't have a family life anymore. And since I've been here, it's as if I've lost my vitality, too. I don't even feel like reading any more, and I used to be so fond of reading.

"Yes, of course, the moment it becomes possible again, I want to go back.

"Oh, but you should see the veld after the rains! We have color slides of what it looked like up here in the hills two years ago. One unending stretch of flowers as far as the eye can see. And the commotion when it rains! The telephones don't stop ringing, all the lines are busy. Then everyone flocks down to the bridge to see the river in flood. Last time there was such a crowd that the police were called in to control the traffic. And then when the water has passed, we race to the next bridge to watch it all over again!

"But these are hard times, Sir," Mrs. Nel relates. "I can tell, you see, because I'm also working in a shop. The farmers are buying only the bare necessities: salt, sugar, oatmeal, coffee, tobacco. No more luxuries."

You ask the same questions over and over again, you try to find solutions, and always you get the same questions back again. The farmers sit in the corners of this townhouse room, in the flickering shadows of the lamplight, and they seldom look up. This is not the first evening they're mulling over these questions, these are every day's questions of existence. They look out of place here, stocky, brown, too large and awkward for the walls of the village.

As Mr. Conradie says: "Even the grasshoppers die here from the drought. It may be that some of the farmers are responsible themselves for the erosion. But what can you do? Convert the farm into something else? No, I don't think it's possible. There are people around here who wanted to be karakul sheep farmers. Have you ever seen the way a karakul tramples a piece of ground? I mean, they don't spread out, but huddle together in one spot. You can tell at a distance where there are karakuls grazing: there's usually a cloud of dust.

"And what's more, the idea of killing those young lambs puts me off."

But why go on then?

"What else can we do?" Mr. Conradie asks in reply. "You are born a farmer. And you retain your contact with nature. Today a lamb is born, tomorrow an old ewe dies. It's nature." And he tells us how his young daughter, on her return after being discharged from hospital, had simply sat down on the side of the road and had thrown stones and gravel up over her head for sheer joy.

And Mr. Nel explains how you can lock up finches in a cage without a tree, and how for generations they will nest on the ground, but just try hanging a couple of branches inside the cage and leave them a little grass, and in no time the descendants of those original birds will start building a nest in the branches.

"Each day is a challenge. You have to plan it from dawn until dusk. Try a different type of work? At our age? Go out into a dark world which is beyond our comprehension? Then give me, instead, the darkness ahead, on the farm."

For how long will they be able to go on like this? Twenty, thirty years? And then?

Above the koppies the Milky Way glitters like sparks spewed from a volcano. At night the veld still smells. Then it's almost as if there is little mercy.

This is barrenness itself, and alien, and not to Yolande alone. Man can come and vanish again and no trace of him will remain.

Yolande is amazed at the multitude of stars. Everything is dispro-
portionately big here: the distances, that the sun is always shining,
every day . . . . That everything is so bare. She wonders how the
people really live, how many times a day or a week they eat meat,
what do they read?

Before we leave the area the following day, my brother takes a
few more shots on Fish-water-hole at Mr. Alwyn Nel's. He asks us in.
The living room is dark and cool. There are lynx hides on the floor.
Yolande studies the ancestral portraits, oval-shaped and tinted,
hanging from the molding on the wall.

Mr. Nel is like an old tree growing stronger and stronger with
age. Sometimes his eyes roam the yard. What is he looking for?
Whether something is amiss at the barn?

"Yes, man should not speak out against nature, but it must be
one of two things. Either there is less and less water, or the veld is
growing poor. We used to be able to count on a good year after a leap
year" (— and he enumerates them, year by year, from the turn of the
century, and they are a mere handful too —), "but 1949, now that
was the last one.

"But the rain stays away. Some people say it's because of that
man who went about chopping the heads of the little karakul lambs, I
don't know.

"And the days of trekking to better pastures as before are over.
The roads are all just paths nowadays, and anyway, where would we
take the animals to?"

We say good-bye and turn our vehicle to face the Swartberg
Mountains. The horizon shimmers like water caressed by the wind.
It's silent, the silence of stars also present by day.

the shrubs are smoking kernels
the only fruit growing
the sun

eyes burning wet with searching for rain

dust you are
like everything under foot

and in the shade
of the subterranean cool
you will huddle waiting

to be allowed to form part of
the sun
but then at least in the shade

(footnote)

But the history of this land is a history of drought. Throughout the years, through each year runs the theme the thread the elegy of drought. Every summer it grows large and red and ripe. And sometimes it just runs right through the year and through a few subsequent years as well, until the earth is a fire, and the dust is smoke. Our farmers, generation upon generation, are weary people leaning on the lower halfdoor and gazing far into the distance with red-rimmed eyes, on the lookout for clouds. And the names of the farms bear witness to this, the bitter farmnames like tombstones: *Courage Lost. Stone-fountain, Sourmarsh, Cheat-pan* .... You only have to look at our literature!

As my brother says: "One of these days they'll be riding camels in Bloemfontein!"

And speaking of camels. This thing, drought, is creeping across the length and breadth of Africa at present. They say that the Sahara, like the Karoo, encroaches each year on an ever-wider area, creeps forward mercilessly like a glacier on a downward journey. The proud and independent nomadic peoples of the Sahel countries — Niger, Senegal, Mauritania, Upper Volta, and Chad — the "Blue People" (Tuareg) and the Peul, they who walk upright with a sword at their side and a veil across the mouth, the rulers of the desert, robbers and toll-gatherers, they who walk ahead of their own herd of cattle as a means of proving their manliness, the "sons of the sun" — the drought drives them southward to the contemptible villages, and there they are forced to wait for a little flour and sugar from the government, and their children perish from the unfamiliar diseases of the village, and the skeletons of their camels lie in the desert like the masts and rigging of ships run aground, covered there by time and sand. And already the drought is beginning to eat into the more protected zones of Ethiopia and the Sudan.

Hell*

In the old-old days, long before our time, even before man became a baboon and then discarded his tail and most of his hair again, there was a graybeard Chinese poet who went to live in seclusion on his estate, far from the roaring laughter of the court and the clamor of the capital's wooden carts. Tao Ch'ien was his name, or Tao Yuan Ming — old Tao the Boozer. He was one of those philosophers who sang the praises of the simple rural life and valued it more than all the fame and honor and the intrigues of officials; who wanted no more than an occasional chat with the neighbor across the fence, a jug of green wine, and a little late-night music. And sometimes a poem. And this existence, such philosophers believed, stripped of the embellishments and appendages of power and station, divested of that sickly little bird in a cage — the ego aided by remedies and brews and potions of this and of that, would place immortality in their lap. And yet, until now, it has always remained just beyond reach.

One day, so Tao tells us, he went for a walk along a mountain stream, and through a crevice in the mountain (or perhaps it was a cave; I don't recall exactly now), he found himself in a marvelous valley, heavy with the fragrance of peach blossoms. Among those peach blossoms he encountered people who were indeed immortal. After a while, however, he had to go back, and no matter how hard he tried afterward, he was never able to find the valley again. And from that time on even the slightest allusion to "peach blossoms" in a

*A fertile valley virtually cut off from the "outside world" because of its situation (see *Notes on Persons and Places*). Properly *The* Hell (from Afrikaans *Die Hel*). The Author no doubt intends all its meanings.

123

Chinese poem was sufficient to conjure up again before the mind's eye enticing images of that sad lost paradise. Immortality is a peach blossom . . . .

When we went in search of Hell recently, we knew that the valley was no longer as lost and cut off from "civilization" as before. A road to it existed, in fact, for a good ten years now — well, just call it a road then! "Truly, Sir," one inhabitant said, "now that's one thing I would have liked my father to see before he died — that road. If I had told him that something like that would be coming down the gorge, he would have laughed at me."

The miracle has happened. One takes the Swartberg Pass from Prins Albert: the gravel road climbs up the slopes of the mountain, higher and higher, flanked on both sides by the most formidable rock formations and ravines. There are abysses and outcrops and ledges in the mountain-faces, and a multitude of colors — fever-green, red, purple — almost as though the Lord were very dissatisfied here and simply swept this little lot aside.

A signpost at the top, pointing to the right, reads: *Gamkaskloof*. Hell. The Other Place. Scribbled writing indicates that we have another 22 miles to go from here.

The road to Hell isn't that wide at all; on the contrary, they say it was made singlehandedly by a certain Bossie van Zyl, with a bulldozer, that the bulldozer later careened down the mountain, but that the road-maker was able to enter into matrimony, at least, with the teacher who lived down there. It's understandable — the tumble down the mountain — because the fall of an eagle with only one wing could hardly be more broken than the way in which this road plunges to its end.

On the way there, rhebuck and even an impala duck the kombi, only to stop again a few bounds away, as tame as dogs.

We stop on the last pass to look at our destination: the valley, a green paradise, lies at our feet. A warm wind thrusts upward along the slopes. Immediately in front of us a hawk circles slowly, higher and higher, seemingly unaware of our presence, then hangs motionless (like breath suspended), it's whole attention focused on a reptile or small veld creature far below and invisible to our untrained eyes, waits, and suddenly plummets down like a dead weight. Below us Hell wears a monochrome blanket with a contrasting patch of

124

cultivated soil here and there. The valley is not very broad; at its broadest probably no more than four hundred paces from wall to wall, but a good fifteen miles long from east to west, and obviously fertile.

A road coils silvery up along the contours of the valley in the dying light. On both sides the mountain-swellings tower, and further back, more mountains, row upon row of them, misty as ancient history. From here our gaze meets the setting sun so that the landscape is hazy, a filmy faded blue. Chinese ink drawing.

"All rightish, eh?" my brother says, and I hear the shutter of Yolande's camera *click-click, click-click* behind us. The wind has made its nest in her hair.

The view almost wants to go on endlessly, like *on and on forever,* a poem by Li Ho:

The white glare withdraws to the Western hills,
High in the distance rise blossoms of sapphire.
Where will there come an end to old and new?
A thousand years fluttered away in the wind.
The sand of the ocean turns to stone . . .

Because the valley stretches in an east-west direction, it stays light here until late, in the summer at any rate, although the walls around Hell are very high. Thus small embers of sun are left among the long since burned-out shadows, when we reach the bottom.

At the first sign of life we stop to ask if we may spend the night on the owner's property. A couple of black-headed sheep and a goat lie groaning with dreams in the yard, and a huge old pig is rooting about under a pepper tree. Mrs. Anna Mostert is sitting on the porch of her house, built, like all the houses around here, by the occupants themselves. A dignified woman, upright, with sky-black hair and larkspur-blue eyes, and, when you least expect it, a sudden shyish smile.

We deliver reading matter, for journals from the "outside world" always arrive three weeks late, and ask how things are.

"No, not so good here either. Not a drop of water in the river and we have no wells. The old man has just gone to do some watering. At least we still get a trickle from the spring up in the mountain which can be diverted through pipes."

Drought's trail of death lies here too. The farmers have long since destroyed their cows and donkeys, and only one farmer still owns a horse or two. The drinking water comes mostly from the gôrês, the wells or holes dug for seepage water in the riverbed. A shepherd points out to us that the showers which have nevertheless fallen, are not enough even "to wipe out a spoor." Even those sheep they have managed to keep have grown too emaciated to be slaughtered and, like the villagers, they are now obliged to get their meat from the butcher.

And whether the countryside has changed much around here since the building of the road and since the telephone has been running across the mountains? But, apparently, the isolation is just as great as before. While we chat the telephone rings shrilly a couple of times, short rings followed by long ones. "It's a party-line, you know, Sir. And the other people join in so loudly in the listening with you, that you can't hear a thing. You don't see many strange faces here. As for me, I always like to see one. Some families have moved away. My brother-in-law's gone off, too, only yesterday. But others have moved in. A railway worker, Cordier, from Beaufort West, up here in Kafferskloof, with children at least, for otherwise the school would be forced to close down . . . ."

A one-man school is not allowed to have fewer than ten pupils if it doesn't want to become a farm school. At present eleven little mites fill the benches. In France there are foreigners, too — Spanish or Portuguese migrant laborers mostly, as long as they have children of school-going ages — much in demand in some of the smaller communities, and for the same reason.

There are nine farms in the valley and not one of them is really large — the one owned by Uncle Henk Mostert, for example, covers twenty-six morgen — and eleven families, i.e., roughly forty people. Almost all of them share the same family-names: Mostert, Marais, and Cordier.

Mrs. Mostert with the lively blue eyes tells us about the earthquake which tore through the mountains "like a heavy storm, over thataway, twice. The little clods rained onto the roof." Involuntarily we glance up at the thatched ceiling.

Also about the landslide higher up the gorge, close to the Jouberts where a slice of mountainside caved in and slid down, and how for a long time a waterfall then bubbled forth from there. A miracle one might say. The geologist has said that there is another such fault above their house. "That's why they want to sell the land now."

In a natural kraal a little further on we pitch our tent and grill our meat over a fragrant fire of guarri and thornwood. Around us are the sounds of the evening: children bringing sheep and goats back to their shelters, dogs trying to scare the dusk with their barking, baboons virtually right next to us on the ridge — very excited.

The darkness brings with it the stars, big and fiery and clear: the Hunter and his belt, the Lesser Dog, Aldebaran the Bull's Eye, Canopus the diamond, the Greater Dog with Sirius, Betelgeuse . . . . From here it's as if you're lying on the bottom of a dark boat so that the stars stand out even more sharply against the night. Look intently, and you'll see how they rock. That's how it's always been, I suppose.

But a little later the full moon makes her appearance in the entrance to the gorge, especially and exclusively for Hell alone. So pale, so tangible, like dough from heaven as I have never seen her before. And later still a truck passes our camp with a few people singing lustily and playing an old folk tune. It's Saturday night's bit of merrymaking. They draw up at the Mosterts' — where could they go beyond? — and a mouth-organ wants to start on a mournful ditty under the all-embracing and prehistoric night. But then it doesn't. And we go to sleep.

One is greatly tempted to see these people, these landowners — "but if it can't be helped I'll just sit on a stone then," an old man said — as freaks of history. That they certainly aren't. It's true that they live in isolation from the outside world and probably exactly the same in many respects as much earlier. It's also true that they were an independent group of people, and still are, and that they don't care much for strangers playing innocent here. That an intruder will occasionally be driven away, still holds true. An old man, questioned about the drought by complete, though interested, strangers, replied hotly: "I have nothing to do with drought!"

In bygone days, so the story goes, it was much harsher. "There are a whole lot of skeletons lying around in these mountains. Every single one of the old farmers knew each of the others' tracks and a stranger was rapidly hunted down. Usually it was a brown man. They would tie him to a tree and by evening they would give him a plate of tasty food. Then they made him dance the reel right through the night just for the hell of it, until the following morning when they would jump onto their horses and drive the fellow from the gorge by firing a few shots over his head from behind."

It would seem that they are afraid people might want to investigate too closely the "illegalities" — justified pleasure as far as I'm concerned — still practiced here. It's certain that mead is still being distilled with the good old *kareemoer*: "drink some when it's been distilled three times, and you'll keel over on the spot." Although — the bees are few and far between this year; flies there are in bunches: "and may the good-for-nothings burn to death!" But if you believed all they say, you'd swear there's not a drop of mead to be had in the entire valley.

And the game then? "No, it's game fit for a king . . . but we don't have a king, do we?"

"They say," confirms a farmer, his watchful eyes darting in all directions like the eyes of all the farmers around here really, "that the hunting season is never open, but the muzzle of my gun is never shut."

"But," his wife covers up hurriedly, "we valley-people never go hunting, it would give the valley poor air." (And later we dig into her game-biltong with relish.)

It's difficult to get the real story, and that's the way it should be. When there's trust and when the amber tongue-loosener has made the rounds a few times, then the truth is blown up a bit and conversation sparkles.

They are the first to laugh at their own antics. "Folks used to think only baboons lived here in the gorge. Then one of our men went to buy stamps in the village on the other side of the mountain. And the guy in the post office asked him, So when did baboons start buying stamps? And he said, Only since they started employing monkeys in the post office."

Anything the other side of Calitzdorp or Prins Albert lies beyond the frontiers of conversation. Unknown visitors from the outside world are either learned Afrikaners — "and of course we don't speak a 'high-brow' Afrikaans," one lady mistakingly contends — or

English. And to speak English is an act of heroism. "When the man was still some way from us, Sir, I could hear at once . . . but that's English he's speaking, isn't it?! And the next thing I knew, I was left standing there all on my own. Heck, and I only manage a word here and there. But, Sir! we did have a good laugh at each other." Even Yolande was "the English girl" to them.

Another tendency is to think of the people here as living in the Land of Cockaigne. True, the soil is fertile, and what it produces is probably sufficient to keep the inhabitants alive — all kinds of fruit, beans, tomatoes, potatoes, sweet potatoes. And they export raisins, and dried figs. In the interests of truth I'm obliged to mention also that we saw on more than one occasion a farmer lying flat on his back under a shady tree, fast asleep and dead to the world. But their existence is one of poverty. Their houses are picturesque, but the facilities meager. The people are tough and strong, even at an advanced age, but the men invariably go around in the same faded working clothes, and the women in the same old bonnets. The children probably enjoy taking their time about going to school, but for some of them it means a four mile walk, lugging their books along in small flour bags on their backs. And there they sit in one and the same classroom from Sub A to Std 5 under the supervision of a friendly young teacher, Mr. Liebenberg.

Besides, quite frequently the people are very easy prey, evidently, for traveling salesmen and peddlers. One old man bought three gigantic rolls of "French" cloth — crease-resistant and flameproof! And on the day he wore his first suit, his cigarette burned a hole right through the material and after a while the baggy knees were doing *this* (and he demonstrates with two gnarled index fingers). We learn too how people from outside carted away truckloads of fine old family furniture in exchange for trashy modern junk — and to add insult to injury, they are then asked to pay extra to "square" the deal! Because one lot is old and the other new, you understand.

One hesitates to claim that it gets hotter here than elsewhere, but by early morning the sun is already clinging to every tree and shrub. (The temperature would rise that Sunday to nearly 36 degrees centigrade in the shade.) The valley literally teems with birds of every description — finch, pigeon, boubou shrike, starling, crow — and they all squawk and whistle and grunt and cry and warble.

We travel around the valley for two days with a bottle of moonshine at hand. There is much we want to know. How long have the people been living here, and how did they wind up in this inaccessible gorge? The first generation has already died, and the second, and the present generation too is getting on in years.

There is no community graveyard. Each family buries its own dead. "As a matter of fact, my father's grave collapsed just the other day," a farmer informs us calmly.

Originally, so they say, the gorge was discovered by farmers in pursuit of Bushmen who had raided some of their cattle. A small group of families made their homes here, and from then on they have all been interrelated. For years the only way into or out of the gorge was on foot. Essential supplies were brought in on the backs of donkeys.

Even the Boer War made little impact. At least the hollow trunk of an elephants'-food tree, fortified with hoops, was mounted as a cannon at the entrance to the gorge. Then it was packed with gunpowder and 500 muzzle-loader bullets. Only much, much later, long after the end of the war, was the cannon fired, and the surrounding countryside, apparently, is pitch-black and bald to this day. It is said that the gunner vanished into thin air right there.

And throughout the years government and law have been abstractions. Often there was dancing, and music too. "I remember," relates a lady, "how they used to drink mead. There was plenty of it then. A barrel was made simply by driving four pins into the ground and stretching a hide around them. One fine day, when my late grandfather was drinking from the barrel on all fours, he lifted his head and saw an enormous banded cobra swimming toward him on the surface of the beer. So he just blew it a little to one side and went on drinking."

Or the one about the dog-tax collector who arrived here wanting to make people pay for their dogs, can you believe it! One old man, blessed by Providence, kept seven of these creatures. First he pelted them with stones and yelled at them to shove off, because "what the hell are the whole valley's dogs doing in my yard again today?!" But when that didn't have the desired effect, he pointed his gun at the poor tax-collector, an emaciated little fellow with a goatee and boots, and made him spend the whole goddamned blistering day up on the ridges digging out stones, "so that you can see how damned difficult it is to raise little dogs."

"And by evening," recounts Uncle Henk Mostert, "when he arrived at our place to stay the night, he was all snot and tears. And he never came back again either."

When did vehicles first make their appearance in the valley then? "Well, that was long before the road was even built. Two Van Zyl brothers. They wanted to be the first. And they had the thing carried in here — across sandbags in some places — without a scratch, an old Ford Pop. All the folks from the valley helped. You see, the Van Zyls were distilling a lot of must wine at the time. Well, anyway, later they sold the car to an old guy by the name of Marais." And then? "Then? Well, Marais didn't know how to drive the thing. But he did start it up once or twice, and then he took the wheels off and made himself a nice donkey-cart."

We wander further up the valley, past farmsteads, some deserted already, where prickly pears grow against a wall, where pomegranates are starting to turn yellow, and where Adam's figs hang, heavy and black, bunches of shade.

The farmers are working in their vineyards. When we ask one farmer Marais whether there is any game left in the area, he turns all his attention to an imaginary thorn in the calloused palm of his hand and tells us quite irrelevantly about the "rubbish" he has been hoeing where the grapes are "swelling." Extraordinary how much the people remind one of characters from Bosman's stories!

We say hello to Aunt Sankie Marais. Her complexion is almost translucent and her cheeks as red as a doll's. Her gaze travels thoughtfully up the heat-shimmering hills: "There's not a thing left on the mountain for the animals to eat anymore." And on top of that, one face of the gorge is state property too. We used to have commonage rights there before, but the farmers had a strongly worded letter recently. No, we can't see her husband, Uncle Andries. He's with the goats and the goats are pretty nervous of strange people. (But we're sure he is peeking at us from behind the nearest shrub.)

And then we are back with the Mosterts again. Yolande is impressed by the natural elegance of the farming people. To her they are just like the Italian small-holders — devoted to the soil for so many generations, and so close to nature that there are no airs and graces, no ostentation, but an inborn courteousness and hospitality.

Mrs. Mostert offers us a slice of sweet melon. She contends that it has a fairly bland taste, but to my mind her sweet melon would win hands down at any agricultural show. Yolande asks about the dishes enjoyed by people in the valley, and Mrs. Mostert tells us about their delicious country fare. She is not familiar with traditional Cape foods like *bobotie*. She tells us that her one great desire is to be able to ride on the train some day.

Later we also hear what befell her just before Christmas. Of how she had downed a full glass of brandy and had then started running — she firmly believes that if you have had one too many and don't want anything to happen to you, you should cut out and run like the devil. They finally caught up with her by car near the old log — a good few miles further on. "And where should I run to on the train now, Sir?" Afterward the neighbors held a hop-dance on the sand in the moonlight-yard . . . and at fifty-five she's getting on, after all.

The same moon rises again and bathes the same countryside in a detached light. Mrs. Mostert shows Yolande the family album and her daughter's embroidery in English (which is a very emphatic Afrikaans). We have a last nip with Uncle Henk and listen to his ghost stories. When we leave, we are the ones who are thanked for the entertainment, for how we have made them laugh.

Then we walk back in the eerie moonlight. Only among nations where the deceased are never really absent is one so afraid of ghosts. At the root of our way of life in this country lie many of the relics of the ancient-Khoisan-people: their words, their remedies, their customs. Though we may not bury our ancestors near the fireplaces, though our graves may collapse, something of their blood keeps haunting us, and *in* us.

The various sweet and sharp scents of the veld are borne toward us on the night breeze. I think of the tale of the man who hanged himself in this gorge. Was he brown or white? What does it matter? Death does not discriminate. The noose was just as short. And how the locals refused to touch him. A doctor was obliged to come from Prins Albert to take the corpse down, easily three days later. What had it smelled like by then?

This is immortality: that flimsy thread running from generation to generation. That we must all die, that is what links us to the eternal. And that cold moon giving us goosebumps now, that moon has remained just the same. Like a peach blossom.

as on the highway along the Langeberg Mountains
just outside Swellendam, the earth dark, just after the shower
so cool

hands in pockets
a moon clambers above the blossoming of hills and folds
moonful of moon

in the vineyards
under the vines
among the leaves
hang bunches
of black-wet
sweetness

wholly carefree. or else something infinite
like clouds cowing over the slopes of Zululand

stalk through the land
hands in pockets:
the sun hisses, a rag-float with streamers and banners
and a band of drums and strings
a cloud of dust
sent up by people dancing
behold the skipping — jubilant
brown children in rags and tatters

January 23

Suddenly the past few days have stopped being nice. And yet, "sweet was the road/ in the land of the rising sun" — or so it should be, with a place for everyone. Which is not the case.

Yesterday we left the Gamkaskloof. We seemed to be the only travelers on the road. The weather was beginning to turn, and at the top of the mountain pass, just before starting our descent toward Oudtshoorn, it rained a little. Other than the odd pine tree and sugar bush now and then, the mountain ridge was naked. ("Naked we came into the world and they'll strip us to the bone before we leave it again," one old laborer groaned.)

Do you know what the pine trees dream about? They dream that they are the masts of ships. That's why they strain against the clouds like that. That's why their leaf-branches are like bulging sails and why the dead needles lie around there like raveled threads, and their pine seeds like the excreta of seagulls. And the wind is hung from the trees like a flag. Every tree stands erect like a mast, hoping to be noticed, selected by the trained eye of the cabinetmaker. And in their reverie they echo the sounds of the sea — the murmur of the sea, the grinding and creaking of ropes, and now and then a flapping sail. Sometimes, in the night, you hear a soft weeping.

But they don't all dream of voyages. In the mountain range bordering the sea, on the highest slope giving you your first glimpse of the sea when you come from the interior, stand other firs. They are fossilized travelers, warriors, explorers. They have been standing there for so long now and are slightly stooped as though peering at the watery horizon. They wear large green hats and jackets a little worn at the elbows, for here it is often cold, and a mistiness leaves a thin layer of moisture on the peak. These trees are mute and yet filled with expectation; it seems as if they want to smell something, want to hear a distant sound. And when you listen with your ear to the ground, you hear a mumbled moaning sometimes — like a sigh it gusts through their ranks: "Thalassa! There is the sea! There is the sea!" Will they be able to drink some of the intoxicating mead too?

In the afternoon, late, we reached the village of Oudtshoorn. We registered at the Holiday Inn — just as hideous here as elsewhere in the world. Later on in the evening, artificially separated from Africa around us, we had a few drinks in the air-conditioned night-club of the hotel. There were several soldiers in the building. One officer with red eyes — in addition to being a soldier, he belonged to the Security Branch — addressed me non-stop as "sonnyboy" and tried to prove that he was well-equipped for his task as he had even read Mao. In the smaller hours of the night he gave unbridled vent to a blood-thirstiness bordering on insanity. But that's what his job is all about, isn't it? — to keep an eye on borderlines.

They wait. They wait for the day of reckoning, and meanwhile it's as if the waiting is driving them crazy. Do they realize it's inevitable? Do they realize nothing will ever prevent the majority from coming to power? But how many will die trying to stop the inevitable?

Today we visited the Kango Caves. And first thing this morning I learned of the murder, the death of Amilcar Cabral. Not only was the man a leader of his own people, but he was also an example to those who never knew him personally. I met him only once — one twilight evening in a street in Paris; he was the kind of man you don't easily forget, no matter how brief the encounter. One of the things he used to quote sticks in my memory — an old saying: "If you spit up in the air, you're only soiling your own face."

Poor Africa! When is the outside world going to leave you alone? The repeated murders, whoever commits them, of those prominent leaders directing the nations of Africa against the humiliating neocapitalism — are they coincidence or deliberate policy? Lumumba, Ben Barka, Mondlane . . . . And where is Luthuli?

We walked through the halls of Kango Caves where the light of so many centuries — transience itself — is caught in stalactites and stalagmites. Time is ancient.

And later we called at an ostrich farm where the most battered old birds are turned into racing horses. Jockeys, dressed in gay silk costumes, mount them, grip the helpless wings and then race up and down for the amusement of tourists.

Clouds lay upon the skyline, piled high, white-unusual mountain chains. Back, to the Boland via Riversdale and Heidelberg. When it started raining, the drops were fat and clumsy like wet moths against the windows of the kombi. We drew up somewhere and bought prickly pears at the side of the road.

From January 31

Thus one month has passed. We have seen much already, but never enough, and our bodies are acclimatized — glide easily again in this warmer air. The impressions gained each day have a cell-structure too, of course, and naturally the presence of that structure (a foreign body in the body? essential fuel?) determines and alters the body. Gradually the cells of old impressions are replaced by those of new ones. It becomes quite normal that there are mountains waiting at the windows every day when one gets up, that the sun sails through the blue sea making little white waves, that every cloud is a potential hat, that a wind the color of dust stirs the tops of the trees in the afternoons.

Only the press can't get used to our presence, still believing that we might, one never knows, be worth pressing for a story. Life is beginning to settle down comfortably again. Chortle — though she avoids going out because of the way people stare at her — has already established her own frame of reference. For hours she busies herself with Ounooi's plants and flowers, inspects and arranges the stones and thorns and pods she intends keeping as mementoes, cuts and sews garments out of the local cloth, pages through journals with Meintjie — Mietjie's daughter — and is still spoiled by Oubaas.

Sometimes, in the small hours, I still wake up suddenly afraid and seldom knowing what woke me. At night, when I shut my eyelids, my eyes — or rather the small black antennae of the eyes which are light-sensitive, and insatiable — fly from the room next to the back verandah where we sleep. I never know where they go and what they do there; the agreement between us gives them free rein to fly and to walk and to tumble and to strain wherever they wish while my eyelids remain closed, but when it is time to see again, they are expected to take up their positions. They are like foreign sailors on

136

board a vessel calling at some port and allowed to gallivant and make mischief during a night out on the town. And on occasions when I have to find a hold (somewhere in this alien night without my antennae, I am as blind as two bullet holes.

two spots drew near to me
two spots drew near to me
two black spots

then two black spots drew nearer and nearer
then two black spots drew nearer and nearer
the night is speckled

two specklespots drew nearer unto me
two specklespots drew nearer unto me
ever nearer and smaller

two black speckled spots
ever nearer and smaller
then I saw nothing

On the evening of the 25th we went to see the play, Siswe Banzi Is Dead*, in the Space Theatre in Cape Town. The theatre itself is evidently one of those loopholes (escape valves?) which are allowed to exist, like the odd multi-racial restaurant perhaps. Its existence is a good thing in the sense that it keeps a small flame of human dignity lit, an illusion of normality — a place where you are not humiliated into accepting the laws and restrictions of the regime. But it is bad, too, because naturally it preaches to the converted, because it soothes the consciences of the limousine liberals (one wonders how the people who come to see this play treat their servants), and because, when all is said and done, it's ultimately elitist. I don't want to say much about the play itself — I have little experience of the theater, and

*Play (1974) by foremost (controversial) South African English playwright Athol Fugard. Deals mainly with the pass laws and influx control which severely restrict the freedom of movement of the black people in South Africa. Play is for two characters, and the parts were acted by two black South Africans, John Kani and Winston Ntshona, who also toured Europe and the U.S. with it, where it was well received.

137

besides, what struck me was not that it is a play, but rather than two black people are locked up in an arena, forcing us, the onlookers, to listen to them. And because of what they have to say, and the fact that they say it, we are in a quandary. Yet what they tell us about is the terrible everyday existence of the slaves in this land, and that is a tale we could hear everywhere if only we cared to listen. We don't dare listen, because then we would destroy the foundations of our domination. What these two actors brought to the Cape was the message that they are people — and relentlessly we were confronted with that fact. Such theater deserves the designation "heightened reality." And afterward? Isn't it a kind of morbid gratification to sit and watch the agony of another like that? Only, this agony has its offshoot in society — for it's an existential agony which is intensified and controlled by the white man's laws. The only means of breaking away from this hell, is to break the powerful hold of the white man.

From tragedy to farce. The village where I completed my school education now has a new high school. But some of the old teachers who were around in my time are still in harness. Peaceful, Nollie, Kampies . . . . Dear, good people who will always have my respect. The new headmaster duly approached me with an invitation to address the senior pupils. I couldn't refuse of course, if only because my acceptance would please my parents who want so much to be proud of their son. Even when I was still at school some queer fish would arrive to address us from time to time; mostly it would be a globe-trotter or some such, and one whom I remember particularly well was a cowboy, a Bill something or other, bedecked with tassles and the owner of an imposing Harley Davidson. Among other things he came to brag about the — more than likely insignificant — parts he had acted in Westerns. And on another occasion Gregoire Boonzaaier, sporting a beret of the type artists are supposed to wear, demonstrated his talent to us by creating a naturalistic master-piece in pastel-crayon on the stage in two shakes of a duck's tail. (The work still hangs in the school.)

Thus every peddler must have his special act. Well, I really got down to business, and having rigged a blanket across the window to create the necessary air of conspiracy and subversion — Col. Huntingdon's agent across the road, the henchman whose duty it was to keep me under surveillance, almost tumbled out of the palm tree in his hurry to get his camera, bugging-devices, and notebook ready — I carefully built a portable barricade with a red flag on one corner and a black one on the other. I would pinch an old rusty sickle from Pa's storeroom, and brandishing that and a hammer, I would leap onto the barricade in full view of the innocent little lambs and whisper the "Internationale" at the top of my voice. I would probably have to make up the words here and there, because it's a lengthy song . . . .

The moral vigilance of the village vigilantes should not be underestimated, however (or is Mietjie's young Dawid who constantly keeps one squinting eye on me from under the table also one of those brown sell-outs in the Branch already?), and the school authorities were informed that the village was not prepared to allow me to indoctrinate their offspring; I was the turd in the sparkling drinking-water of secondary education, so to speak. Then the headmaster came to jilt me gently and it was mutually agreed that Jopie and I should have tea in the staff room during the tea-break one day instead. (As teachers are harder to corrupt!) And it turned out well. It wasn't even necessary for me to make use of my collapsible machine gun. The headmaster—a champ among the Brethren*, I'm told — opened the friendly proceedings by asking me briefly (a) whether I accept the Calvinistic doctrines, and (b) what my position is vis-à-vis the terrobberists†on the border. I replied hurriedly lest my cup of tea be taken away from me again. We had delicious cake and biscuits, and Jaaplamb was given a box of dried fruit, while a set of cups and saucers bearing the school crest and motto — "Aim High" — was presented to me. In my time we used to say: "Aim High and bend low." I shouldn't have dared to aim at all that day, since half the staff are burly physical education teachers with fists like stones from the Hawekwa Mountains.

Dear Mr. Lochner, Mr. Burger, Mr. Aucamp (and you too, Miss Goosen and gentle Mr. English Master), if you ever get to read these words: it gladdened my heart to be able to see you again. The years which had fallen into the water of the little Stink River and had

---

*Members of the *Broederbond* (see *Glossary*).
†Terroberists: Properly terrorists. Refers to SWAPO guerilla forces in the northern border of South West Africa-Namibia which is the southern border of Angola.

vanished under the bridge at the old Masonic Hotel, no longer counted, and in the village of memories which I cart all over the world with me — which makes me a privileged plutocrat — you will always hold positions of honor. Because those memories are associated with a brighter era, and you are the means by which I recall the wonderful treasure chambers of a language, remember the fresh smell of planed wood and strange atlasses with green and red and yellow countries.

One day, when I am young again, I will try to write about our years at school.

That same afternoon we left for Onrus with Ounooi, taking the route via Paarl and over the mountain at Franschoek. Beyond the mountain where the countryside turns yellow, yellow and hilly toward Caledon, we stopped to have a look at the soil and the sheep, and we saw a tramp on horseback, wearing a broad-rimmed hat, and behind his back he carried a rolled blanket and his saddlebags, almost certainly full of biltong and dried peaches and a tin of liniment and acid drops. A small golden cloud of dust whirled under his horse's hooves. Over the veld too there were whirlwinds occasionally — "dustdevils." Evening came at Onrus and there was a breeze from the sea.

when I want to get up at night
to get rid of the water that has become too sharp and superfluous
I must walk back cautiously, tiptoeing
from one floor to the lower
through dormitories where small bundles in white attire
lie sleeping:
I can see the paleness of the dark
for moonlight shines deeper than the earth
as I tiptoe back past all these moments of my self
taking care not to wake the little corpses

in the courtyard I will fertilize the earth
and return to my bed up there:
the moon is a silver key
to a door which does not exist

It was night The gray walls around us We made our way from the cells to the courtyard No moon but light enough nevertheless to see The warders have evidently not smelled a rat yet All quiet We must get over the wall To the outside Freedom It's my fault that we're all locked up here I incited them to rebel against the Authorities I spoke of light Said that man was more than just a selfish and exploiting animal Because they trusted me they cooperated *They* are going to break us like one does with crabs to get at the soft flesh *They* have the time *They* have the power To break one To a small heap of vomit To make you want to puke at your own brokenness. Your desire to go on living We are the guinea pigs I must take the lead Someone has left a ladder in the courtyard Grating sounds heels and soles of shoes on gravel Carefully and quietly now Ladder propped against wall and we climb upward one by one with rasping breaths From here it's easy to get onto an adjoining roof Then through a garden onto the street and down narrow tunnellike alleys into the city with all its buildings and streets Gray brainmatter No word or sign of guards Carefully over the adjacent wall onto the roof below and then free Freedom We start running How the back is almost a magnet for bullets Look back Warders are black etchings against the night sky Floodlights suddenly shooting through the streets As seen coming toward the eye And we run But no one fires Freedom No one gives chase Until we realize suddenly That it isn't necessary The city

     the entire world
        our goal
   is their *gaol*

A very aged young girl said to me: *life is a trip;* agreed, but *si sconsiglia nettamente di comperare trips, dato che sono quasi sempre di qualità incerta. A Goa Sono numerosi quelli che hanno fatto un brutto viaggio e sono flippati . . . Spesso non si ritorna più indietro, o si ritorna dopo diversi mesi . . .).*

When Rimbaud was a mere child he ceased writing poetry. Perhaps poetry became itself an obstacle in his quest for a systematic derangement of all senses on the way to prophethood. Perhaps he realized that you can't poke a hole in water with a sword. (So we have been taught by the history books.) Be that as it may, whether out of despair or because this was indeed a liberation, he laid down his young sword — though that blade had already had a taste of blood, too. (Billy the Kid.) By then he had traveled the length and breadth of Europe on foot a few times. His friends, in fact, had nicknamed him *l'Hottentot* because the soles of his feet had become like leather. And after making a detour to include the Far East, etc., he discovered his destination: *Africa*. It is true that he had previously predicted — and indeed therefore created — this destination in his verse. In Africa he wandered around in the Red Sea region for a bit. If I remember correctly, he even wrote two accounts of his travels and submitted them to some Geographical Institute or other in Europe. To them the name Rimbaud meant nothing, and to those with their silver-silk-thread-embroidered waistcoats in Paris salons who knew him, he was already dead and decaying. That was his first death. (Death comes to you in due time, is your due, like an ocean between one Continent and the Other.) They wrote to him that the Institute had insufficient funds at its disposal at present to be able to make use of his contributions, but that he was welcome to write to them if he should come across something worthwhile on his peregrinations. He went to the mud-village, Harrar, to manage a trading post for a French adventurer. By this time, it seems, his only ambition was to make a lot of money quickly. With a caravan of camels and mules he started smuggling arms for the Abyssinians. Everyone should be an arms-smuggler at least once in his life. The buyers — and the sellers too — swindled him something terrible. Not only did they rob him on one occasion, but in addition, they almost stoned him into the bargain. Meanwhile, it is claimed, he took a wife and maybe even fathered a child. But a veil is drawn over that episode as it is drawn over the faces of the ladies of those regions. In Harrar he became intimately acquainted with cold and heat and loneliness and hunger. Wolves, demented with hunger, invaded the village from the desert. When some epidemic or other mowed down the inhabitants, the corpses were placed on the walls around the city. Then a stench of decomposing flesh would rise toward the open furnace of the African sky, gray clouds of sand would be borne forth by the wind from the deep desert, and small smacking sounds, when the growling wolves cracked the bones of the corpses with strong jaws to get at the sweet and rancid fat. At one stage he injured a knee; I think he fell from his horse. The injury simply refused to heal and grew more and more painful. Gangrene, that cold fire, began to smoulder in his fibers. He had a young lover, a faithful native who stuck to him like a little tail and more than likely didn't care a fig for any "poetry" — and rightly so! — but the lover couldn't put out the fire. It became necessary for them to transport him back to Europe for an operation. In Marseilles the leg was amputated chop-chop. From there he returned to his mother's farm near Charlesville, where idiots grow old and fat, to convalesce—get onto his legs again, so to speak. And now his one overriding desire and ambition in his life was to return to Africa as soon as possible. (Even though he knew that nothing rots a person as effectively as the sun, and therefore, love.) He had practically nothing at all. He had decorated his room with the few rugs and strings of beads he had managed to bring with him in an effort to re-create Africa in these strange parts. He tried to keep crickets alive in a clay jar and watched how they continued to scurry around even though they were maimed. At night, when he couldn't sleep in spite of the pain-killing drugs and perhaps because he was afraid too of the gleaming sword of his dreams which could sever the stars from the branches, he made music on an African stringed instrument, and the farmhands and neighbors came to listen beyond the circle of light (like deaf wolves) to this strange incantation, to the lament of a small bird without origin or station across the dunes. He did not rally, but his determination forced him back. His sister accompanied him on the long journey by train back to Marseilles. It was hot and smelly in the compartment. He saw Paris — where they had given him the raw deal to begin with — through the window of the train, like a stranger with a gray blanket over the stump. In Marseilles it was chop-chop back into hospital with nuns and nurses. The ante-chamber of the breath-preparing-for-a-journey. From his sickbed he made preparations for the passage to Africa. The fever came to sit upon him like a wolf with wings. He started growing delirious. Brought up old verse, piece by piece, and perhaps new verse also, but his faithful sister did not record anything, just as one does not try to pin down the symptoms of scandalous death. Even on the day before the last he dictated a letter to the ship's captain to ask to be allowed to embark early the next morning before the other passengers, because he would have to be carried on board and he did not wish people to see him in that lamentable state. Then, that's how it has been recorded, he accepted the Christian faith once more and kissed the gallows and immediately his mouth was poisoned. (Sometimes one pays dearly for death.) And he left his body lying there and gave them all the slip. That was the second death.

What the history books do not record, is that he disappeared a day or so later when he felt better. His family never wanted this mentioned. Let sleeping wolves lie was their approach. His life had always been a blot on a clean page. Absconded from school at an early age; raped, perhaps, like a whore, by a detachment of soldiers one night during the Communion days in a barracks in Paris — and thus romanticism was drilled into or out of him; his so-called poems which caused the good citizens to pull the sleeves of their jackets down over their shirt-cuffs with thin lips and firm gestures (in those days there were no professors of poetry to separate the good from the subversive yet); his gay days with Verlaine; the fortune he didn't make, and so on. It's not certain whether he managed to get passage on the boat he was meant to have sailed on. The transportation of the remains to Charlesville where Ma Rimbaud would have had to pick him up in a small horsecart, was sure to have held up everything. What is clear is that the track traced by his single foot was later noticed in the desert. He vanished without trace, gloriously, like a white line on a sheet of white paper. Africa is a reality. And in Africa you cannot die. In the way mankind has been doing for centuries in Africa, Rimbaud gradually began to migrate southward. When you start nosing through history you sometimes lose track of him. Dunes shift, and rainy seasons wash away the roads or locusts eat the stones to shreds. All the same, at times he turns up as a big-game hunter here, as a bartender or a mercenary there, as a snake farmer suddenly, or in his capacity as second officer on a riverboat where he wore out the deck measuring it with his stump. What is a fact is that he made his appearance after a cycle of years in the Kimberley area and staked himself a claim there on the mines. Poor Rimbaud! He should have realized that he could lay claim only to Death. But what, after all, is Death's six by six compared to the Big Hole?* He made no money—we do know that, because his mother died of poverty. His little stones, no matter how shiny the compressed experience of years and years had made them, were toxic — so the people whispered. He turned transport-rider and bought himself a dog with the name of Jock, and it was probably on one of his peddling trips that he met Eugène Marais and talked him into killing himself— with the tragic result noted down in history. Thereafter we lose his shadow again. It looks as if he went to settle in Namibia near the Etosha-pan. There he laid out a small garden with the object of attracting the animals to the bit of moisture on the leaves. His artichokes wouldn't thrive there, and strawberries or cherry trees were completely out of the question, of course. They knocked up a kind of platform for him in a tree, and in the evenings, when the sun steamed far across the plains like a train, wrapped in clouds of blood-soiled billowing dust, his valets carried him to the tree and propped him up in his lookout. Here he spent his nights watching for the red eye-sparks of the desert wolves. Then he would occasionally shout "Harrara! Harraar!" like a frog with slime in its throat, old as water itself. He was a very old man by this time, the stump of his leg small and shriveled like something purged by fire, like something to be ashamed of, like something you take along with you everywhere and won't get rid of simply because it was a gift from your mother, just like an extra penis. Now I gather from the newspapers that there's arms smuggling again these days off the Skeleton Coast. A leopard might change its hair and its name and its glasses, but not its spots. If ever an occasion presents itself for the holding of a respectable writers' conference in this torn country of ours, writers who carry their skeletons about inside them like arrows pointing the way in a desert devoid of roads, Rimbaud should be invited to give a talk about the French literature of the last century, and to pass judgment on all the rubbish which has been written about him since.

Trouble is that the Security Police would probably arrest him in the event, because they dislike cripples, and *their* death is another matter altogether . . . .

*A disused open diamond pit in Kimberley, more than 1372 metres in diameter and over 2743 metres deep, excavated entirely by the most primitive methods employed by the early diggers in the last century (1870's).

("I don't want to stay here
for here is nothing of me" —

the heart goes dry with pain
like an asshole
not in use)

(*Onrus*)

 quite naturally I believe in a hereafter
I will die and adorned in my gown of paradise
                                   come hither
on vacation
   here
where like a sun-carpet the sun
lies over everything
           to walk this road
around this corner where the milkwood
and the redthorn grow
            against this spirited sky
the mountain far ahead and the sea behind
up the lane —

I will live with the cats in the brushwood
and walk through the walls
through time setting in matter every now and then
until it flows again and rots to life —
and when you come to rest here
I will be sitting keenly in your company
staring at the grownups
and at night rummage for rusks in the biscuit tin
(don't blame the mouse)

I will not disturb you
but you will know I am here
               for
by day I shall make the sea green and blue

and in the evenings light the stars
with my eyes

The self-image in the eye of the I

(I am an Iconoclast.)

The concept I am trying to convey implies not a "visible and tangible
representation or imitation . . ."; nor is it a depiction or likeness or
idol or model or reflection or portrayal, but more of a mask. Perhaps
imago comes closest to it: "1. Final & perfect stage of insect after all
metamorphoses. 2. Mental picture, fantasy or idealized image of a
loved person formed in childhood & persisting in adulthood."
    We all know *I.* 1. (ī), pron. & n. Subjective case of 1st pers.
pron. (objective *me,* poss. *my;* pl. *we,* obj. *us,* poss. *our*); (n.,
metaphys.) *the I,* the ego, subject or object of self-consciousness. (See
also *ibis:* stork-like bird with long curved bill found in lakes and
swamps of warm climates . . .; *ice:* frozen water . . .; *icing:* sugar etc.
coating of cake etc. . . .; *idea:* archetype, pattern, as distinguished
from its realization in individuals . . .; *ideal:* answering to one's
highest conception . . .; *ideate:* imagine . . .; *identify:* associate
one*self* inseparably *with* . . .; *identity:* absolute sameness . . .; *ideology:*
visionary speculation . . .; *idle:* (of action, thought, word)
ineffective, worthless, vain . . .; *island:* piece of land surrounded by
water . . .; *isolate:* place apart or alone . . .; *isotope:* one of two or more
forms of an element differing from each other in weight of atoms . . .;
item: article, unit, included in enumeration (properly not the first)
. . .; *itinerant:* traveling from place to place . . .).
    It should be realized that these words must be explained *ejusdem
generis.*
    What I would like to get at is that all of us live behind projec-
tions of ourselves. With the writer — because his self-consciousness
is intimate material — this probably happens more consciously. We
project an image of ourselves. That projected image, which is an
intermediary, is more than likely not the one observed by others. (I

see my image from behind, the "others" see it from the front, because I look through my eyes from behind.) But to the degree in which others react upon that image, that image exists, that image has a right to existence. (Without banks, a river is not a river; without language, concepts will not exist. And vice versa.)

That image which is created — sometimes its creation takes place over a period of years — and is then projected, undergoes the influence of the community, is determined by it even. I create an image of myself as I *ought* to be or as I would like to be — should be either in my own eyes, or in the eyes of others. Moralistic considerations may play a part here. (Hemingway with his he-man image, Fitzgerald, the "swinger.")

The image may be a substitute for the "I" or may be used as a kind of shield for the "I." (Invariably we accept almost instinctively that a "real person" must be hiding behind the intimation of a personage experienced by us.) Image both as a means of contact and as an isolator.

Can that construction be used as a "chair" to climb onto — out of yourself, away from the "I" — and so on? Is it possible to have direct contact with the "other" without intervention from the respective images? Can an image of the "I" exist where there is no "other"?

What seems clear is that the image is not organic, that it cannot extend and grow and relax over the years, that it becomes a mask, that little by little you become a prisoner of that image and run the risk of being smothered by it. A struggle may then ensue between the "I" and the image. You may rebel against it, may smash yourself on it. You may become one with the mask, until that form is molded. (Perhaps the image is the sum of your scars.) The image as swathes of the mummy; the futile attempts to embalm the "I" within, to immortalize it. Creation of an image as a quest for eternal life. The image as mirror. Image coffin.

But the creation of an image (therefore?) as a desire for self-destruction. The fixation of certain I-attributes against which there is rebellion afterward because it is false and imperfect. (And bound with time.) (Every word is an image. Every word is false.)

But what leads us to suspect that there is a fixed (waxing and waning) "I," that there is an I-I, you-I, she-I, we-I, it-I? Is "I" not the absent construction, the lost master-key? (I created an image of myself and was then dissatisfied with it because I realized how relative it is, how dependent upon the way others see that image, how it is a "household" object, has become a means of contact, a language.) (For that reason — on account of what memory of purity? — I decided that an alternative must exist, an unrecognizable "I." The perception of the self creates the self.) (In relation to others I exist. But because I can never put myself entirely in their place, I am unable to identify that "I" objectively. Therefore I create — like water from water — an image of the self, a certainty. Image-making is holding on tight where there is possibly nothing to hold on to. To hold on doesn't mean that there is something which holds, or that it is the same something holding on from hold to hold.) Consequently there is interplay, dialectics, between image and "I." I create Image; Image makes "I." But for every observer there will be an image. The mouth utters a single word, but every ear hears something different, something which is unique, *exclusive.* (Prism. The prism of the prism. The rabbit produced instantly from the magician's hat.) Does image determine the nature of the self?

An ancient tale of which I am often reminded and which I have retold many times, is one by Anna David-Neal. Young Tibetan novices, she tells, are made to wrestle with their own "creations," projections or images or phantasms outside on the plain. They are not allowed to leave their seats. The projections must acquire a life of their own and then be destroyed — physically! And apparently it has happened that travelers passing by or staying in the hills nearby could hear the shouting and the crying and the whistling of the combat. And it is not unknown for some of the youths to be beaten — slain even — by their own projections.

I want to project a fire. A fire which will light up like a burning tree before my eyes no matter how thick the snow lies; which will scorch the all-embracing darkness (the absence?) into me!

(When last seen, he was heading up the hill toward the moon like a tree ablaze.)

Perhaps it is all, all this scribbling, nothing but a phantom growth.

(Con calma!)

February 13, 1973

The waves come again
        come white
and blue
from the blue of the ocean they come
breaking here against the rocks where the gulls
        cry horror
there comes a dying from the sea

O Cape
O Cape where are you sailing to?

At Sea Point old shriveled men sit arguing
each behind his paunch
about how cold New York is now
sit struggling against death
still trapping from time to time a boat in the corner of the eye
in the distance en route from Lemuria to Atlantis
and they are brown
from accumulated sitting waiting:
as for us, we side with the sun

In Paris the snow is knitting gray sweaters
        over church and home
In Paris the city's underwear is fraying
the light will be lying lost in the street
and little old men wrapped in gray bodies
        snare a sun in their wine
en route from grape to the shine
    of a hangover

O Cape
o nest of the sun
I must lie down to pray under the blue
terrible heaven

Watch over me be merciful
     in food and drink
Amen
     yes
          Amen
Watch over me take me with Thee Amen: CAPE:

There comes a dying from the sea
comes breaking on rocks where the gulls are crying
comes from the blue with the burning white of the waves
comes
came
will come
come
forever and ever

A View from Outside*

It seems that each of us is to have a turn to speak, or rather to preach this
week. Mine will be a funeral oration — a very extremistic funeral
oration — you will simply have to bear with me. But death makes me
fighting mad. Particularly when the corpse of this young writer from
the Sixties is not completely cold yet. Consequently you will have to
make allowances if an excess of emotion is brought out into the open, or
onto the paper. Emotion is always superfluous and intrusive; does not
recognize its limitations. Surely you weren't expecting to get a cold
analysis from me . . . .

     André Brink intimated the other evening that there might be a

*The title of a controversial paper read by Breytenbach during the annual Summer School of
the University of Cape Town in January 1973. The Summer School attended by academics,
students, and the public usually lasts for about a week. Experts from all over South Africa
and abroad are invited to deliver papers in their field at symposia and lectures, and there are
plays and poetry readings as well. Breytenbach delivered his paper during a symposium on
the so-called *Sestigers*, i.e. the Afrikaans writers, poets, and playwrights of the 1960's whose
avant-garde writings are generally regarded as having put Afrikaans literature as a whole on
an "international" level. Since these writers broke with many of the traditional political and
religious tenets of the Afrikaner, they were — and many of those who have continued to
advocate change in both a literary and a specifically South African sense still are —
controversial figures.

resurrection of us Lazaruses. I wonder. It sounds somber, doesn't it — all these references to a motley many-colored funeral. As a matter of fact, one of the things I specifically want to ask this evening is whether there is still some life left in us, or are we totally mummified as a result of our petty bourgeoisie mentality? I mean, are we so bogged down in our hire-purchase-lives — that life we'll be paying off for life — that we have to get permission from the insurer for every brusque breath or wind passed? Are we scared to death, then, of life?

Going by recent definition given by a national leader* — I am referring to a White National leader, not a national one — I suppose I am also one of the "agents of a spiritual and moral contamination, operating in the dark like a plague and having already brought the Western world to its knees, one of those layabout louts with Samson-like hair, but minus his strength."

Strange, that predilection of the plague for darkness, for what is black and unmentionable, for the terrifying unknown, for the night when, like Samson of old, we can yield to the touch of each other's bodies — what a glorious plague! — before the day betrays us. But we carry the night around within us, don't we? What we are able to see on the outside, is day — the dimension here inside is night, is the infinite.

Just as well then that we find ourselves here in Africa where the sun is always shining, and not in the Western world; and in Africa I want to call a spade a spade. My talk this evening, here, will be regarded as politics. And so it is, unavoidably. Like the work of art which is politics when it alludes to the reality in which the public finds itself. All talk in this sad bitter motley-funeral-land is politics — whether it is whispering talk, talking shit, spitting into the wind or speaking in his master's voice. It's not a choice the writer has, it's neither using nor abusing poetic license (and why should the clown be allowed more license than the factory-hand?); no, it lies in the very nature of communication. Together all of us have industriously and

---

*Breytenbach does not name this "leader," and with so few clues it is not possible to identify the particular person in question. On the other hand, it is very likely that this "omission" was deliberate, in order to stress the high incidence of similar speeches made by the politicians of the day. The views expressed in the quote were held by many influential speech-makers, and could be heard regularly from those pulpits, political, university, and business platforms intent upon maintaining the status quo.

blindly as ants, dragged this country to the last abyss before hell. Now we can talk, can't we, talk so loudly that we can't distinguish the crackling of flames from the chattering of our teeth.

I said I was not going to pretend to be objective. Not because each case has at least two sides, an inside and an outside, and because I recognize both possibilities, do I dare to say I am "objective." The only objectivity is a skeleton in the ground. And even then you have to allow for the ghost . . . . To return to what I was saying before: some of us are already emasculated, objective. Others are still kicking up a wisp of sand. White sand, of course. On a separate beach under a separate sun!

I am biased. I take sides. Because to me what is at stake is the establishment of liveable conditions in our community. Because to me what matters is a quest for, an opening up toward a society in which *each and every one of us* may have his rightful share, within which we may accept responsibility for each other *on an equal footing.* Because, to me, it's a question of combating those institutions and edifices and myths and prejudices and untruths and idiocy and greed and self-destructive urges and common stupidity which render such a community impossible. *That's* my loyalty. *That* is the substance of my South Africanhood.

My talk is entitled *A View from Outside.* In one of his poems Hart Crane employs a striking metaphor when he refers to someone — probably an impervious simpleton like myself — looking down into a tin can trying to discover the image of the moon above him.

I'm glad I don't have to speak about a view from above. There are few phenomena I find more loathsome than the elitism of those who think in terms of a small privileged group — those who regard their vocation as writers and poets as sacred, and who deign occasionally to plunge into the warm crawling masses — in search of "material" — to surface again in the cave, for fresh air. The purity of their whiteness shines like leprosy.

A view from below, with the southeaster about, could certainly prove interesting; a view from inside, alas, no longer possible for me. Therefore I want to walk around that view and try to say how I interpret this title: an attempt to indicate what the afterbirth of the Sixties — our own private Frankenstein — looks like from the outside; an attempt at placing it against the background of South

Africa and the South African cultures of which ours is but a tiny component. That backdrop, you would probably agree, is one of conflicting cultural currents of political stench, of social unrest, of discrimination and detention and censorship. In short, of a fermenting cauldron. But also one of conflict.

When I speak of "us" this evening, it is as a whitish or off-white South African to others of the same kind — with a few notable and non-representative exceptions. What exists in this country has been perpetrated in our — in my — name, in our — in my — language. Although, therefore, I am no one's delegate but my own and that of my fleas, I cannot and will not dissociate myself from this mess.

I am convinced that the salvation of this country, if such an evangelistic word is permissable, is almost exclusively in the hands of my black and brown fellow countrymen. Thus has the line of division shifted and have *we* become the bastard race. As a group we have had our chance, and babbling away we allowed it to pass — clutching martinis, as it were, and gazing all the while upon the melancholy sunset over the Karoo, on the look-out for immortality . . . . Now they alone can improve our common lot by first liberating themselves. And just as I respect the black man trying to improve the dispensation of his own people, just so, I believe, will the black man respect me only to the extent that I am prepared to work for the transformation of my own community — and not if I attempt to tell him what he ought to do.

In other words, to me this symposium has been concerned from the very opening address with the acts, and in particular, with the omissions of a number of younger writers writing in the laguage of the tribe in office, the group in power, the rulers — and who bear a particular responsibility, therefore; who like all Afrikaans writers occupy a privileged if unenviable position in the tribe, even if only by virtue of the fuss made about them, because so many of that tribe's aspirations pass for cultural aspirations, because the identity of the so-called Afrikaner was originally one of language. It is concerned, in the same breath, as I see it, also with the work of a number of writers who began to query certain tenets on which the vested interests of the Afrikaner tribe are based. This questioning kicked up so much dust, in fact, because trifling with the institutions and taboos of the tribe inevitably poses the danger of gnawing at the status quo. Touch the Afrikaner and you touch the state. Whatever our high priests may say, no one can exist in isolation. The continued survival of the "Afrikaner" as he is defined by those in power and by those who preserve the tribal taboos, can only be ensured on condition that we do not accept our South Africanhood in word and deed.

Of course, within bounds, a measure of rebellion on the part of the long-haired and/or eggheads will be tolerated; it is seen to contribute, even, to such suppleness as ensures a lively glow of health. And what we did was to confuse that forbearance with freedom.

It's good, they say, that you wish to concern yourself with the freedom of the Afrikaner. But to meddle with the freedom of man, of the individual, which would necessitate an about-face within the framework of society — that's a horse of a different color, so to speak. That's subversive. That is not of our people, but alien, they say. And it's not realistic. You're dreaming. Come back, Brother, they say, to the hard reality of the African territory. Thus we attack each other under the banner of "reality."

What they really want to say is: don't stop us from jumping into the sea.

I remain convinced that I can only be free to the extent that my fellow man is free.

Now you will probably contend that I am over-estimating the social responsibility of the writer, relying on the easy publicity which we — the little writers — obtain from the pulpits and the news media — particularly the predominant purple press in this country of ours which, red-nosed, never stops looking for sensation, or is quick to cry wolf! wolf! or is too scared to do its own thinking — except when, full of bravado, in pub or closet — and then make use in a cynical manner of what others would have said, implying that they too, perhaps, may occasionally have thought along the same lines. Maybe you are right. But part of my argument this evening is just that, is to demonstrate, in fact, by making use of the perspective you have promised me, that the "anomalies" whereby the writer benefits in the realm of publicity are inherent in the pattern of affairs here. And that those "anomalies" which are to us, the Afrikaans scribblers, an existentialist agony — but to five-sixths of the population are a hard everyday humiliation and frustration of self-fulfillment — do not exist to the same degree anywhere else that I know of.

We are a bastard people with a bastard language. Our nature is one of bastardy. It is good and beautiful thus. We should be compost, decomposing to be able to combine again in other forms. Only, we have walked into the trap of the bastard who acquires power. In that part of our blood which comes from Europe was the curse of superiority. We wanted to justify our power. And to do that we had to consolidate our supposed tribal identity. We had to fence off, defend, offend. We had to entrench our otherness while retaining at the same time what we had won. We made our otherness the norm, the standard — and the ideal. And because our otherness is maintained *at the expense* of our fellow South Africans — and our South Africanhood — we felt threatened. We built walls. Not cities, but city walls. And like all bastards — uncertain of their identity — we began to adhere to the concept of *purity*. That is apartheid. *Apartheid is the law of the bastard.*

But, to bring play into our otherness, to safeguard the material benefits we enjoy, we were obliged to give rope, to decide that others also may acquire dignity, may enjoy some of the sweets of life — as and when we grant it to them. That is why we first determined the nature of way of life and their aspirations, and then prescribed their future accordingly, from now to eternity. That is what we grandly call the policy of — not development, please note, but separate development. That is what we call the dispensation — not of liberty, please note, but of similar liberties. Then we are not only realistic, but magnanimous and Christian as well, are we not? So much, then, for the black man, though we remain to him *baas, BOSS, master, meneer, moroeti, sir.* But as to the fate of our body-own shadows, the brown people, we are at our wits' end.

And these walls, the Apartheid, this "purity" and separateness, this *verkramptheid* (narrowness) and *verligtheid* (enlightenment) is the scope of our suicide, our self-destruction, our death. We are going to the dogs, and it seems that in the process we are prepared to drag the whole of Southern Africa with all its people down with us.

Nothing I say here this evening will sound new or strange to you. We all know it. What I discover myself means nothing. What

156

we realize as a group, as a society — that is important, for that is a shared possession, it has true value because it is on the way to truth. We are all involved in this tragedy together. It truly won't help to adopt a head-buried-in-literature pose.

And our writers then? What, in the meantime, has happened here inside? Our jaws are still jabbering, before long we will even be protesting yet again new and smarter censorship laws, we will be soured . . . then lightly turn once more to mutual buttering up; we keep moving — not the continuous moving and making of noise which is love — but the spasmodic noisemaking such as this week's, here, of wandering dead. We helped to build the walls, we maintain them; now they have become the walls of our prison. Occasionally we climb up onto the walls to see if the night is not about to break yet. One moment we think our literature is comparable to the "best in the world." The next we slink about with both tails between our legs, we tear our own breasts — because we are snubbed and booed everywhere. We are in Africa and we are not Africans. We go to Holland, France, and we realize suddenly that they've been lying to us. We are not Europeans. We go to England and we discover that we are Boers trying to live like Englishmen here beneath the Southern Cross. Whom can we measure ourselves against? For whom do we write our distorted, pretentious, nouveau riche works, other than for a couple of university pals lending such work a right to existence by assigning it? We are stark-naked and we don't even realize it. We endeavor to knit ourselves little blankets with big words and even bigger concepts grown out of other cultures and of which, in any case, we don't understand the first thing. What do we know of the rest of South Africa? Do we have any knowledge other than the fearful knowledge of the master? Does it ever occur to us that our country is attached, irrevocably, to Africa? Is it not amazing that the golden age of the Sixties, that time of harvesting our nice fat prizes and of wanting to fight to the bitter end about who should get the Hertzog-Prize,* that it coincided with a period when more and more unread, therefore non-existent, books by fellow South African authors were

*Named after General J.B.M. Hertzog who was prime minister from 1924-33, this is the most prestigious prize for Afrikaans literature. It is administered by the Suid-Afrikaanse Akademie vir Wetenskap en Kuns, and is awarded annually in rotation for prose/poetry/drama.

being banned? Does your mouth, too, have that insipid taste of shame? And here we are gathered now, ruefully looking back at the damnall we have done. And being proud of it.

I contend that our literature, no matter how clever sometimes, is largely a product of our stagnation and our alienation, and that it cannot be anything else, given the framework within which it originates.

Do we have alternatives? Are we nothing, then, as writers, but the shock-absorbers of this white establishment, its watchdogs?

The day will dawn when we, the present generation, will be hated by our descendants because we have bartered their birthright. Because they will be forced to live under the yoke of ailenation which we are now engaged in creating for them. Because we are instrumental in denying our fellow citizens their rightful birthright, here, today. Call it the sins of the fathers . . . . Call it *karma* if you like. It's all the same.

A young girl, one of the ones already being manipulated in our high schools, trained in fear and the hatred that goes with it, wrote this terrible thing a few days ago in a letter to the *Burger**. "We have sown Apartheid and we will reap a white man's land." What a tragic blindness! It's true, we have sown Apartheid or allowed it to be sown, and yes, fear is germinating, and despair, insensitivity, hypocrisy, superficiality, terror, perversions, intolerance. And blood.

Already we are part of that situation, here, now. Are we aware of that? We inherit our own sins. The black man wants to have less and less to do with us, he no longer pleads for his dignity like a "responsible" convert, he simply takes it without a by-your-leave, he seeks allies and arms. Why on earth has it taken so long? Why only now? Is there anyone who believes that an end can be put to this process of consciousness? How long did we tolerate the yoke of British imperialism, and what did we do then? Or have they less reason? Are they less human? Do we think sufficient time can still be bought, somewhere abroad? Time to do what with? Fragment the country even further?

And in this night we now enter, the fires of nationalism will be fanned, will flare up even brighter and more destructive. It will be

***Die Burger* (Citizen), leading Afrikaans Cape newspaper.

158

said that it is "us" or "them" — without our knowing who "us" is, without our *knowing* "them." That side which we are going to have to choose, is it going to be a knowing choice, or a desperate tribal choice? Will we even have a choice? The expectation will be that something will be defended. What? A Western civilization? What Western civilization, and whose? The white man's sole right to decision-making? The white skin? Only death's skin is an unblemished white. Afrikaans? Whose Afrikaans?

This is where the future of each of us will be settled, since way back when. If we would only take a peek over the wall, we would see, if you pardon the expression, that the camel's back is buggered.

One would like to believe in a miracle. One would like to believe that it could be possible to write in this country for and about people as people. But the poison of racism flows so deeply in our veins. Even in our language, our beautiful language, our wonderful vehicle. We speak of man and woman, of boy and girl. And when these are not pale enough? *Kaffir, nigger, coolie, blockhead, "uncle," ayah, kwedin, maid, wog, munt* — yes, one of our foremost writers from the Sixties still refers to "skepsels" (creatures) in his latest work; to his credit I suppose I had better add that he does not speak of "skepsel"-females or "skepsel"-ewes. Some of those terms were dropped under the pressure of growing consciousness, but will we ever accept the full and equal, self-evident humanness of the "others"? We stick now to a smug *Bantu* and *Colored.* By defecating others we defecate ourselves. Then ours becomes a fecal language. Is it so difficult to address a person by the name he uses when referring to himself? Do we later want it said then — in this land of sunshine, there were two species of *homo sapiens* — man, and white man?

A society without a feeling for history, without the stability of tradition; the human being with ahistorical identity who lives only for the immediacy of the present moment — if the above is humanly possible, it means that we are here this evening to celebrate the death of the memory, and worse still, that of all hope. It depends on us. I have said all talk is politics. Similarly, in the final analysis, all struggle is, in my opinion, a class-struggle. And there is no "culture"; there is class-culture.

As Pasolini put it: "In denying the social implications of a work of art, you lock yourself up in a romantic idealistic asylum which no

159

longer interests us, and it is futile either to consider or destroy such an attitude. As futile as being angry with the dead."

And Roman Jacobson: "In language there is no private property. Upon contact with the public, each work of art becomes social."

I do not like the terms "work of art" or "art." When making poems became the art of poetry, it lost its teeth. It became an aesthetic thing referring to itself alone or to other literature; we place it on a shelf between safe covers where it cannot bite, now it is food for lizards and academics; it is a threat no longer to the status quo, a tool or weapon no more.

In the words of Godard I submit: "The bourgeois system manufactures art which propagates a bourgeois ideology and values: detachment, political ignorance, and passivity . . . . Today's laws want us to write only advertisements on the walls and not poetry. But I believe that we are short of poetry, and it must grow out of a social practice!"

To write is to communicate, to eat together, to have intercourse, a communion, all of our blood, all of our flesh. We are men, writing for men about men, and therefore about relationships between men. Our first dimension is man — in his sameness and in his otherness, in his humanness. Where there is something seeking expression, the language will expand where necessary to give expression to that something. And vice versa, a language, a channel, will evoke the thoughts it can transmit. Such are the dialectics between concept and language. Sooner or later the water will flow where those channels exist — in spite of our water bailiffs, the censors.

As for myself — I want to try to write for *here,* for *now*. I want to come as close as I can in my work to the temporal — not the infinite; that has always been around. And infinity says nothing. What hurts is the ephemeral, the local.

I think that by taking cognizance of the nature of the struggle we are involved in and share, by making that struggle clearer — and even more: by taking a stand based on this knowledge — we expand our humanity and our language.

Then only will we be freed from the traps of Apartaans, will we speak Afrikaans: one of the many languages of Africa!

Viet Nam, and America is the name of death

if I had the power I would summon the birds of heaven
and all the small beasts of the veld
that like the night they may bear witness to your struggle
the struggle of heroes;
even the beasts and the night and the birds
are confused and poisoned,
but Viet Nam will live
supported by all nations!

and were Africa at my command
then you would find asylum there,
I grant you its riches and sanctuaries and comfort
so that you need never tremble again under the earth
never again kneel in the dust before bombs;
but Africa too will have to raise the shield
against metal-white wings of death;
you have demonstrated: man can go on living
with heart and lungs, with eyes of resistance,
and the nations will support you

o heroic nation of Viet Nam,
where do we find the words
to grasp your wounds,
to interpret your struggle?
but this you know already: every sun
is a dark bell tolling
in memory of the body of a child
embalmed in napalm, every moon
is a mournwhite turban round the head
in memory of the beloved who are rotting, and also
of the brighter flame which conquers
and through you we too grow stronger, more worthy,
with an option on the future
for the barefoot children of the earth

you forfeit your lives so that we may live:
where you die now freedom will grow,

those bloody fruits
for us all
for you, warriors where destruction falls from heaven
ripping open the graves
and blackening the grass
you are the heart of all mankind:

Viet Nam, o Viet Nam . . .

O Viet Nam, Viet Nam . . .

Space . . . (For my whitish fellow writers)

There is a ring at the front door, a dainty ting-a-ling sound. We are in
Wynberg in temporary quarters — for our week in the Cape for fun
and games of the summer school — owned by a kind friend, K.
Naampie opens the door. I had been dreaming at the window. The
window has a view of the football-ground cum athletics field of a high
school, and the children are running round and round the field —
some boys are giving it everything as though they really want to
become athletes, others seem wobbly in the knees, no doubt the
smokers and the jerk-offs; the girls come in all shapes and sizes too —
some have substantial bottoms and thighs like bowls of dough
bulging from their rolled up bloomers and things which leap up and
down crazily under their blouses, some of the others have pimples and
bouncing braids and mouths full of giggles. My dreams, their
dreams. Are my dreams equally visible from a distance? When they
move across the small area of field covered by the teacher's seeing eyes
— the teacher born with a whistle in the mouth — they sprint like
the devil or suddenly limp rather conspicuously, but during the rest of
the round, the lazy and the podgy and the garrulous and the lovers
huddle together. Nampti opens the door with its ting-a-ling ring. A
large figure shuts out the light. Behind him you would be able to see
tall trees. They're the trees of the wind which draw rain in winter.
Above the trees basins of clouds shake unsteadily. I was just about to
start writing a poem for K. with these trees in mind; I wanted to

162

write that he should think of us, and of our passage here, later, when the trees will be sad, full of autumn, and we will be far across the sea.

"*Chef*," Gamso announces, "*il y a un drôle de type dehors qui demade à te voir.*"

Naturally I get up to see who it is, fearing, as you probably expect, that it must be a Security man. I get up with smile and right hand in readiness, and if I had had a tail, it would have been wagging already. And, heck, I don't recognize him, not at first. He has grown older with his long hair bleached and deep grooves running mournfully down either side of his nostrils. There are spots of dandruff on the shiny collar of his jacket — even from the front I can see how his jacket bulges at the back, and as he enters the living room I see that one of his legs, the left, has apparently been amputated at the groin — it has been replaced by a wooden leg which taps as he walks. No, you can't guess who it was. He comes into the room where there is more light, and with the awkwardness of having to walk with a rigid piece of wood strapped to his hip, he turns aside a little, and I start when I notice the two stunted and *naked* (for hairy) wings behind his back. But I conceal my horror, because you're not supposed to let the disabled feel uncomfortable, and with a helpful hand supporting his elbow I pilot him toward a chair. Yes, and only then does it fully dawn on me who this is. Panus!*

"Panus!" I say, disconcerted. "Great Scott, where in the name of God do you come from?"

He gives a little embarrassed cough into his hand, nods in the direction of my wife, and mumbles: "Well, I live just around the corner in Mowbray† now."

This then by way of introducing what I am actually about to write. To make a long story short: Panus learned where we're staying and he also saw the fuss in the papers. It can't be said that the two of us are very fond of each other, but what with one thing and another our lives are considerably entangled. There was the bone we picked a few years ago — an incomplete report was published at the time —

---

*Author's "alter ego." First appears in *Om te vlieg* (To fly) (1972), a "story" recording the observations and experiences of Panus, i.e. Breyten, and Sosê respectively. Sosê, signifying "So says"/"Say so," etc., is a clever Afrikaansification of the name of the old Chinese philosopher So-chi (Afrikaans So-sjie).
†Suburb of Cape Town.

and ever since we have been in the same organization. Shall I say I was pleased to see him again! No, I'm much too indebted to him for that. Be that as it may, his visit today has a purpose. In view of certain statements and things made, he wanted more clarity on such aspects as (intentionally?) have not been cleared up yet. And in his own way he has become a kind of seer: his disability on the one hand has certain compensations on the other. Thus he had foreknowledge, as it were, of the reactions my remarks were to elicit — he predicted (only now) that people would be writing to me to say "piss-off" and "good-bye." Well, we shall see. I tried to write our conversation down — or at least the most significant points arising from it. It will form the first part of this piece of writing. A second part will deal with the broader context of the whitish writer *in situ,* for, having put the two together, it seemed on reflection that the issue under discussion was one described in more winged language as "poethood." (God have mercy on us.)

"I don't want to talk to you about absolute things. You know, since I've been living in Mowbray — and although I still spend some Saturday afternoons strolling up here on the Mountain too — I don't believe in the absolute anymore. And for me there is no past and no future. Also — it may sound strange — the image you see of yourself in the mirror is not an image, it is *you!* Having taken that into consideration then, etcetera, I wonder nevertheless how you see yourself. Fine, you arrived here with much uproar. All right, you were not to blame, still you have known for quite some years that your . . . poetic 'activities,' shall we say, are confused with all kinds of other stuff. That evening up at the campus you gave vent to a whole lot of unoriginal stuff. Was it your deliberate intention to abuse your position as a poet to attract attention? Sometimes it seems to me that you see enormous warts on this country because you evidently feel that you have been personally — I almost said physically — injured. Almost as if you want to say that what has been done to you — and please don't exaggerate, but granted then that you have been staying abroad for a stiffish little stretch already, more or less dissatisfied with your situation — almost, I was saying, as if you feel this shouldn't happen to a white man. You were generalizing. I have the impression that you were trying to act the part of the prophet of doom. The newspapers came up with all kinds of comment. Including, as Schalk Pienaar says, that you were out to create a specific effect. But to whom and for whom do you speak? Haven't you wedged your ass between two chairs? Because the whites regard you as a nigger-lover, and why should the blacks ever accept you? I mean, thanks for the kindness, but what do you know of the experience, the emotions, the seen-from-the-inside life of a black man? And you, a poet within those inconsistencies — you can't want to cry like that in a language — inextricably interwoven with a specific group of people, warts and all — while simultaneously wanting to scold and reject the whole caboodle! Are you a masochist perhaps? Or is it just for the anarchical kick of excreting on your own back stoop? What exactly were you hoping to find here?"

"I'm afraid I can't be of much help to you. You're right — and I'm aware of it — there is a knot of paradoxes here I haven't yet been able to resolve to my own satisfaction. Perhaps, by going even deeper into the thing, I am in search, in fact, of an agonizing kind of solution; one tries to transcend oneself. Knowing, of course, that you will never get away from the paradoxes ultimately. But isn't that the case with all other people, too? And is it necessary then to bring about — in our old Calvinistic way — this reconciliation? Let's pull a few threads. There's a definite analysis which can be made: in short, the anomaly, the in-between position of the let's say intellectual (the head-and-sometimes-heart-too worker) who wants to fall in with the oppressed, who wants to side with the proletariat while belonging, both by birth and by profession, to the privileged. Particularly in a country like ours where the conspicuous outward manifestation of indentification of your 'group' — skin color — is a sign which can't be erased. Take my case, for example: I want to do the seemingly impossible: by means of the narrow and exclusive language of poetry (poetry too is only a language) I want to try to say things which will affect as many people as possible. First objection: the medium (verse) does not lend itself to that; secondly, even less so the Afrikaans language, since we have no tradition whatsoever of socializing usage; thirdly, it's a language which has been branded as a tool of and an excuse for oppression. It is therefore rejected by the very people who are going to rebel, and the way in which you want to use it, is rejected also by your 'own people,' because it does not give expression to

165

something they share or believe, does it? Another contradiction — as you know, I find myself largely in foreign parts (in more senses than one) while wishing to remain involved heart and soul with an everyday and *possibly changing* local reality. And yet, and yet, I am going to boast now, but I have the feeling that I give expression fairly accurately, somehow be it by an almost organic crack in my nature, to a feeling of being between the devil and the deep blue sea, which is experienced by a considerable number of Afrikaans-speaking people.

"As for your other remarks. I believe that I'm not interested in provocation for its own sake. I convince myself that in my way I am doing my bit for change. Yes, but what must be changed? Ultimately the attitudes and relationships of people, of course. How can these be changed? Now there I'm pessimistic, because I don't think moral considerations are going to pull it off; it can only start happening once the balance of power is altered. And by balance of power I certainly do not mean the power of literature. Though the power of the word should never be underestimated; words may help, for instance, to bring underlying problems into the open. A pal of mine once said: 'Culture is a gun.' Another poet argued that the so-called expression of culture helps to identify the enemy.

"Why do I feel so strongly about it personally? Because I believe that I too — like all the other powerless Afrikaans-speaking whitish people — have, by force of circumstance, been placed in the humiliating position of being subjected to a discriminating system I despise; on the one hand this system with its laws and structures and things forces me into a specific kind of relationship with other South Africans, while preventing me, on the other (or at the same time) from evolving to my fullest potential — within this set-up it is impossible either for us or for the blacks to become full-fledged and useful people for our country.

"What was I hoping to find here, you ask? Yes, well, I'm not sure I always know myself. I wish I could write as well as the West Nkosi play, especially that guy, I don't know if you know him, on the Marabi bell.* I'm not sure I know what I'm trying to say with this

*There is some confusion about identities here. West Nkosi is in fact a black Soweto saxophone player, while Marabi refers to a (long dead) African dance and not to an instrument: a Marabi bell as such does not exist. Perhaps this sentence may therefore be interpreted as follows: West Nkosi signifies the *band* lead by Nkosi, while "that guy . . . on the Marabi bell" refers to Nkosi himself playing Marabi dance music on his saxophone (which contains a bell).

166

exactly. Let's put it like this: those men play *naturally*. If they had been singers, I would have said when they open their mouths sounds emerge. And right away — but that's another story — it's a godcrying shame that some of the best talent in our country is chucked away so afterbirthishly. We mess with people. In later years we will look back on this period and realize how much was not or could not be utilized during these intervening years.

"I came back to cut myself a new cane, to wash my ear in the language, and to stuff my eyes with mountain and sea and desert and flower. To be *there*, not just with-it."

"Let's take it back for the moment to the social dimension. I still don't quite see where you fit in, although I too believe that literature — or let's say art in general — most certainly has a social function. Indeed, one function specifically is taking cognizance, and such cognizance as is inherent in the writing process, so to speak, must be communicated, disseminated. To me 'power to the people' means that the people are provided with the means to knowledge of self, knowledge of others (maybe that's the same thing), and self-determination. To give the people back to themselves. Writing, therefore, is not *possession*. What you have shared out, or have helped to create, is no longer controlled by you, and they who have eaten it, can do with it as they please. For instance, we, the South African nation — we are not a people yet, and in addition the bosses are intent on breaking up the one nation we were on the way to becoming, aren't they? — we have yet to learn what we are, we have to get used to ourselves. You were trying to thrash a few things out a moment ago — that you would deplore your work being nothing but an act of *mea culpa*, that your little clarion is cracked, but that you want to contribute to the possibilities for real transformation — economic and political transformation, I suppose, which would lead to cultural transformation (and *not* the other way around). It is true that our society is on the brink of revolutionary change. Is art an effective means then with which to occupy oneself?"

"That depends on the content you are attempting to give to your work — and that isn't something you can determine on your own. The mechanism of 'being a writer' is by its very nature another aspect entirely. Broadly speaking writing starts for me with resistance — first of all resistance to death. 'Is death not cruel enough that life must copy it?' Who said that? I don't write for the cessation of

167

Afrikaans — we cannot afford the luxury of suicide — but expressly for the continued existence of certain 'principles' (the re-evaluation?) even though they be alternatives — I mean, even though they must replace existing principles — also in Afrikaans.

"Then, after that, we come to the things the writer is able to attempt within his profession. It's high time that we band together to exert pressure on the publishers — that we band together as the body concerned — so that they will start looking after the interests of the writers, and really and truly become 'bearers of culture' too, instead of lying down in the dust like dogs at the feet of parsons, politicians, and policemen. It's high time we band together to refuse to see our work being used by authorities with whom we could never agree. By refusing to publish we can see to it that the censors disappear into deserved oblivion; we can — by boycott actions or more fighting against censorship laws; we can oust the yes-men and the tail-waggers from the faculties; we can take direct action to make sure that the banned work of fellow writers, fellow countrymen, dissidents, blacks, and English is printed (even if we have to do it ourselves) and disseminated. We can, or we could, but we won't. In truth the Afrikaans writer is a sop. We can, or could, extend the frontiers, be little pariahs in our own right. No dice. You know yourself how it is. Our talk smells even worse than our writing. Liberalists we are indeed — privately, of course, just like the rest of society. But what the hell, one shouldn't get upset.

"The trouble is, as I have tried to point out before, that the means of combat (writing, language) is itself so ambivalent. All art is artificial. I could say, in parenthesis, that we are too much concerned with art as shit and not as yet sufficiently with the possibilities of shit as art or a form of artistic expression (arse poetica). But writing cannot be a direct means of communication. Writing comes between and hampers saying and hearing (or understanding). What is written and described is the act of writing itself. The banks determine the river. I have tried to indicate that there is a connection between content and language. (Language is content.) Maybe — that is how it seems to me — all my fumbling and puttering comes back to relationships: those between inside and outside, between man and man, between saying and saying, between thing and perception. The historical 'I' then becomes a lookout post and an observation point — the point where 'inside' and 'outside' cross, where the best study can be made, therefore, of the relationship between the two as well as of the point itself — the point which only acquires significance because the two cross there at that specific moment. Then I think: I do not really believe in irreconcilable paradoxes after all; rather in the relationship between points of departure, in tension between those paradoxes. Out of those relationships, and spurred on by that tension, come new attitudes which in turn conjure up new contrasts. Or am I talking myself into a tangle now?"

"No, I wouldn't say you're talking yourself into a corner, but your remarks can't be described as containing the wisdom of King Solomon's coachman's second cousin from Gurglefountain either. (And *that* was well before Yeshu Hannorsri's time!) This little game of relationships is interesting, however, or middling to half-interesting. And yet every writer has this kind of foreshortened view of himself and of his own work. We are not even touching now on the true reasons — if any — for writing activities. Oh, I know, some write because they suffer repeatedly from *pruritus ani*. You who are so obsessed with the outward if obscure manifestations and appendages of the power of the Central Authorities (or their watchdogs) like crew cut soldiers and whiskered public servants, you hadn't even noticed that one of them was specially delegated to keep an eye on your activities. A gregarious animal, that's what that is (sporting university degrees instead of a degree of universality!) and there you are now: you have your case of someone suffering a bit of discomfort with the above-named affliction who is not allowed the glorious relief of a good scratch; only the other night up there at the university I saw him slobbering and shifting about on his *ani*. For other geese the thing which must find expression is a silver needle in the brain, and sometimes their etchings leave little traces of blood behind, too. (Though it is occasionally the poem itself, that which is a snail, which wants to maneuver across the skin on razor-edged ice skates.) To this category of scratch-and-writers Petőfi's words apply: '*Le désespoir est une chimère, c'est ce qui le rend si semblable à l'espoir.*' But for most spillers of ink the word-and-concept poem = thought.

"Leaving it at that for the moment . . . tell me rather how you see your own work, what value you place on it; I mean relative value, naturally."

"To begin with just this: I have already attempted elsewhere, some years ago, to explain what I try to achieve with my poetry — as seen from within that poetry itself. It was the flesh of a little essay entitled *Monologue through an Anus* (perhaps it should have been *Aneus,* who knows). I must warn you that I intend to write down our conversation and to submit it to the Boss, and therefore you should know that anything you say may eventually be used in evidence against you.

"My worth? The reply to an obscure question will naturally be obscure. It's difficult to evaluate and to place my work according to 'purely' literary criteria. It's difficult to do so with anyone's work, especially in times of crisis or transition such as these. 'Culture' is the realm of the bluffers. Literary values or criteria, seemingly impartial and harmless, contain, or even are, the translation into words of social criteria. The cultural manifestations of any group of people exist also to portray and to protect their interests. Culture is class-culture. In our country it is at present — I'm talking about the Afrikaners — a bourgeois culture. That's why it's conservative and bigoted. At the same time we also have a small minority trying to grope their way to an alternative, probing, questioning view — and that, indeed, is where we should be careful, extremely careful, because even our questioning — our loyal resistance* — may again be swallowed up by and adapted to the prevailing culture; we become, in turn, fringes and frills, having contributed at best only to a renewal of the old. In other words, in other words, ladies and gentlemen, the question is whether our aim be adaptation — reformation even — or transformation, and to achieve the latter, also the takeover, therefore, of the cultural levers by people not representing the current ruling bourgeoisie. That's just one side. For what is a work of art? What is the act of creation? (Pardon the lofty curse.) Is it not an attempt, in actual fact, to transcend oneself, for whatever reasons? (And

---

*Reference *inter alia* to a volume of critical essays entitled *Lojale Verset* (Afrikaans equivalent) (1939) by the great Afrikaans poet N.P. van Wyk Louw (1906-1970). The sub-title of this volume reads: "Critical thoughts on our Afrikaans cultural aspirations and our literary movement," and it bears the motto: "Revolt is just as necessary in a people as loyalty. It is not even dangerous that a rebellion fails; what is dangerous, is that an entire generation may go by without protest." In the main the essays attack the stagnation of Afrikaans literature and literary criticism and the smugness and lack of self-criticism prevalent among academics and writers alike.

transcendence has no reasons, I know; I only mean — some people want to go beyond the limit of being in order to encounter other stations of being and other hordes of humanity, others again desire immortality by writing in the dust.) And while it is true that the appraisal of a work of art is based on considerations determined by group interests, while it is a fact, therefore, that a work of art in that sense has no 'value,' it is nevertheless true that it should be able to satisfy certain requirements, if only because a work of art has its own, I'm tempted to say, biological life, its own cell structure. It must be admitted that these requirements weren't and won't be the same for all time — or more precisely, these requirements are manifold and probably always present, but different 'times' highlight and emphasize now one requirement and then another.

"Take *my* work, for instance. It's probably damned difficult to separate the chaff from the wheat because any evaluation is suspected of having ulterior motives. A little more distance would sort that little matter out, however. Then it would become clear that my 'contribution' to whatsoever was relatively slim. Only a few of my poems are wholly satisfactory; too often there are dull patches and untidiness (denseness instead of density). In defense it could be argued — if one wanted to — that almost every poem should be seen as a component of a whole or of a cycle, or reflecting a facet of an all-encompassing non-reality. That's splitting hairs. The work frequently gives an impression of *collages,* scrap-work: pieces picked up here and there (references, quotations, other 'realities'), seldom digested and absorbed by the mother-thing, the poem. That's why my shorter bits are better than the long ones — and the very best, being a synthesis also of my poetic credo, was this one, included in I don't know anymore which volume:

on the whole I'm sitting shitting on a hole
expressing myself abundantly

And yet, it's not up to me to make rash and subjective judgments. One thing is certain — in due course it will become very clear that my work will be worth much less than the relative uproar of the past year would lead one to suppose. Also that the few poems which are interesting date from the earliest 'period' (taking into account that there was not much variation in the oeuvre). My last work, like this book, for example, has a moralistic tenor, even a preachy tone. It sounds shrill, but inside it's more limp than limpid. In addition, it is without real roots in a given environment, and it's doubtful whether it is acceptable to the people to whom it is addressed."

"Once again you speak of 'last.' On more than one occasion now you have indicated — threatened? — that you are working on your last volume; not forgetting, of course, that you then tried to postpone that deadline with the odd publication here and a little translation there. I understand that there are two hearts beating within the breast of the writer, so to speak, or two beats of the same heart: the creative impulse or the making-public, and the suicidishness, the death wish. I can understand that a certain amount of scope for variation between the two is necessary. I can understand that the one always gets under the skin of the other. I can also understand that you are then expressly going to create for yourself an appearance of death, of truncation and cessation where it does not exist — an ersatz-death. But in this game of self-destruction, aren't you weaving threads in which you are going to get yourself entangled? The game may become deadly. And my questions are: Are you not merely engaged in making yourself interesting? Do you want your friends to demonstrate their affection by talking you into going on? Or are there insoluble problems in your work? Are you then running away from both the social (of which your mouth is so full) and the personal responsibility? Or is it plainly and simply that you have dried up?"

"Panus, old chum, your questions come close to the bone — and it's difficult to accept such presumptuousness coming from a border-line case. . . . I must admit that elements of the answers are already contained in the questions. There are many other possible answers left. Half in jest I must say that I'm going to stop because I've announced it — and that's not at all as silly as it sounds. Perhaps I felt the need to subject myself to an *arbitrary* decision? All good things must come to an end, even pleasure. I never said I was going to stop writing — that can only happen once I know why I write — but except for the last collection, for which I want to make advance publicity now, DEATH-CHAIR, it means the end of the publication of new work.

172

"There are good reasons and there are bad reasons. The bad ones — *inter alia* that I put quality on a par with limited quantity; also that I want to see poetry as associated with youth, and I have left youth behind; that there are promises and expectations which I cannot fulfill; and so forth, of course. The good ones? To finish, to pass on to something else. To go on living is another form of suicide, also to take the mystique out of it; because I have become attached to an absence; because I occupy a false and loose position within the Afrikaans community and the Afrikaans literature; because I have had my say. And the hell with it!

"You won't miss your excretion. Too much sod, too little god. This is how Kafka put it in *A Report to an Academy:* 'That progress of mine! How the rays of knowledge penetrated into my awakening brain from all sides! I do not deny it: I found it exhilarating. But I must also confess: I did not overestimate it, not even then, much less now. With an attempt which up till now has never been repeated I managed to reach the cultural level of an average European . . . . But do not tell me that it was not worth the trouble. In any case, I am not appealing for any man's verdict, I am only imparting knowledge, I am only making a report. To you also, honored Members of the Academy, I have only made a report.' "

"If I have to stop lying, I won't be able to create another thing.

"A cessation is inevitable. Do you still remember where the beginning was? All well and good, one also wants to stop *to prevent me returning, like a dog, to the vomit of memory* . . . . The beginning was different. We launched forth because our tails were nice and long. Two poems I still recall from that time. One was in English: 'Visiting a friend, I was surprised when his cocker spaniel came to meet me/ wearing a hairnet/ I was told this was to keep his ears out of his food.' And the other one with the vulture name of *Culture:*

like miserable medlars
          bloodied in snow
like white wardrobes
like a firm denial
like hearts
like a fox on Saturday

173

like a fox on Sunday
like a fox on Sembleday

"And at last, Panus, it would only be fair in the grasp of an
ultimate gasp, while the wound opens and the juice flies away, to
make a final bequest. I bequeath the following titles to any writer
who thinks that he or she or they can do something with them.
Naturally they may add to these what content suits them.

THE PROFITS OF PROPHETS (the testament, perhaps, of a
poet with a vocation?)
A TAIL IN THE TELLING
LEAVING THE SECURITY RANCH — WHO TWIGS?
THE MIRROR AND ITS IMAGE
LIFE-MINE (an autobiography?)
BY THE WAY (an account of a journey)
FREED VERSE

Once again, this legacy is for any writer who wants it."

The afternoon, meanwhile, has grown old and bent, and
shadows which had fallen from the clouds had become heavy and had
started dragging on the earth. Always, even though they may be far
away, one is conscious of the presence of mountains and of vineyards
smelling warm, of trees catching and keeping the sound of the wind.
It's a wonderful world. With some effort my visitor had got to his
feet again. He is a living paradox. I saw him to the door. It was agreed
that we should spend an evening together again, before the departure
and the autumn and the isolation, and in the presence of Jan Blom*
next time. I asked him whether he wanted a towel to throw across his
wings, but he said no. When he had disappeared around the corner
with much pain and discomfort, I sat down to pen/pin down the

*Pseudonym Author's volume of poetry *Lotus* (1970) appeared under. (Afrikaans *blom*
flower.)

174

above and to tie it to a language. Thereupon I pondered the nature of
a poem some more. Here is the fruit of my meditation. Afterward I
wrote part 2. (Every cloud is a potential hat.)

this thing has the required length
and as for form it looks
(though somewhat disjointed) as it should;

as it is lying flat we shall not
be able to estimate the thickness

on the one hand, what is visible is is —
I mean the jerky patter
that hopes to deny beginning and end

and thus through refusal to refer beyond itself
proclaims independent — hence incomprehensible — existence

what would be audible if eyes still heard
on the other hand are sounds related to one another
since rhythm, or rather, components

caring for one another
are the tokens of organic life

certain elements are possibly repeated
even though it may only be to fill gaps
and thus wrest meaning from its context

but in this manner the delusion
of completion is sustained

e.g. the higher and previously discovered white-self
returns and now exists in painful certainty

so take this thing between thumb and heart,
hold it at an angle against the wash of the light,
and call it if you must: a poem

Two quotations to begin with. First, two lines from an old poem by Andrei Voznesenski:

*"It is a poem's function
to be Shame's sensual organ."*

And Mikis Theodorakis who says:

*"Resistance
is a purifying fire."*

As philosopher, painworker, researching the agonies of the mind — man is a cripple in a sense, or underprivileged at the very least. Politicians, officials, clerks may be flexible and compliant; the "creator" (the organ of belching and breaking) never has the freedom of being allowed to choose between offering resistance or yielding. To him it is neither an ethical nor even a moral problem, but purely technical. The "creator" doesn't dare to capitulate. Surrender affects the very roots of his trade.

The above paragraph sounds somewhat inflated. I'm not trying to say that the researcher is above and beyond any social responsibility and accountability; on the contrary, he has a greater responsibility than anyone else since he is instrumental in determining how those to whom he gives expression see themselves, he helps to formulate the ideals of his people. But he can open up the world by seeing and saying, or he can cover up. And the cover-up — the self-censorship, for instance — causes a certain blunting; he uses his tools to the wrong ends so that the tools themselves are finally affected, for there is a delicate and living balance between word and concept — the word (syntax, etcetera) acting as harness.

Now it is a fact in most cases and in terms of a distorted justification that we are mouthpieces of the Afrikaners in office. Our true identity is limited for us; we are forced into the framework of group interests — and racial or language groups, not classes or stations. We are prevented from analyzing the true nature of our activities. The clearest example of this, of course, is that we cannot or would not see that the liberties of our fellow-writers-of-another-color or another-language are our liberties too. The excuses put forward for this omission, when we had our chance, as you know, included the specific and unique situation of Afrikaans — more or less thus: "We cannot afford to boycott the repressive laws of the authorities, because our market is only a domestic one, and if we're deprived of that, we've had it." That's placing small tribal values before human values (based, moreover, on an unproven argument), and afterward it was ridiculous to try to dissociate ourselves from the authorities. Another point of departure — equally cowardly — was that the Government knows what it's doing, and when people or their work are banned, it's for a good reason which we don't need to know.

Who are these authorities from whom we wished to dissociate ourselves? The Government, of course, is the Government, with all its administrative (and sometimes — and more and more often these days) . . . policy-making branches like the Security Branch. The party monopolizing the political power is the Nationalist Party, National Christian in the way that that other one was National Socialist. And the pillars of this party-government are the Christian Nationalist Churches, the Afrikaans Academy, the *Broederbond,* and other cultural and secret or semi-secret pressure groups. Their combined power, as manifest through faculties, student organizations, libraries, and what h ave you, is great and bitter and rigid.

In essence the nature of our regime and our policy is suppression and — where and when it is relaxed — paternalism. From time to time we happen to place the accent on so-called enlightened decisions taken off our own bat on behalf of the entire nation (of South Africa); thus it happens that some of us advocate the inclusion of the "Brownman" in some of our privileges, in such a way as to suggest that it's a hell of a favor. Our regime is also one of occupation. Because we behave like settler colonists, we will be treated as such.

It is this totality which we are part of as writers, albeit on occasion a-mumbling-and-a-grumbling.

In most Western or Western-oriented societies the intelligentsia are an appendage of the bourgeoisie . That power which is not undermined is the power of the bourgeoisie — they are the ones who pay, thanks boss — and even the deviations and perversions are those of the bourgeoisie. I will go further and contend that even a concept such as "freedom of expression" is debated only in its bourgeois context and ramifications. The role of the artist — the elite or the

177

clown — is an inevitable outcrop of that class, without the ability, necessarily, to be an integral part of it. Only within the whole of another kind of distribution between the capitalists and the workers and tenants will that role be different one day. Then — but in the meantime too — our art can be a means of struggle, and then we can contribute effectively to the transformation of a society.

We talk to our masters. Our discourse can be a Dialogue, need not be mere consent.

Our blindness is not unique. If our relationship — as Afrikaners — with the other people in our country were not a colonialist one, if the "preservation of the tribe" were not such a leveler, we would perhaps be better able to recognize our own class position. Their imperialism makes it equally difficult for the Americans to see themselves in complete clarity, in the mirror at home.

For our country is on the brink of drastic changes — or, put a better way — revolutions. What will remain of our Afrikaans by the end of the century, and in what context, and who will then be able to blame? We can, said repeatedly and once again: be part of the problem or part of the solution. What will those revolutions look like? No one knows, but the only choice we have left now is the manner in which we want to (and can) take part in the opening up. Whatever happens, it won't be the way we imagine it.

In another country, long, long ago, in a similar but not identical situation, someone wrote to the intellectuals of his time and environment: "Fatheads, babblers, idiots, do you think history is made in the salons where democratic parvenus flirt with aristocratic liberals, where the little advocates from the provinces, yesterday knowing no one, today are already licking the hands of their highborn excellencies? Fatheads, babblers, idiots! History is made in the trenches where the soldier, overcome with the nightmare of the war, plants a bayonet in the belly of his superior, and, hanging onto the footboard of the train, returns afterward to his village to raise a fire in the house of his lord. Such barbaric goings-on stick in your throats? 'Don't hold it against me,' replies History; 'I'm doing what I can.' One is the logical consequence of the other. Do you honestly believe that you determine the course of history in your contact commissions? It's all nonsense, idle fancy, cretinism!"

178

In conclusion — any opposition on the part of the Afrikaans writers to Afrikaans authority will cause a furor and enjoy much attention in the English press. We must not allow ourselves to be put off by that, and the disproportionate interest which our actions will invite won't be for healthy reasons, but is much more likely to be spite from a neutered and provincialistic section of our population (but oh, how strong economically!) — and yet, we may not allow ourselves to be influenced by that. It's high time, now, that we — we with our privileged positions — extend a hand to help our oppressed writer colleagues. If we cannot do it as human beings, then at least as committed colleagues. And not just in our long-drawn and over-cautious statements, but actively, where possible, in the fields of publication and distribution and in our disregard of the censorship laws.

A final proposal and wish: that we may break away, both in our perception and conduct, to a broader South African identity.

February 18

The Cape Town week with all its excitedness and its disjointedness is over. It is not the Cape Town I used to know. But occasionally something I see this time suddenly corresponds to an old dream which I myself had lost, and the coincidence is confusing, and for a split second I am back where I want to be. Some of the pine trees are still tall and wild as always. Graaff's pool is full of boiling foam when the tide comes in. Yesterday evening, at the end of the last of the confusion up at the university, some friends took us along to the cabin owned by someone living on the steep slope above one of Clifton's inlets. The guests were all outside on the lawn above the sparkling sea. The moon was large and silver white. Suddenly the landscape — the nightscape — was virgin; eternal as it will always be. We little people drank much and deeply, and our conversations, though we may remember nothing of them today, hurt. Linus was there, and Ampie and John and Fanie. The waves of the tumultuous sea, those swollen silver things, boomed and broke continuously on the sand, and the stars came sliding down like drops. We were so small that we were almost shy in each other's presence. We'll never stand together again like that, not the same people. The dark wine, the smell of the sea soaked into our clothes and into the house and into the hedge where a drunk had got himself entangled and the night as dark as safety, and the moon which speaks Afrikaans — and all the other languages of Africa. At home behind the Mountain I dreamed.

last night, I don't know what time it was,
halfway between the days of Satyr and Sun
the sea opened before me,
a word became thought,
our sea, my sea, sea, a blue
tumbling tumultuous sea
white with excitement —
the waves were steam engines made of glass
filled with water
which for no reason
on the beach
broke crashing;

I am a god and the sun never sets
the sea never sinks,
only its surface grows somber at times,
from a remote yesterday I have summoned my friends
to share this conversation with me —
Daan, John, Ampie, Faan:
"let us squat here in the sand —
"the wailing of the aircraft we shall
"not hear
"above the sound of the exultant sea"

— and perhaps it was already too late

180

Today we had the honor to be invited to a wedding — the wedding of Farieda, youngest daughter of the late Mr. A.G. Brown, and Yusuf, eldest son of Gaironesa. We missed the Nikah in the mosque in Long-market Street,* but went to the reception afterward up in Scotches-kloof.† As is customary, the receptions of the bride and her groom were held in two different places, and like all the other guests we drove up and down several times. We even went along to the park where a deaf and dumb photographer took the photographs of the couple and their retinue. We weren't always in the right place either. "They (the married couple) have just gone over *there*," it was explained to us, "but they'll be coming back *here* again shortly."

It was a dignified ceremony, with an occasional touch of nostalgia. At the bride's hall we were treated to a variety of delicious Malay dishes. The bride and her bridesmaids sat at the top of the hall on a decorated dais, and we, the guests, at long wooden tables laden with delicacies. An elderly aunt — Kanalla — across the table from us, saw to it that our plates were never empty. I couldn't keep my eyes off the pretty and mysterious young girls. At the door the barefoot children from the neighborhood jostled each other. Just inside the door sat an old man who was so wall-eyed that we didn't know who else, besides us, he was looking at as well. Daantjie was convinced it was the evil eye, and as protection against it — it's supposed to help — he twisted one of the buttons on his jacket right off. His own eyes were stiff as a poker and his face bright scarlet. Suddenly the guests, led by a chanter, started singing — some of those sad wedding songs. The heart was carried away.

Who else did we see in the Cape? We dined with Gatsha Buthel-ezi and his wife and Sonny Leon and a few other people, and an evening or so later Gatsha and one of his associates paid us another visit. It's almost as though the man enjoys his tricky position — or possibly he only laughs to give himself courage. And it's as if he himself believes in a fatalistic way that he will be disposed of sooner or later. In his inside pocket he carries a ridiculous little pistol as pathetic self-protection.

*One of the oldest streets in the heart of Cape Town.
†Part of Malay Quarter in Cape Town.

February 20 - March 9

The closer you get to the end, the faster it goes. To the extent that I have had the feeling during our travels across the country that we didn't really stop anywhere. And what we brought back is somehow very little, too — a few impressions, a handful of verse, bruises and corns.

Left Wellington February 20th in Pa's car. Yellowish wind pushing angrily across Dutoitskloof Pass. On the way up the mountain one passes a farm — a winery — on your right. It's called "Klippie." Be warned, a strange man lives on that farm. He runs up and down along his fence with a top hat of highest opinion on his noble head, and with alternating little please-sounds and desperate little curses and his tongue poked through the wire, he struggles to get at the passers-by, be they nationalists or ex-nationalists.

Hurriedly we reached the sea. A long way up the coast, close to Knysna, we dug into the provisions Ounooi had packed for us. And here the wind was a raging white presence; spray and small blobs of froth were thrust inland. When you drive for a whole day and cover hundreds of miles and get the same terrible wind from the front during the entire journey, that's when you begin to sense the immensity of this continent. (In Europe it would mean experiencing one and the same element of nature from Paris to Rome.) We turned inland at Port Elizabeth and on the first evening, by half past eight, we found ourselves in Grahamstown with Andre and Alta.

Drawing up at the front door (in the twilight) — at least the rain had cleared, for along the sea of the Bay* it has started raining great fully grown drops of water all of a sudden, which splashed against the windows until our view was covered in streaks and smudges — drawing up in front of this gracious home (even more grandiose inside, we would later discover, a splendid place, old Settler dwelling, as old as the hills in the South African context, that is to say, over a hundred years old, of colonial simplicity, but homely inside all the same, though it does have a waiting room next to the study, and in the study of the maestro there is a desk. God be my witness, which is a disguised ark, one can't tell when the tall waves of

*Port Elizabeth.

182

destructive reactions will sweep across the archipelago, with a top fit
to skate on, two by two) — drawing up at the front door (hand-brake
on) a quotation flashes through my mind. "Quotations," some other
fellow alleged, "are when your own breathing has dried up and you
start relying on someone else's." It is — the quotation, I mean —
something said by an old Spanish author during a writers' conference
— an auction of worn-out ideas — in which the man (I can't think of
his name just at present) explains why he sees his work within the
broader context of a people's struggle (or a part of that people) for
social and political freedom. Absolute freedom of expression (say I) is
a bourgeois illusion, a claim (a concept) made by the arrogant elite.
Why can't we, the little writers, see how and where our activities
could fit into the construction of the "nation"? Because we have a
hierarchical view of matters; we are afraid we may be "demeaned"; we
have a zap-one-time-fartass-smell-of-corn — and in the final
analysis, sterile — opinion of what we're worth. We are not useful,
we are value-incarnate. "Freedom," a toothless Portuguese
contended much later, "exists only at the moment when you are
fighting for it." (That's it, Brother! Chew it to bits!) The quotation
— it escapes me for the moment — was longish and an historical
review of this kind of problem in itself. In short, a clarification giving
meaning to one's trade. I wanted to quote that as we entered; I sorted
the words out in my mouth; if only I hadn't forgotten for the moment
where exactly I had read it. It was used, however, by another quoter
in a little book with a short title which was published recently in
France. Leave it at that. (And no more.)

Brand River Rietpoel and Klipdale,
Riviersonderend Soetendal and Matroosberg,
but Adamskraal Muishond and Groot-Keerom,
Suurbraak, Lemoenshoek and Sorgvliet —
also Moordkuil This Area Enlarged The Baths
Pakhuis Waenhuiskrans Mooimaak and Darling;
yes, Goergap Paleisheuwel Dwarskersbos
Moedverloor;
yes, Tra-tra Nougas Height Biedou Mountains
Gannakuils Kanarie and Renoster —

CONSTABLE!
CHAIN!

No, that's not the road we took. It's just because. Besides, when you're afraid to be alone in your sleep you should dream like mad.

At five o'clock on the day of February 21st we left Grahamstown and by 10 that evening we were in Butterworth where we stayed in the Masonic Hotel. Butterworth's streets were full of buttery mud since it had been raining hard and without let-up. What were we up to? Nothing. And early on the day of the morning we made tracks.

It was still quite early when we called at a Dutch Reformed Mission Station near Umtata, where a cousin of mine works. It would be too easy to pass judgment here on the activities of the people there. The only thing which is clear, is that they believe in what they're doing, and that it's pointless. I myself would never take on such a task — for what has the D.R. Church in S.A. to be proud of? Whatever the wonderful people performing the basic work of conversion and education — out of personal conviction — may feel: the Church is an appendage and an instrument of an inhuman racial policy — the deadliest poison against any true Christianity.

We spent the whole morning driving through Xhosa-land*. A reservation, a reserve. Fob-off-land. But also a land of stunning beauty. God's finger merely brushed here and there so that the country rose wantonly. God's fingernails occasionally scratched and red and bloody lie the dongas. Xhosa-land: this land a continuation, a tenacity, a clotting of the ocean. The wind is brackish, beneath the clouds the seagulls moan. The air a sheet of blue paper, and crude with many spatters and blotches the cloudy white writing. Read: Xhosa-land.

Qumbu, Mount Frere, passing Kokstad, the town of the Koks and the Griqua — *Voortrekkers:* Pioneers. We were half-expecting to see the Drakensberg Mountains coiling step by step to port like blue smoke in the sky, we expected to find indications of symbols — the tracks of bare feet, rusty spears, wagon wheel scores in the rock, the skeleton of a San man hanged from a branch, shards of beer pots, a

*Land of the Xhosa, i.e. the Ciskei and Transkei (see *Notes on Persons and Places*).

184

Royal Dragoons flag torn to shreds — but there was nothing — our expectations were put to shame, and only clouds tumbled from the symbolic heights. By four that afternoon we had reached Pinetown next to Durban, and Cowhide and his wife. Cloete was also there. We had a curry in the city that evening (with Roargrumble de Vries) in a restaurant where people of all South African race groups were present in the most normal way in the world. For, dear reader of twenty years hence, please don't laugh, get up from the floor, hold your breath, and listen to me: in the dark times of 1973 it was still against the law and inconceivable that, let's say, Dumile, Jakes from the Cape, Skobota Msezane, and Violet and I would be allowed to sit down to a meal at the same table in a public place. Our land, you see, was a kind of laboratory for all kinds of perverse laws and human relations — with but one theme in common: that they were based on fear and hatred and ignorance (and greed).

The curry was hot as it should be, and after a few more nips at Rumblegrumble's home we went to bed. At that stage we left Ba-sjan sitting cross-legged on top of the table with his pitcher of wine alone in the kitchen.

Durban, so say the history books, is the capital of India. Indeed, Durban is an Indian city. Possibly because one comes across the same delapidated Victorian architecture here as in Bombay or Calcutta — a generalized Brighton in the colonies. The vast majority of the Indian population are as poor as church-mice of course, but there are also sections of the city where swanky homes owned by extortion-rich Indians tower. Durban, melting-pot, but also city of extremes. On the beaches the whitish-skinned lie washed up on shore like half-dead fish; the people in the street are generally black; the rickshaws you see are not drawn by the grotesquely dolled-up Zulu "warriors" of the advertisements, but by grayish men in tattered clothes with a couple of bits of string and things draped around their legs for the sake of the image; here, supposedly, the Afrikaner is not the cock of the walk, but mostly the bus driver or the railroad worker; the street is full of handsome black women — indecently dressed; a suave young Indian, apparently mistaking my hair-and-beard appearance for that of a bleary-eyed hippy — and not perceiving that it is the apparel of the suffering ascetic, the bloody artist — tries nimbly and in whispering tones to sell me a stick of marijuana. That good "Durban poison."

What a strange land we have! Before emptying the cup of consciousness last night, before the sleepfumes were able to overwhelm me, I thought again of the Cape and of that wedding the other day, how gentle and friendly it all was, of the brass band and the bagpipe players and the marchers who poured up the hill at one point during the marriage — all wearing Scottish kilts, of how the Mountain's own cloud was on duty. And then also of how one of the wedding guests showed me where the Imam Abdullah Haron used to live. Do you remember Abdullah Haron? He was one of the ones who slipped on a cake of soap in jail and in so doing knocked life out of his mouth. And later an inquest brought to light all kinds of burn and scorch marks on his body. The body is an ashtray. (Friends, if you ever happen to wind up in jail — and that's not hard — just stay dirty then, rather than to be killed like that.) And what became of his wife and children after his death? According to my informant they were compelled to vacate the house, because she and her deceased husband had been married in the mosque only, and not before the magistrate, you see, and, so I hear, she was not entitled to remain. And if that's true, and I shouldn't say it because it will create problems for my publisher, but if that's true, then I will and must say: the officials responsible are dogs. May they rot before they die!

Around noon we advanced in a northeasterly direction. First along the shimmering and flowing sea past places where famous patriarchs are buried — Shaka, Luthuli — and then turning sharply inland where we were swallowed by sugar cane plantations, green, majestic, tall like waving capital letters. Occasionally the road was like a dry riverbed between high green banks. The road itself was strewn with gray stalks. The Indians we encountered here were much poorer and blacker than their Durban cousins, with huge white eyes. Now and then we could see a primitive temple structure at the edge of a sugar plantation, a collapsible temple painted in bright colors on the outside, presumably erected for some god or other who must have come from India too, and is no doubt also having a tough time on this bitter continent. Once we spied one of the faithful, virtually naked and smeared with dyes, perched peacefully on one leg in the shade of a big tree. At first I almost mistook him for Panus, but he had no noticeable bumps on his back.

Higher up in the hills we stopped to buy fruit from a small African boy. All he could offer us was a saucepan full of guavas, and the only word we managed to get out of him was "fifty cents." To the extent that we began to suspect that that's what the fruit is called in Zulu.

In Vryheid, at the police station, we asked for directions to our destination, a game farm called Shamanzi ("Beat-the-water"). A constable introduced himself and told us that he too was from the Boland and that he was so homesick that when he saw a "Colored" he had to stop himself from grabbing him around the neck and kissing him.

Dusk caught up with us before we were able to reach the farm. In the dark we found ourselves at a big gate, and in the car headlights we were able to distinguish a perfect Zulu hut beside the gate. Xhosa houses are square or round — mud walls decorated with patterns around the door (white-faces) which often face the sea, and supporting a thatched roof; Zulu huts don't have straight walls but resemble domes put down on the ground and thatched with grass or reeds. A man clad in the khaki great-coat of a forgotten world war, crawled out of the hut and came over to the car, erect and proud in spite of his age, so that we could sign the visitors' book. From here the dirt road followed the course of a donga to the main buildings below.

A half-tame lion passing for a yard-dog, growling, and with eyes like silver-winged moths, came to nibble at us before we were rescued by the people of the house. Two families of bosses live on the farm — Douglas Graham and his wife, Martha, and Mamba-eyes* De Villiers with his wife, Catherine, and their small son, Uys. The whole place was still under construction, but we would only see that properly the next day.

After a few stiff nips we ventured out into the veld the same night, in the back of an open truck, hoping to shoot a buck for the pot. Near a dark kraal we picked up Manyatella. Manyatella is the senior game warden and tracker among the 12 families of Zulus (of which altogether 23 work on the farm) in the area. He looks and he

*The Black and the Green Mamba are highly poisonous snakes, confined to the northern parts of South Africa and the eastern coastal belt.

sees in the night as if it were broad daylight; in fact, going in search of game with him is an unnerving experience — a couple of days later when we were out hunting with him again, he would stop every now and again to indicate the presence of some animal or other, and for the life of me I usually saw nothing but shrub and tree and faint horizon; I learned then that I am blind in more ways than one. But that night, in spite of much patience and a plodding search through wet grass-seed and under trees whose branches slapped you spitefully in the face, we didn't see or shoot a thing, not even a stray terrorist.

We slept in two isolated rondavels which also happened to be inhabited by bats, mambas, and mosquitoes equipped with the most up-to-date arms supplied by the French sanction-breakers. At daybreak we were able to get an idea of the size of the farm — after 10 months of putting up wire around it, 22 miles had been fenced in. The Igazi, a rusty red river in which we swam with palish buttocks, runs through one of the gorges, and an airfield was still to be laid out on a plateau. The animals already present — some indigenous to the region and others imported from other parts of the country — included: zebra, impala, wart hogs, gnu, bush buck, mountain antelope, mountain reed buck, gray antelope and red antelope, leopards, black-ridge jackals, hyena dogs, striped (Cape) polecats, honey badgers, civet cats (Genets), white-tailed mongooses, mercenaries, African tiger cats (Servals), rock rabbits, African ant bears, bush babies, porcupines, hares, cane rats, red hares and go-away birds, and other affairs emitting heartrending cries high up in the sky. There are several species of tree and shrub too: thorn, Cape teak, tamboti, matumie, red ivory, marula (elephant's food), wild olive (don't ask me what it looks like), umbrella tree, kaffir tree, wild fig, wattle, and so forth. Even the aloes weren't just any old aloes; they were Bolinii, Bainsii, Superfoliata, Candelabrum, Marlothii, Umfolosiensis, and Arberensis. And as for the liquids, they included: Johnny Walker who couldn't find his way home again, Haig, Black and White, Separate Development, Teacher's Kentucky, Three Stars (or Treestar), Scotch, Common Whisky, Shame on you, and Cane Spirit — the latter are Catherine's father's favorite heartdrops.

In the evening we would offer our bodies to the mosquitoes and other flying, creeping, or crawling insects outside under a lamp — a signboard for the blood-suckers. (Toward the end of our stay one of

188

Douglas' arms was swollen red and stiff, and the diagnosis was either spider-bite or alcohol poisoning.) Or we would sit indoors, depending on the temperamental generator throbbing faintly in the distance, and play monopoly: to be diddled disgustingly by a fellow named François, a budding capitalist. And when we complained (because we were being fleeced) he replied: "Yes, here I sitteth again in the midst of the scournful between the Philistines and the Pharisees. But I shall advance. And he laughs last who laughs last!"

A third joint owner, and some of his friends from Johannesburg turned up on the third day in a Mercedes: Andries Retief Potgieter Piet Pretorius Hendrik* (called Captain Bligh). In the interests of better human relations and mutual respect (which he believes in) the Zulu laborers were ordered to dance for us toward dusk. After the workers had obligingly given their slow version of the jerk, Captain Bligh drew himself up in all the glory of his white shirt and trousers by the collective light of Africa's skeleton-white moon and the flickering barbecue fire, and with arms raised and fists outthrust, he began (through an interpreter, for a chief, though he may now be white, must speak through an interpreter) to address the dark hordes in their sneakers and tattered vests and plastic beads from up there on the terrace. The effect was marred, however, when one of the Dutch lady's breasts popped out of her dress and Catherine's father's tonic drops exploded in his hand.

On the morning of our second to last day on Shamanzi, Cloete and I went hunting with the laughing Philistine and the old hunter who guards the gate. Without his khaki coat, wearing only a skin around his loins, and armed with an assegai and a knob-kerrie, the old gentleman was like a phantom from the proud past. Apparently he is well into his seventies already, but his strong and smooth body wouldn't let you think so, and to our shame he outpaced us easily and lightly of course. We made our way along, down the outer fence, through a dip, and up onto a ridge which was densely overgrown. A small herd of impala leaped up ahead of us and Francois shot one down — a small ewe. The old hunter slung the buck across his shoulders and was back at the gate where the other guests and Nosmas, my wife, were waiting for us, before we had even got

*The satirical significance of these names is lost if the reader is unaware that these were all names belonging to famous Voortrekker leaders and heroes.

halfway. From a distance we indicated our return to the trigger-happy heroes at the gate, to stop them from taking a potshot at us by mistake.

death

when the grass was still green and damp
in the undergrowth
the imapala was shot —
little she-ewe leaping its first and last brown-white
quick as an eye
with lead in the liver
— the others darted off blindly
  into life —

and up near the gate she was slaughtered,
the skin peeled off:
small stiff legs,
small white teats —
the red of blood and blue of veins,
the leanness of flank,
and then, in a sudden spill:
the whole bag of entrails, folds of slime —
but the eyes

death absence:
the eye thick and green like motion:
the veld hunching: the sky shining:
every eye a green intimate meat-fly

On Monday the 26th we left the farm with a gift leopard-skin in the trunk. Near the border with Swaziland we reached the highway, and we took the route to Joh'burg via Piet Retief and Ermelo. It became evening and night once more. Somewhere along the way a police patrol flagged us down with torches at the side of the road. I was at the wheel. It was a routine check. An elderly-ish sergeant with cap and regulation quiver-mustache posted himself at my window and asked to see my license. I handed him my French driver's license, and he unfolded it — I must explain that it is a sizeable pink concertina. The sergeant's mustache gingerly hovered about the unknown, and I could see that a question was struggling under his cap. Now would he ask: "What is your orientation?" I thought. But no, the question was: "Is *this* a driving license?" And when I said yes, he was happy, and we were able to continue our journey.

Arrived in Johannesburg late, grubby and tired and almost kicked out of the Victoria because we looked so down and out. But our names in the visitors' book caused the Italian manager to change his mind quickly (he must have heard a bell somewhere, ringing distantly) and the following morning we were surprised with a bowl of fresh fruit with the compliments of the management.

I don't want to say much about the Golden City. There must be several middle-sized cities in America which look the same, I imagine, and that's why I have no desire to visit America. Freeways, cars, sky-scrapers, and police around the houses or offices of those people you would really like to meet. Except for Diagonal Street, where the witch doctors have their shops and the stench of semi-decayed ape carcasses is barely disguised by the heavy fumes of incense.

When Cloete had left to go back to the Cape on Thursday, March 1st, we moved in with Ampie and Stella. On Friday I spent some time at the University of the Witwatersrand* where I read some of my poems (and it was a flop) and attempted to incite the non-Afrikaans students to full-scale revolution. As you discovered for yourselves from the newspapers, it was so successful that 16 student leaders were detained at once. In the subsequent confrontation 34 students were devoured by dogs, and 16 law-enforcement officers suffered heart attacks, but the press kept this quiet.

We were invited to lunch by Ernst van Heerden. We spent a few pleasant and peaceful hours with him at his home, so crammed with works of art. We had genuine Cape food, a fragrance from the Boland and of old customs when there was still love in the pot. We left with

*Largest English university in South Africa, located in Johannesburg.

precious memories of a hospitable and sensitive (in the positive sense of the word) host, of a modest man who in a quiet and almost diffident way feels deeply involved with his fellow citizens and with what is happening in our broken land.

already it was almost dusk
and the rain like green growths in the sky
when beyond the city he
squatted at the top of a hill, naked

and glistening as though covered in slime —
the landscape undulating before him
and the city remote,
his body a quivering fork
excreting eyes —

melancholy raw eggs
with the color of love,
to stare blindly into the gloom
like reflections without presence
like echoes without origin
like mankind without man

Saturday, March 3. Early in the morning we join Ampie and Stella on our way to an airfield from where we will take off in her father's plane for their bushveld farm. The pilot's name is Mr. Bird. He is a frail Australian, long ago — long, long ago — he must have been a fighter pilot or some such, and for many years now he has been flying all over this part of Africa. He is partially blind and only manages to hear thanks to a hearing-aid clamped to his ear. When he laughs, his dentures sag a little and expose the innocent red gums. But fly he does fly! High in the foaming clouds, everything white around us, nothing but a peak now and then popping its head up above the clouds (like elderly colleagues sharing a steamy sauna) to see where the angels romp. Over the Lowveld, close to the boundaries of the Kruger National Park*, we begin our descent. The merciless landscape which is unfurled beneath our wings; the gray and brownish green, the bloodstains of the earth in between, and sometimes, straight as a small jet of spit from a deft and experienced mouth, a dirt track from here to there. The farm on which we are about to land is one of a series of six or seven (called Timbavati) which are privately owned and nestled against the game reserve. How Mr. Bird is able to recognize the small landing strip on this flat earth devoid of hills or water-courses, is beyond me. But we land with a jolt and a bump, and with his hand Willem Williams (Billwillempie) steadies the wing of the small craft. It's his job (and his family's) to look after the homestead and the outbuildings.

After lunch we pull the jeep out of the garage and, armed with a gun against the lions, we drive off into the veld. Ampie claims to know which end of the gun should be held against the shoulder if a lion should suddenly decide to join us in the open vehicle, and I believe him as hard as I can. We pay a visit to a certain Mr. Roos, the game warden for all these farms collectively. His workers are employed at that very moment in cutting up an elephant — one or two are hollowing out the grotesque feet (like cushions). Whitish red meat. Not for eating purposes, though the meat is sweetish, apparently, but to make ashtrays out of the gray molds for the nouveaux riches. Its severed head lies a little farther away from the house. Even from here we see the crowding of vultures. They hardly move as we approach; clumsily they hop around, jostling and bullying each other to get at the pickings. When the flesh has been devoured and the bones are clean, it will be easier to saw the teeth out. Roos explains that this was a lone rogue elephant which had trampled and flattened anything and everything resembling fence or field in its path. We agree to return when it grows dark in the hope

*One of Southern Africa's most famous tourist attractions, this game reserve is situated in the Eastern Transvaal Lowveld adjoining Mozambique and covers some 2590 km2. The country is most typically lowveld, i.e., with thick bush and long grass; in the north there are mopane forests, while the Limpopo river is bordered by dense and sub-tropical vegetation, with scattered baobabs. The bird-life is particularly rich and varied, and one is likely to see a large variety of game in all parts of the park (its principal attraction), including elephant, lion, and rhino to name but a few species. (*Mopane*: the shrub or tree *Colophspermum* or *Copaifera mopane*, sometimes called ironwood, an important fodder tree in low rainfall areas. *Baobab*: African tree also called monkey-bread with enormously thick stem.)

of seeing the hyenas which are bound to put in an appearance at the feast as well.

The place is alive with game. When we take another drive later on in the afternoon, we see giraffes and zebras and, at dusk, two dark humpy rhino, mastodons galloping away ahead of us, regardless of trees or shrubs — silent train engines causing the earth to vibrate, yet sporting silly little tails sticking stiffly straight up in the air. On the far side of the high fence enclosing the game reserve we see a gray elephant too, huge as a thick and creased stage curtain. And surrounding these beasts everywhere, are thousands of flies with nasty bites. We are obliged to chastize ourselves with leafy twigs to keep the pests away from our bodies. Among the trees the ants have built red and golden-yellow castles. This is not a part of the world, may the gods be listening, where I would wish to spend a night on my own.

Later in the evening, after a meal of barbecued meat in the open, it begins to pour rain. At intervals the distant muffled groaning calls of lions can be heard. Roos told us earlier of an attempt to import ostriches and get them to take to the area, and how the lions had eaten the experiment. The womenfolk eventually go to bed, and until late Ampie and I talk and try to find solutions. He is far more desperate about the future of the Afrikaner than I dare to be. And in the small hours I see the fiery eyes and the grisly mug of a hyena against the wire screen of the outer door. The creature's laugh sends cold shivers across the land and its people's problems. But we doze off again. This self-destructive continent. (I suspect: I'm a barbarian on a journey through Africa.) Sleep is a stream of water. And all the conscious thoughts, the impressions of the day's events, the last problems — these are the banks which are being dug out by the water-course, which crumble and tumble into the water and are dissolved — which certainly modify the composition of the water too, but become water nevertheless, water which continues to flow to nowhere, relentlessly, immutable, and never the same again.

When we leave on Sunday, one of Billwillempie's (William Willemse's) children has to chase the gnu and such-like from the runway before we are able to take off. And when Mr. Bird has flown low over the farm once more, with wobbly wings, as a parting gesture, we make off, back to Johannesburg. In Johannesburg Mr.

Bird takes off his wig to say good-bye to us. (Tap-tapping his white walking-stick, he himself disappears around a corner of the arrivals hall.)

The time, I think as it grows dark over this city of glass and concealed poverty, the time draws near when we must turn our steps toward home:

I will die and go to my father
to Wellington with long legs
shining in the light
where the rooms are dark and massive
where the stars are perched like sea gulls on the roof
and angels dig for worms in the garden,
I will die and with little luggage
                    set out
across the Wellington mountains
through trees and dusk
and go to my father;

the sun will be throbbing in the earth
the waves of the wind causing the joints to creak
we shall hear the tenants
shuffling overhead,
we shall play checkers on the back verandah
— granddaddy cheats —
and on the radio
listen to the news of the night

friends, fellow dying
do not hesitate; life still clings
like flesh to our bodies
but death does not leave us in the lurch;
our coming and our going:
our legs will be intimately acquainted with freedom —
come along
                    into my dying in into going to my father
to Wellington where the angels

dangle worms to catch fat stars from heaven;
let us die and perish and be merry:
my father has a boardinghouse with many rooms

But our business, if I may put it that way, in the wicked city, is not finished yet. On Monday there are things we have to do in the city center again. I pay a visit to one of those places where Colonel Huntingdon's mustaches hang around all day in a car in front of the entrance. With telescopic cameras. As the cameras have sensitive ears, we go up to the roof for anti-security reasons before conspiratorially inquiring after each other's health.

(Once that has been disposed of — the affirmations of health — one of the wretched tormented immediately proceeds to more secret matters. To illustrate, he tells me of a friend by the name of Flapass — on account of the long movements he makes when he stands up, gesticulating madly, at activist meetings.)

During the lunch hour we have the good fortune to get in touch with Pooh, Thingamebob's wife. Thingamebob has been locked up in jail for years now, and the authorities do everything in their power to make life a misery for Pooh, too. They tried to cut her off from the community; the restrictions placed on her force her to live completely on her own at times — easy prey for nighttime evildoers; in her work, too, she is harassed ceaselessly, to the extent that it is seldom possible for her to remain with the same employer for more than a few weeks at a time; her fellow workers are encouraged to spy on her; all of which is presumably occasioned by the small-minded vindictiveness of leeches, the pettiness of stink-horns (*Phallus impudicus*). In spite of all that, she remains proud and convinced of eventual retribution and justice. She's invincible. And I must own that, in addition, she is one of the most beautiful females I have ever met.

After this brief meeting we leave for Pretoria. About Pretoria I want to say nothing at all. I don't know if there's another place on earth where I feel myself to be such a total stranger. I picked up a cold in the back from the way we were stared at. We spend the night at the Crazy Horse Saloon Hotel. A surreal atmosphere pervades the city: a national ladies' bowling tournament is in full swing, so that the lounges and dining rooms are crammed with weird white-clad ladies of all sizes and sexes, wearing strange white garments and headdress. They also have smiles, glistening throat funnels, mouths full of scoured white splinters. Some of the burly ones bellow now and then and pat the frail ones on the back. (As bulls would nudge calves, though not so that it hurts.)

Back in Joni we have a date with two friends from Paris who are also touring Southern Africa (more Zimbabwe than South Africa really) — Serge and Michèle. To them, with their stored and filed experiences of travels through Viet Nam, Cambodia, and Indonesia and Egypt and goodness knows where else, probably nothing is unusual or strange anymore. We seek a little evening coolness on the verandah of an old hotel on the edge of Hillbrow,* order beers and write postcards to our black friends in exile abroad. In the sinking light the buildings become blunt. One breathes. Sometimes you have to go a very long way to get that breath. That's a survival technique too.

In the evening we decide to have a meal at a place specializing in typical Afrikaans food. Wine is a nuisance, of course, since that must be bought separately at a liquor store, and it's not until we're back at the restaurant once more, that we discover the two bottles of red wine we had asked for turn out to be two bottles of white, once they're unwrapped. The manager of the eating place takes pity on us and when it has grown late enough, he produces a bottle of red wine himself, and later still we are served with good marijuana in an adjoining apartment as well. Loose are our tongues. The black waiter who was serving us a minute ago is invited too, is also included in the company having a smoke, in order to be living proof of his master's liberal benevolence, but he is quite clearly ill at ease and excuses himself fairly early on — or is it just merely because he has to catch the last bus or train back to camp?

By four o'clock on the afternoon of March seventh, having had a noisy loose screw in the carburetor of the car replaced in a garage, we leave Joh'burg to return to the South. We make a wide detour through the Western Transvaal, accompanied by an awe-inspiring thunderstorm. The thunder claps and rumbles, and lightning strikes down not far from the road onto the iron earth. Water pours across

---

*Densely populated, cosmopolitan area of central Johannesburg.

the road, but there are smoke fumes too. I start thinking to myself that it's God, perhaps, none too happy with my activities. But we are saved, the electrically charged atmosphere is left behind, and with evening approaching we draw up at an hotel alongside the highway where commercial travelers eat their englishy food in silence, served by waiters in white jackets.

Kimberley. That was on the eighth, in the morning. What was the weather like that morning? The previous day, as described before, was just passable; much electricity in heaven, tension and threats, and from time to time sulphur's black slashes and small blue flames in the trees. Even that which is most perfect and that which is farthest removed from fire or consumption burns sometimes. The rind of the golden orange, for example, when it is properly dried out, will burn with an intense crackling halo of flames as a result of the oil it contains. (I am troubled by the gaps between sentences, by abrupt transitions — unjustified?) When evening came at the end of the previous day in that small sleepy hollow where they were to spend the night in the hotel where the nomads were eating like puppets, fascinated by their plates, those plates so full of eyes, they went for a walk to where there is a village square hedged with trees, just common village trees, and beyond the row of trees the verandahs of shops and other businesses, sometimes with porch plants in tins; the evening went to lie down farther away toward the desert, in the same way that a huge veld-fire dies down, the flames already too low for the eye and only a tinge of a blueish reflection on the walls of the horizon. By the morning even the last traces of rain had gone, the odd fleet of clouds high up in the sky being clearly not of the water-variety. The desert, though in the background, most certainly plays a part — the heat here is earthy.

Breyten Breytenbach and his wife, Wife, had promised to call on Sonny Leon and his family if they should pass through Kimberley. They phoned from the Post Office for directions to the Leons. At the Leons' house they were warmly received. The house, like those of the other "Coloreds," is situated on the edge of the village. Inside, it was deliciously cool. There were fresh flowers in vases and bowls, and a portrait of our host as a soldier during the World War on the wall. When it was necessary to go and fight overseas, then the brown man was good and acceptable enough for the white man, but now that the

Party which had supported the Germans is in power, now the brown man lives in a political and social ghetto. Sonny Leon is a lawyer by profession, as well as being the leader of the Labor Party. His Chinese extraction is clearly discernible from his features, but he also has the tall upright body and the loose limbs so typical of the Afrikaner, and the flat vowels and marked consonants. B and Wife were invited to stay for lunch.

But before lunch Sonny Leon had to drive to the location to see Robert Sobukwe, and B asked whether he could accompany him. He had always wanted to meet Sobukwe. Of all the historical and still living leaders of the South African people he is one of the very few who was not imprisoned or exiled. The authorities detained him on Robben Island for a number of years, and afterward he was exiled to Kimberley and banned there. The regime is afraid of his kind, and when you meet the man, it is clear why. The slum where he is forced to live — "Bantu Township," I suppose it's called — does not succeed in detracting from his authority. The people respect him and look up to him for guidance. Even the full-time surveillance under which he is kept by the political police is a kind of backhanded compliment. He remained sitting quietly at his desk, and they chatted about this and that. It was almost lunchtime, outside the sun was gasping. As a writer I am compelled to say "this and that" here. For the laws of this unhappy land lay down, among other things, that the words of a banned unperson may not be quoted; I know that the bosses — the censors who move stealthily under cover of literature — are waiting for the slightest pretext upon which to sink their gleaming false teeth of holiness into the jugular veins of the straying writer or publisher, to empty the "unhealthiness" with much tail-wagging, before there's any subversion. Not that they discussed anything else, that is, they didn't talk only about this and that, but also about nothing in particular. Besides, one realizes in advance that what you say in evidence may be used against you, because Robert Sobukwe's rooms and toilet are definitely bugged.

Nevertheless and that notwithstanding, or following on what had gone before, or precisely in consequence thereof — after about thirty minutes of simmering conversation they were interrupted by the sudden and unexpected appearance of someone in the doorway. Afterward B would attempt to give an account of the phenomenon,

199

but it would prove to be no easy task. Now if you would call to the mind's eye some of Fra Angelica's paintings or even Giotto's, with specific reference to the depiction of "the annunciation," you are beginning to get an approximate idea of what happened and what it looked like. Naturally, there are certain differences between the two pictures. B or Sonny Leon or Robert Sobukwe can hardly be described as being either Mary or pregnant. On the other hand, the being in the doorway didn't have the familiar wavy golden locks, but reddish hair shorn to well above the ears, the hair parted high and dry on the head — one cannot blame him, for when all is said and done, hair exists but to provide the hat with a hold. He had flashing little blue eyes and a blunt brush-mustache, like a badge, beneath his nose. In addition he was dressed in a safari suit and had socks up to the knees. At first it was possible for them to think that his name was Gabriel, but that wasn't the case. He held a flaming sword in his hand, for he was Justice. His long wings, with muscles bearing testimony to frequent exercise and a healthy physique, rubbed against the doorframe. "Good afternoon, Major," Robert said calmly, because to him this guardian angel was a familiar figure. His name, so we were told, was Major Haplob. (*Haploblepharus edwardsi*) and he was fighting mad.

The three gentlemen, the blackish, the brownish, and the off-white one, were summoned outside, one after the other, where it was separately and individually explained to them that they had broken the laws of heaven — in terms of Mr. Sobukwe's cross he may never entertain more than one person at a time, and needless to say, Mr. B was not in possession of the necessary permit (which would have to be issued subsequent to deliberations by the highest authorities) to enter a Bantu Township. (The word township sums it up beautifully: a ship on dry land.) Was it hot, folks! Creaking, the glowing coach, the sun, traversed the firmament. Everything could melt, all courage and strength. Several more cars were parked outside in the heat, full of angels as well, presumably to prevent the conspirators from taking off — or had they perhaps all gone for a drive to get some fresh air, to pick flowers in the veld, to have a picnic beneath the shrubs, to make garlands out of blades of grass and watch the antics of the wise ants? Messrs. Leon and B were told to report to the offices whereupon Mr. Leon pointed out that they had not yet eaten and that the two gentlemen in question intended to have a bite to eat before placing themselves at the disposal of the law . . . .

Well, B was quaking in his boots. In spite of his big mouth, he had but little experience at this kind of game. Had the angels decided to hack their victims to bits right then and there — who would have been the wiser? For there is no law to curb the angels, every South African is guilty and doomed to eventual execution unless he manages to make his or her innocence seem attractive to the authorities, in other words, unless he or she is prepared to work for the angels. Sonny Leon, however, tried to reassure B, because for him, God help him, this was an ordinary occurrence, and with an ironic smile he pointed out that B was thus gaining a small measure of insight into the everyday existence of the majority of his fellow citizens.

The delicious Chinese food stuck in B's throat. After lunch they went back into town — Wife as well — to where the angels have their offices high up at the top of the Sanlam building. An escort intercepted them in the street, a big black man who was idly licking an ice cream — "someone has to do the dirty work for the boss." Upstairs they were taken to separate offices and statements were taken from them — of course one couldn't allow them to sit there telling lies in the same office, for then one would no doubt be prompting the other to boot! Striking and telling was the *agitation* of the angels, how they were dying to get at the vermin; like anxious and starved dogs straining at the leash . . . . There were swords and chains and whips and other trophies on the wall of the office where B and his wife were made to confess. After a while Major Haplob entered, looking at B's statement (wings and mustache a-quiver) and then put it to him (B) that he was lying, that they simply couldn't have been talking about nothing in particular, but about *"revolution"!* (Oh, dear reader, please forgive me, sooner or later that big dreadful ugly word was bound to slip from my guts.) And B dreamed; he dreamed of a world in which it would be possible to speak *also* in the most normal and natural way of revolution.

After they had been warned not to say anything about what had occurred, and that a decision as to whether they would be charged or not would be made at a later stage, they were released. Snarling with frustration, the angels snapped at flies, chewed and sucked at the blades of the swords, there were heavy doors closing off one section of the office, an extradited black was on his knees in the corridor trying to erase the scorch marks.

There were a few people on the porch of Sonny's house. Apparently all the people of his neighborhood come to him for advice. B and his wife said goodbye and aimed the car at the long road to the Boland through the Karoo. Every car was suspect. They were convinced they were being followed, that the shadow of the angels still hung over them.

Hopetown, God-have-mercy, Britstown, Victoria West. The world burned to cinders. Koppies here and there, burial mounds. A silence, a vast silence, unbroken even by the wind. Heavy clouds, deep and low in the heavy air, boats with somber flaming sails. Darkness had long since overtaken them by the time they reached Beaufort West, but the village was like a Bethlehem at Christmas — every hotel full up. Nor could they go on, really, for the carburetor valve had been shaken loose again. There they were then, filled with fear and exhausted, in a hostile village in this foreign land. And a man, a stranger, came to them and asked (in English) whether they were having trouble, whether he could be of some help. And when he had examined the problem, he set their minds at rest. And he took a similiar screw from the carburetor of his own van and substituted it for the faulty screw. And he asked no questions, but he too was something of a stranger in these parts really, because he was from the Bay.* And he didn't introduce himself, but he whistled while he worked. And in the night above, this eternal night which has seen so much coming and going already, fat stars sat shining like frogs in a marsh. And the English Samaritan wished them a good journey ahead, and they drove on in the night.

The headlights of another car approaching them from the front from time to time, were sharp and cold in the night, and they could see the light playing across the heights and hollows long before it reached them. The road through the Karoo is a narrow one, one vehicle glides past another for an eternity. Sometimes the dark ribbon is bordered on both sides by sheets of fog occasionally closing in

*Port Elizabeth.

202

completely. Ghosts and spirits, the restless deceased and roaming unborn, move through the dark, wailing across the veld. We South Africans, we will go on haunting the world forever. We are, all of us, slightly nuts, there is a bleeding crack running through each of us. At the most unexpected moments we give in, the flaw comes to light. We are victims of history and hostages of our own fears. We whiter ones are the scum of a civilization based upon injustices. We are alienated and we have alienated the blacks. We are mad, all of us, with rigid faces. We fuck behind bushes and weep in our mouths. We keep revolvers in our wardrobes and bottles of liquor in the drawers of our desks. We eat peppermints to sweeten our breaths and write letters to newspapers under pseudonyms. We pray and we hang people. We are maimed, we are only half human, but we know it, we are mad and realize that we are mad. And we never get away from our land.

Late that night the travelers found refuge in a motel on the road. And early the next morning they descended across the Heks River Mountains down to the Boland, and at home, their people were waiting for them and called out loudly with joy when they made their appearance. Ounooi's hands were under her apron and there was gay laughter and her cheeks were red and the lenses of her glasses sparkled. Oubaas was sitting on the front porch wearing shorts, and he called "Well, what do you know!" and laughed as though it were all funny. How touchingly relieved they were! On the porch with Oubaas was a "client" — old Mr. Palvi who has such a time with his wife and children, who takes potshots at the fruit thieves in his trees, who was so wild in his young days, who used to have such a good time dancing at the Montague hot springs. Mr. Palvi took B's hand firmly in his own, in the way the very old people used to, firmly and for a long time, and he looked deeply into B's eyes as if he were looking deeply into the well to see if the dead rat was still there. The sun put beds down behind the house. Food was prepared in the kitchen. There were letters to be read, letters wishing to draw attention to the fact that foul-mouths and critics and people who marry non-whites belong in Paris, piss-off and goodbye. Wife was quiet. B's back, as I have said before, was absolutely rigid with fear and lying.

203

Journey

(: a hint of death inside me)

1.
ringing out from our blue heavens
but our heavens are filled with living fire
in the trees high up on the mountain
a silvery light and other things which blind the eyes
a sudden taste like the shock of electricity of the
without beginning or end
: a hint of death inside me

from our deep seas breaking round
the sea has lost all sympathy for the white man
the frothy scum comes from Europe
thousands of oil tankers like festering whales
fearfully the milkwood stands quite bent
nothing will rinse the rot out again
: a hint of death inside me

valleys and plains and then nothing but more flies
and then the desert
in the desert you need no name
you are your own name
you are the nameless
Lord, do swallow us!
: a hint of death inside me

when the fire dies the hills are scorched black
up to where night begins
send forth your eyes among the stars
like water irrigating the trees erupting in blossoms
and the wind shakes itself free hiding nothing
the wind a row of empty houses
: a hint of death inside me

game reserves for the wild animals of the land
homelands for tame people

beside the wagon trails we saw a ragged man walking
without thither or thence a skeleton and tufts of flesh
a native an indigenous exile and always
deeper inside there was space enough in his eyes
: a hint of death inside me

come hither oh hither all ye conceivable gods
unity is strength
farms locations villages suburbs
cities like sanctuaries for music
and also dogs that understand only Afrikaans
bred and trained to devour people and expose the life inside
: a hint of death inside me

my land my land oh bleeding anus
and love like constipation within the body . . .
that night we could but drive like blind men
crisscrossing through the land
the flames of heaven licking through the panes
we were blue dying while life lay outside
: a hint of death inside me

2.
the day rises in the east
beyond the blue horizon of the white waves
out of the gentle sugar cane plantations
the day is light

all that lives in heaven
and that below on earth
is born from light
belongs to man

in the mountains there are no more gods
the moon is an empty house at night
the gods have always been human
our love is a realm of gods

the day inflates the mountains
running like fire through the desert
we men reel on, drunk with light
each sheltering in the shade of his own body

over the fertile towers of the cities
over the white trees of the farms
a man calls *oo-aa* to the outside
and another replies

over climates seasons
over despair and harvest
over hill and dale
and hunter and grass

the day blows on
until night falls
on the cold sea
as far as the coast of death

the night rises high in the east
approaching the land like waves
swallowing the vineyards and orchards
the day that butterfly incapable of swimming

oo-aa   a man calls to the outside
and another replies
glorious glorious glorious it is here
death is the very blood in our veins

3.
such is man
such his search for being
such his demand for love
and acceptance of his fellow man
you call out to hear no echo

there is a massacre looming
beyond gardens and streets the blood
torches freedom flags,

vultures over the shining floors
in the air-conditioned lounges of hotels
smiles tearing eyes threaded through a silver needle
there are beetles in the soup

truckloads of soldiers and children on the rooftops
a white god floating white on the surface of the pool
cries shots the teeth are shouting

like large pink breasts wearing socks up to the knees
cows are chewing skeletons houses exploding in dust
sirens wailing

and the mine shafts are occupied by ants
in the factories the orange-trees turn gray
you call and do not hear
such, o beloved, is man
you call and you do not hear
such is death this blood in our veins:
freedom or death,

From March 10th to Sunday the 18th we were in Onrus again.
Serene aunt Susan was there too, and Baby and Spare Wheel. We saw
a lot of the Rabies and Uys, and all of us frequently had meals
together. Summer was nearly over. Jan took us inland one day in his
rattle-trap. Higher up toward the mountain there had been a leper
camp once and there are speculations that that is exactly how Onrus
got its name, that the people from the settlement along the sea were
anxious and were possibly afraid that the river from the mountains
might be contaminated. On another occasion we went to see the color
slides Biltong and Joors had taken in Greece. We were weary, and it
was as if the shadows of our impending departure were already
beginning to impede our view. I wrote a poem.

1.
and the summer too draws to an end
the shadows have no sultriness anymore
the fruit no inner flesh

small clouds molding across the moon
the teeth of the small beasts of the veld gleaming white
the houses cracking

a land forfeited:
it's time to go into hiding

2.
small and sweet and black is my cigarette: *Havana*
and smaller still by nature freedom

and distant the Southern stars:
suddenly it is autumn,
then white and blue with white groaning crests come
waves, the southeaster is in the sea —
Hermanus a whiter boat lies in distress

the gutters are leaking
the moon turns inside out
(in *Havana* the *companeros* dance the cha-cha-cha)
the mountain shrouds itself — spots of rust
will frame the windows in flowers

such is summer's end,
the shadows have no shade any more
the fruit without flesh or moisture
the teeth of the small beasts of the veld
will cause this house to crack like all others

small and black as sweet as my cigarette
and smaller still of freedom nature —
I saw my heart
saying:

"do thus what you still have to do
but do it by all means
with compassion and mercy"

March 18

Believe me, I hesitated a long time before deciding to write this.
Why did I hesitate? Because I and my wife, Sweet-tongue, are young
yet, because I love this world as the eye loves the light, and because
we would like so much to come back here. This earth speaks as no
earth anywhere else, my people lie buried in this ground, I myself lie
in the dust here — must I then be separated from my grave? Also
because my father and my mother grow older each day, ever older and
because I would like to walk with them until the parting. Why then
do I write this down all the same? Because I love this soil, this land
with its people, as the eye loves the light, as a flute loves the last bit of
darkness before dawn when the morning breeze stirs the tops of the
trees and the shrubs and the grass with a primordial warm hand.
Because I believe in the future of this land, because we have a future,
can build a better world together, a better world for the Vietnamese
small-holder and the Indian from South America when he rises from
the folds of sadness and the African and all the other proletarians — a
world where the kind of people I met tonight will have neither
function nor *raison d'être* any more. But to achieve this, to continue to
walk upon the only possible road, we must learn to speak and to tell of
the hideous figures in the shadows. We must not allow ourselves to
be brow-beaten and intimidated one by one and separately. It must
become part of our shared experience, part of the treasure of our
common consciousness — we must recount among ourselves those
methods applied by shady characters trying to force us into the
framework of their bosses' control, so that we may all become
stronger and better able to offer resistance.
   That was the reality with which I had to come into contact.
People of my tribe, people of my history, people of my language,
people who are at the core of my unconscious safety wanted to talk to

209

me — is it from that unconscious and fundamental safety then that I must become alienated? The sting of death lying in one's own bosom. But what is the only true death? It is that which we do unto others.

This land is a screaming hell if only we cared to listen. Even the whitewashing we are engaged in now will not prevent it from exploding one day. We are responsible for what has happened, we are responsible for what is going to happen. Who are the people temporarily keeping the cover on the cauldron? They are the spies in the shadows, the eavesdroppers with the dark glasses in government cars, the agents of capitalism, those who maintain the spoils and the positions of power of the exploiters and the blackmailers, those who believe that the means justify the end — the end has long since been swallowed by the mud of amorality — those who must deny the humanity of their opponents so that every last bit of useful information may be tortured out of them, those for whom no law or code or belief exists, nothing but the obeying of orders, "orientation," and the deepening swamp of alienation, or perversion, or loneliness. For these people the enemy must be hide-bound and simple — and they create for themselves phantoms against which to fight, simplistic threats to justify the pain and dulling (and self-humiliation) of the actions they carry out every day. And so they increasingly lose their way in the labyrinths of asocial insanity, they themselves become victims of the system, they believe that they believe, they believe that they understand, they believe that they are doing good work, they believe that they are sincere and that their children will be proud of them, they believe that they can halt the progress of history, they believe that theirs is the correct orientation, they keep straight. And killing or letting live becomes a matter of choosing the best method, or expediency. Or when their rank is increased to that of advisors, advisors to the puppets in office, then the dirty work is carried out by the mentally deficient, by the psychopaths and the moral monsters, the heavies, the killers. They are the crusaders of imperialism, the servants of the law of the jungle, the soldiers of the Übermenschen. They know how fragile power is, they know how easily politicians may be bought and sold, and they know how to employ any means to achieve their object — be it the other's fear, his love for his nearest and dearest, or even his patriotism. They are the power. They are the conspiracy. They are the corruption. They command life and death. They are subject to no moral or legal obligation. They are the judges and they are the executioners. And the white men of our land have supplied them with an arsenal of laws to facilitate their work. In the belief that it is an antidote, we swallow the poison in increasing doses. Our fear and our greed has secreted monsters and because they hate us for what we have made them they will destroy us — even though that destruction be simply that they turn each of us into a monster too.

Someone, let's just say an "acquaintance," calls me from the Cape and informs me that two gentlemen from Pretoria would like to see me, would like to meet me, would like to take me out for a meal — not in the Cape or in Wellington, but in the heart of the old liberal Boland, in Paarl. And I cannot refuse. If a robber surprises you en route with a pistol, you can't say: "Listen, pal, I'm in a hurry today, try again tomorrow."

I dress neatly and proceed to the agreed hotel with a heavy heart. (Honey-tongue knows nothing about it, nor my parents either, of course.) They are waiting for me at the appointed place. They might have been family of mine. The name of one of them sounds something like Colonel Huntingdon, the other, I think, is called Captain Lamort. (*"Lamort salaud, le peuple aura ta peau!"*) We have a drink. And, in order that we may enjoy each other's company in more congenial surroundings — how considerate and how kind — it is suggested that we have our little chat in a more private chamber upstairs above the dining room. That's where the cat starts playing with the mouse. For nearly three months I've been shitting myself, now the time has come to face the music.

It's all very cozy and homely, "Afrikaans" I should say. We are decent and civilized people, aren't we? and sensible, don't you agree? Yet though the official mustaches crease into smiles from time to time, the eyes remain sharp, the jaw muscles tight. Outside the windows of the hotel room are the first of the oak trees, the first vineyards, and the blue mountains climbing toward a starry sky. It's a beautiful land, it's an eternal land. It's our land.

I'm not going to attempt to reproduce the whole conversation here. Questions are asked about impressions, and inquiries made regarding orientation. But finally it boils down to this:

1(a). You are on the wrong track, Son. What you, mistaken if perhaps sincere, are trying to do with the best of intentions, plays

211

into the hands of tough people who take advantage of you and your kind. You are arming the murderers, and don't think you will have a say in how they will use their arms.

1(b). We know everything about you, whether at home or abroad. We know everything about everything and everyone. (But tell us, how is . . . nowadays, and where is . . . now, and have you been to . . . yet . . .?)

2. We are all-powerful. Your coming here was determined by us. We shall decide whether you will be able to leave again. We must report back. Your parents aren't getting any younger either. See how beautiful our land us. Whether you will ever be permitted to come again will be decided by us.

3. And that depends.

4. So why not cooperate a little then?

It has grown late. In the South, in Africa, the nights are mild and full of life. In a majestic caravan the stars travel across the dark veld. Everything breathes. At home my wife, Heavenly Body, has probably been asleep for hours. And Oubaas is snoring peacefully, more than likely, flat on his back in the dark bedroom between the living room and the verandah. When he sleeps only his eyes peek out from under the blanket, but he doesn't really have to close his eyes because without his glasses they are soft already. Only Ounooi will stir now and then and cough like someone in a hurry. My breast is icy.

We have a few more glasses downstairs in the bar. We are all friends. The cats and the mouse are the best pals on earth. There are other drinking pals too in the pub, though it's way past closing time already, and there is camaraderie, there are bonds uniting us, there is shared mortality. Only, I'm not allowed to say anything. I'm not allowed to cry. Those others drinking are on another planet.

Then I'm allowed to drive home through the night, through the fields of my youth.

Old Pal,

well, we had a jolly time again last night, or what am I saying? I feel a little under the weather and jittery this morning, and you too, I guess. I keep seeing white spots in front of my eyes and soon it's going to be an uphill struggle to try to explain to the old missus how urgent and time-consuming last night's business was — but, hell, it was worth it. I mean, we're still young, aren't we? Sometimes you have to give life a kick up the backside! There's a long death ahead, and it's healthy to let your hair down once in a while before that day when we'll have to remove our caps and wipe our mouths at the gate of the great Dark Place. (And that boss never says there's no work, does he?!) In any event, I promised to write you a book — and I have a kind of feeling that this thing is never going to see the light in our language — so what? — and since you overdid it in the liquor stakes, which shorten (and in any case blur) the road and probably remember very little of our escapade, I suppose I'll have to relate the whole story. That's my job, isn't it?

You were also quite depressed yesterday. Not even at your usual drinking hole, but at a dullish trough down some back alley instead. Full of anxiety and worried with it. That things aren't going well, that the business is going to the dogs, that nobody loves you — and it's a lonely old vale of tears as it is. I tried to cheer you up, but why should I lie to you? You must know for yourself that there are quite a few men in this country who appreciate what you're trying to do. That's not what was bothering you, of course. The aches are older, have been with you, presumably, since childhood. Forgive me for saying it now, I don't want to open old wounds, but I do know that you lost your father at a very tender age, and when depression gets hold of you, you feel the lack of a father's company or even just his nearness.

Please don't take it amiss when I say that I'm so lucky in that respect. I know how deeply satisfying it is to sit quietly and comfortably beside your father though you may talk about nothing in particular. Now that we are back from our travels across country, I realize it once more. There are bonds of tranquility, of security binding you to your father and via him to your grandfather. Strange, I have no notion of my great-grandfather or further back, and I'm not really interested either. But in writing this journal, I came to the realization that I am actually doing it for my grandfather. There were wild things in him, there was something of the vastness of Africa behind his eyes. And, strange too, everywhere I go in this country, this strange familiar womanland of mine, there he is. The report which I write is for Grandpa Jan Afrikaner. For instance, I know he never knew Wellington, because we were still living in Riversdale when he lay down to die, but Pa told me just the day before yesterday that he was in Wellington during our absence a week or so ago, there in Grevilleas, seated in the old armchair in Pa's "office." Pa says he dozed off for a short while that afternoon, presumably — as he is in the habit of doing, though he would deny it — with one fist under his ear right there at the desk while the radio is talking nonsense, and suddenly he woke up and Grandpa was sitting more or less opposite him in the armchair, proudly upright as always, and Grandpa said nothing, just looked at Pa very quietly.

That, probably, is how you yearn for your father. That is why you're so fond of Uncle Martin, and of S. who lives up there on the mountain. And when the need arises, you miss being able to go and sit with one of them, albeit for no specific reason, I understand that. Maybe that is really why we went up the mountain to S. You wanted me to meet the man and to get to know him better, since my criticism of him, largely based of course on the position he holds and on what he does or doesn't do with it, was too sharp and unfounded in your opinion. And I wanted and had to see him. That experience with the angels the other evening had upset me considerably, and then the papers — that wonderful feigned enlightened *Burger* of yours — said that Robert Sobukwe might well be in trouble as a result of the visit I had paid him. Now that's what I call "leaked news" or "inspired reporting." I wanted and had to do something about it — because how could Sobukwe be held responsible for an unexpected and unasked-for visit? — but the question was how? I was hoping that S., relying on his access to high-ranking ears, would possibly be able to intervene.

S. lives in an attractive house on the slope of the mountain. I have to admit, he is much more pleasant a person in private conversation than I had imagined. It was hot in the city, with the oppressive heat of late summer. S.'s brother, a retired military bigwig, as far as I could gather, was also present, legs and stomach in a pair of shorts. S.

214

wearing longs but no shoes. We ripped into the brandy-and-water. And S. is a fine human being, sensitive hands, clearly a first-rate brain, even though he messed it up and chucked it away on rubbishy compromising. From sidestepping to shadowboxing to looking the other way, we reach, each in his own way, death, "when the last bell rings." I broached my subject and he listened and I'm sure he'll help if he can — and I'm grateful to him. You, old pal, were suddenly talking wildly in all directions. But that was fine too.

We were rather tipsy by the time we left the house, that's no maybe. As sick as he is, he walked with us to the cars outside in the street, in his socks. And when, by way of saying goodbye, he tried to make a little joke, raising his hand with a: "Well now, how does it go — heil Hitler" — the pathos was poignant.

The sun was still shining fiercely, I could just have made it home in time for supper in the kitchen when there is confusion between bats and stubborn swallows, between patches of shade and blotches of night outside in the yard — I suppose I could still have, and yet I couldn't have really, and we continued our wild pilgrimage. You wanted me to meet some more of your friends, we weren't spent yet, like true good-for-nothings we'd go and annoy the people, we'd go and beg a little tobacco for our pipes and wine for our cups.

First stop was halfway up the mountain at Kobus van Zyl and his wife's — "I drink *my* wine to get drunk." No sooner said than done. The transition between day and night went unnoticed. We possibly even had supper there, I wouldn't know anymore and you certainly wouldn't either, since you never eat nothing, do you.

Some time later we crossed the mountain to Camps Bay*, to someone else's place. The sea lay groaning there somewhere like a contented cow, and the whitishness of the moon washed up wet on the sand and reeked of bamboo. Now what were those people called again? I vaguely recollect that the master of the house had furnished a special little room around the back of his house somewhere for drinking purposes, and is it my imagination or were there really fish nets and others flotsam on the walls? His wine was first-class. Everyone talked loudly, about — can you beat it? — Lawrence Durrell. Perhaps it's true, maybe the Cape does have a touch of the

*Picturesque bay and beach on west side of Cape Peninsula.

Alexandria of old, something of the disintegration of a port, and of the anchorless characters who wash up on that kind of island, rich in obsolete and irrelevant knowledge — culture freaks! Inevitable, I guess, that the conversation should turn to the problems of culture and politics and the relationship, if any, between these. Kobus with a big face trying to tell me that I'm only going to be taken advantage of anyway by the political people, and relating with much bitterness the experiences of his young days, of how committed *he* had been, and how disillusioned afterward. There's someone (and as sure as the crowing of the cock he surely knows it's himself) whom he simply can't forgive for the fact that he, Kobus, had to become a clerk. I also learned that Cape gossip has it that I am a "card-carrying" Maoist . . . . Such an undeserved honor knocks me for a loop! After a while you close your eyes and start reciting long monologues from *Hamlet*. Flickering shadows of ghosts against the wall. It grew late. We had to go home. Such nights go on for ever. It's as though we want to protect ourselves against eternity. Or put another way, we are like farmers watering their fields in the night and heaping up earth walls to channel the water of eternity this way and that. The streets were pitch-black and wet in places so that the yellow street lights sometimes found reflection. A proud (but paltry) fortress is our Cape.

We took the road to Somerset West. We had left your car somewhere. The night would never end. Oubaas' car doesn't have a radio, but you were fumbling with some imaginary knobs on the dashboard and when you got to the right wavelength you sang as though your heart were a broken record-player.

A gentle drizzle was outside. I dropped you off at your home, the early workers were already up and about, and I stood on the accelerator of Pa's car to get home before the occupants would start stirring. And in the nick of time, too. When I turned into the backyard Mietjie was already in the kitchen. The water was still falling from the sky and the ground was heavier. If I had gone to bed then, I would have given the game away. In my heavy intoxication I went for Pa's garden hose and diligently began to water the lawn in the rain.

P.S. This postscript is really meant for André. It's in connection with the quotation I wasn't able to pinpoint the other day. Now I have it. It's from a speech delivered by Antonio Machado in 1937 to an international congress of writers in Valencia. "When someone asked me a long time ago whether I am of the opinion that the poet should write for the people or should remain ensconced in his ivory tower — that slogan was fashionable then — and devote himself solely to aristocratic activities in cultural circles, accessible to a refined minority alone — I replied to him with the following words which will sound very clever and evasive to many of you: *To write for the people? But what more could I wish for? I had such a desire to write for the people that I learned as much as I was able to from them — much less, all the same, that is clear, than the people know and are aware of. To write for the people means first and foremost that you write for people of your origin, of your patch of earth, of your language — we shall never be able fully to appreciate the inexhaustible content of these three things. But it is also much more, for to write for the people we are compelled to remove the barriers around our country, it means also to write for the people of other origins, of other earths, of other languages.*"

Rachel,

You can't get away from your own past, even if you wanted to. And you can't tie your own people to you, no matter how dearly you'd like to. Crying won't help. You can't escape the future either. Man's first dimension is that he is mortal, and that he knows it. That he sees it reflected in everyone and everything around him. To be integrated is to be mortal; to be involved is to be pervaded by a sense of the transient. The rising sun has the terrible glow of hell, of a perpetual flame, of eternity. The moon at night has the wonderful comfort of a white flower one throws onto a coffin in the grave, and each morning you wipe out the grave with clods as red as sparks, and quarter hour by quarter hour the tendrils of the flower climb upward again. Or sometimes, so I feel, the moon is just a porthole looking out onto a light and cold universe. You see, to me the moon remains a metaphor — and the fact that the Americans walked on it, makes no difference, because the Americans also walked on the earth and didn't grasp the first thing about it. Technical know-how means nothing in itself. Even power doesn't mean much. For the moment the white man is still king of the castle in Southern Africa, in Gondwana. Ten years

217

ago it was possible to imagine that it was going to stay that way. And now we know already, now we see clearly that the supremacy (or the guardianship) of the white man, will not last out our century. And in fifty years' time it will be ancient history, like the British domination of India, and this period we are living through so painfully at present, will be condensed into little black letters on a page or two of a history book. The temporary domination of the white man will be remembered only as one of the obstacles in the struggle of the black man — that is, the majority of the population of the land — for liberation and representative government.

But man is eternal and immortal. You and I are directly related to the people of always just as we will be family of the last. And every human being, in his or her hovel or palace, is bound to us. Col. Huntingdon and his henchmen — can we claim that they aren't human beings, even though they are monsters? The man with the short back and sides and the tie who tortures his fellow man to squeeze the necessary information out of him — who tortures *in vain!* — that fellow who speaks Afrikaans and who has children and who has a hard time sometimes because there are so many things he feels like doing (and because his mentors and teachers have made his understanding so narrow) which communal morality won't allow him, who sometimes does it anyway and then feels guilty toward man and God, and for that very reason strikes harder still perhaps, because he does it in the interests of the people and for law and order and survival, that man who violates himself and his victim and all of us, he is related to us. And the man who is tortured, who may be shot, and one morning early when the day is about to break — *break* — as though the day were dawning so clearly and so innocently over the sea, who is hanged with the day — is it in Johannesburg or Pretoria? — so that a last black breath escapes from him like a sigh or a cry — but like a bird of freedom that man is our brother. His breath is ours. The black pain and the even blacker joy enters us yet. Man is indestructible. Because while I remember, those hanged will live on. That is the staggering, the intoxicating knowledge. And that's a responsibility.

That's not what I wanted to talk to you about. We talk so little to each other really. And yet, sometimes you recall small events which you could not have experienced. Because they belong to the family as a whole. Perhaps I too remember things I could not have known. I'm glad I came back. I'm glad I could show my land to Flame Lily. It's *my* land, isn't it? It's private property. The hideous new constructions in Cape Town, the squandering of such a unique nature and human treasure, the fascist evacuation and desecration of District Six — it pains me, and I will have to bear the brunt of it. Yes, posterity will shake its head, spit on the ground and grind the spit into the dust with the toe of a shoe, and say: "The swine! The vile senseless cowardly greedy gluttons!"

And that's not what I wanted to talk to you about either. I'm not trying to hold the pen this evening, it writes by itself. Why must one always keep oneself in check? Why must one wait for the colder calculation, and the ensuing diplomacy, of tomorrow? Like our petty bourgeois writers. Like those who are knee-haltered; hamshackled by the positions they hold, their little government jobs, their debts, their overwhelming fear. They are not writers, they are tattoo marks on the wrinkled skin of the leprous, they with their Waterkloof* and their Koffiefontein. They shiver in their private swimming pools and feel the cold breeze in their huge cars. They have problems with the servants! Then they fingerfuck with Death and masturbate on the manuscript in the bottom drawers. They are family of ours. I love them.

When you're in foreign parts the friends and family of your youth gradually become phantoms. They become legends, caricatures, myths. They decompose and are reconstituted in other combinations. And then you return. And now they are both as they are and as you had imagined them. And your imagination has possibly made them. Maybe they are prisoners of your imagination. Maybe I am nothing but the monster of the imagination of some lunatic or other.

"We Breytenbachs," that's what he hears from Uncle Jors, said Uncle Koot, "we Breytenbachs have many talents; but we keep them to ourselves." Uncle Koot paid us a visit yesterday afternoon. He was neatly dressed, with a little green hat, and in the band around the hat was a partridge feather. Uncle Koot walked very carefully because he was wearing new shoes and they were pinching him. I was surprised

*Fashionable, predominantly Afrikaans suburb of Pretoria (see *Notes on Persons and Places*).

at how small and slight and slender his hands and his feet are, like the most delicate fins of a clumsy fish. He was somewhat indignant because we hadn't looked him up yet, he reproached us for it, said presumably we were too smart and too important now for the likes of him. Strange, how much bitterness there is in our family. We always pretend to be the underdog. Not without reason in his case. *Le malheur s'est abbatu sur lui et sa maison* — disaster descended upon him. He lost his wife, Aunt Baby, and his only and adopted son, Johan, within a few months of each other. He recounted, and his hands trembled a great deal, and then he wept. Of how Johan had left scratch marks on the wall. On the white wall. Because of the pain. And of the clothes which had remained hanging in the wardrobe. And of how thin Aunt Baby was toward the end, so thin that they couldn't even inject an anaesthetic into her during one of her many operations, but were compelled to cut into the living flesh. Where does our journey really take us? I have read that there are two ways and kinds of traveling — like Ulysses who assimilates, who experiences, for whom the world opens up from unknown to unknown; and like Rimbaud who shuts himself off, to throw himself into the unfathomable abyss of the self — in search of a total vision, a complete perspective of the world, the perceptible, the being. But there is also Amos Tutuala's kind of journey, a journey where all boundaries are suspended. Freed by fear. And there is Mini's kind of journey in Pretoria's Central Jail, the hanging jail. And Han-shan's journey while sitting on the Mountain, and Master Dogen's . . . . Yet all journeys *are* the same. Like the sea lion treading the globe while remaining in the same spot.

I sat listening to Uncle Koot's conversation, to his flowery expressions, and I tried to put my thoughts to his words. I thought: Western man has created one God for himself because he was so alone, and now he is lonely because there is a God. And I thought: Each time a rose falls, I stop at the same concept: predestination. While Uncle Koot gazed through the window and heaved a great sigh: "Dear, dear, the thunder has passed again." He took his words from his mouth as though he wished to bequeath them, but he has no heirs. He took his words from his mouth as though he cannot bring himself to take such a good set of dentures to the grave with him. He blew his breath out as though it would ease the load on his chest. There was a lump in his throat. His body was aching. And he'd rather

220

not smoke because "cigarettes just muck up your nerves." And to add to all that, he felt he had a cold in the brain as well. Yes, and that his eyesight was going. That he was suffering. That that was normal on account of the state his glands were in. Such wonderful words emerged from his mouth: words long forgotten; when false teeth used to be hand-painted. When you've been in a dark room for a long time, you're amazed to rediscover the tiny hairs on your hands in the daylight.

Then he told us about Grandpa again. He repeated all the fine things and he wept and Pa wept, too. He laid his words down like wreaths upon his broken life. How Grandpa lay down to die in his little room without an ailment and was just simply worn out. I *know* that the hard stony hills of Bonnievale were right outside his window. You never knew Grandpa and yet you remember him well. Grandpa is not dead. I want to give him to you as a gift. Grandpa died of grief. "He saw a *long* way . . . ."

I listened. My thoughts whirled about. I found a word: Godsickness. I wanted a miracle. My language is shit. Uncle Koot talked about the drought. "Yes, the ground is so hard that you have to die three days before your death if you want the grave-diggers to dig a grave." I started. Uncle Koot was going home. When I kissed him, his mouth was very wet. He has a clever dog, a collie. Her name is Lady. All his dogs were called Lady. Basjas will inherit Lady. "You shouldn't be ashamed of your people . . . . Our late Pa saw a *long* way . . . to the other side of the mountains."

Night approaches. There are hundreds of swallows in the sky, as in Paris too, sometimes. I am lying on the side verandah on a cot, more or less underneath the arbor. It's too hot for blankets. I have a sheet over my body and I imagine that I am dead. Or does one imagine that one is alive? The night is filled with sounds. Those noises are not memories; they are much more a part of me than sounds. The church bell peals the hours, the half-hours, the quarter-hours. For hours days months we keep hearing the frog-song/croak!/croak! Far below at the station a train calls. Moonlight. A veld. Gray smoke. Boers on horseback with rags wound around the horses' hooves so that the English can't hear them galloping off. They doze in the saddles. My Grandpa stands up in the stirrups and checks out his men. It reminds him of the Russian campaign, when with Napoleon whom he had met in St. Helena he tried to salvage what remained of a once proud army. I am laid out under a white shroud and the sounds shock through my body like tremors. The sky is star-spangled. The field of night is strewn with dead soldiers with gleaming buckles and buttons. Glistening ripe grains of corn. Tomorrow the stalks will turn blue. The only place in the world where one is not a stranger. The cement porch floor is covered with cracks. Near one of the yellow-painted pillars ants appear out of the ground like syrup, thousands, hundreds of thousands of ants. They emerge from the cracks in the porch floor. They pour up the doorframe. Early tomorrow Ounooi will come and destroy them with a poison spray. Then they will cling to the wood and the cement for just a little while longer and suddenly lose their hold and fall one after the other. (Be killed in action.) And when they are dead, there are small white specks lying about everywhere. I don't know if that's their little balls of food. Apparently they're Argentinian ants which are gradually ousting our indigenous species. Imperialism in all spheres. How did they get here from Argentina?

Still the day does not break. More than thirteen years ago I lay curled up on a blanket on the lawn on summer nights to look and look at the night and to follow the strange and lonely revolutions of the first Sputniks through the realm of the stars. It was still possible to discern letters in the stars then, thus to read into the future, thus to recognize the name of one's sweetheart. Some of them still hang up there above the rooftop, even though they have become so bleached with age that they have grown invisible. There were plum trees in the garden then, and a trellis vine against the bottom fence. French grapes. The season's first and sweetest. There was water in the pond then. Now half the property has been sold off to the Municipality and the garden is full of soil. The small pond where we used to swim in the dark, because that was the only time our wart-ridden bodies perhaps resembled stars (reflections?)—Christo and Anton and Jan and I — is filled with trash and cans and cartons. On the lawn grows a small willow tree. The night is not over yet. But in the distance I hear the voices of early factory workers. I hadn't realized that the first shift starts so early. Or possibly they are grape-pickers on their way to the farm? Their voices are shrill. The voices of young girls and young men. Their feet walk along the streets. Colored laborers. "Colored"

— what a dreadful word we have tried to burden them with. As if there could ever be a non-colored, a norm! There goes the factory siren now. Now is when the night puts down her soft and ephemeral gown of dew. Now the night is naked. Only the stars are like small holes. The African night. Primeval woman. Egyptian princess.

Do you remember, Ounooi told us that Oubaas, when he came to court her on Saturdays, so upright and proud on his horse, always wore a pair of white trousers? Those white trousers were spotless and without a crease or fold. I see him on his trippling bay in the dusty veld among the rocky hills, and his pressed white trousers nestle in Ounooi's heart. There they will remain and be ours. Such is love. Cheers and cherries.

saw hidden in love a vision which moves the eyes:
Bonnievale the sun walking without stick or noise like smell
through the land the earth red and heaven blue and clouds
white flying carpets cicadas making a glittering sound
clods have shadows tomatoes are soft hearts the river
a slurring tongue whispering deeply across boulders and bulrushes
beyond the ridge the people of Happy Valley fling their sounds
against the koppies my uncle Nick is standing in his garden
chewing grass and caressing his pumpkins as he gazes
at what is growing from his earth counting his blessings my
grandfather's delightful dust lies warmly in the hills for
God sits dreaming in a tree with glasses and a book and
a mug of coffee and a chunky slice of bread gazing at
the imprints of His hands the orchards the water courses the mules
and clouds and dust
and in sheer joy He blinks his eyes

how wonderful the things one sees behind closed eyes!

Wednesday, March 21

Also, we had to go to Bonnievale. A few weeks earlier, on January 23rd, on our return from Hell — and the worse hell still of Oudtshoorn where the Pretoria Guard receive their training to defend the Republic, and in so doing dig a huge communal grave, they are people whose lives can be directed to one dénouement only: to die for an ill-considered cause, without the least hope that that for which they die could ever remain standing, for they are the defenders of injustices, the body-faithful dogs, the muttering self-murderers, but who in the hatred and the despair of their frustrated lives, and wasted lives, will try to destroy as much as possible before they too are destroyed, Oudtshoorn like Pretoria a lair for Col. Huntingdon and his henchmen, Schicklgruber and Dröhl, where he can lower his mask and lick his lips and let himself go to a bubbling up of muffled little moans, for his heart which he can't get at burns and itches with a terrible rash —

a few weeks earlier, on January 23rd, on our way back from Hell, we had already returned to the Boland via Bonnievale. Then it had been almost dark and the sky had been threatening; blue clouds had lain piled up like mountains above the Langeberg Mountains as we drove into the village along Bushman Road. Why Bushman Road? Presumably that road had been a footpath for the old San people in former days, or had it been the scene of skirmishes between nomadic farmers and hunters? Whatever the case may have been, the road enters the village next to the station, and just to the right of that, even before you take the main street, stands Uncle Jors and Aunt Hannie's house under a gray iron roof. It is on level ground now, but when I last saw it at child-height, it stood on top of the hill. Things wear out. Recollection is a pair of glasses making everything smaller: return is a leap of the dream's eye to the eye-eye, a new perspective, a seeing smaller. (The station is important. Even much later when we moved to Wellington, we grew up beside the railroad tracks and I doubt whether it agreed with the sweet potato shoots. A train, its whistle in the night, a station and steam — when and wherever in the world it will rip through the flesh of the present to the very bone of nostalgia — away, forward, into the unknown!) But we were in a hurry last time, and it was the hour of the

224

wolves when the light must vacate the day to make room for the other kind of light of the night, and we didn't stop. (The sky was overcast. C. Pama writes: "Stars never featured in the symbolism of the Boer liberation.") Just drove down the main street, knock-knocking over the wide joints further along where it is made of cement — and saw the blue lamp of the police station on the far left side of the Breë River where Uncle Rooi Daan's land ended at the time, also the cheese factory, the clumps of darkness in the gardens in front of the houses with their verandahs and sturdy pillars, the green abundance of vineyards on both sides, thinly spread at first but then in unbroken succession, and higher and behind the village also the tiny lights of Happy Valley, the location. After that the road took us through Wakkerstroom, Oubaas' birthplace, if I'm not mistaken. Just this side of Klaas Voogds (or as we thought, Klaasvoegs) the roads meet in the main street to the Karoo and to the North, and we took a lefthand turn, via Robertson and Worcestor to Wellington.

But today's the day for a special trip to Bonnievale. To show Moonchild where the rot started. We commandeer Pa's car — he can't come along and waves goodbye with a final word of advice, but Ounooi comes with us. We buy flowers for Grandpa and Grandma's grave at the side of the road. On the other side of the mountain where the Bainskloof Pass starts descending toward Goudini, I have to stop so that Skippingmoon can take a picture of the proteas. I suppose that's the kind of idea which hardly ever occurs to our inhabitants. And a little further on as well, to photograph the laborers in their red and blue shirts, carrying bushel baskets full of grapes on their shoulders, in the vineyards.

Not long after Worcester we're in bush country. It's not the desertlike barrenness of the Little Karoo yet, but already it is arid and has the yellow and red colors so typical of drought. Not too bad, though, for the Breë River is one of the few rivers still showing a sheet of water, and on its banks the sunlight flickers in the tall poplars and the leafy green vineyards start.

As we enter the village, Ounooi is quick to point out who lived where — Uncle Hannes Band who has been bedridden for such a long time now, though he isn't really ill, just wobbly since Uncle John's death, Aunt Bettie and her family, and so on — and then, in particular, the houses in which we used to live: where the thatch-roofed cottage stood near the cement canal and has since been pulled down, that's the one-room sharecroppers cottage where my two elder brothers were born at the time when my father was working on the canal and during the week the workers stayed in tents along the waterway as its construction moved farther away from the village. Ounooi also joined Oubaas there in the tent, with children, bedsteads, and cooking pots. Gypsy life. And then she wants to show us the house where I gave my first discordant and treasonous cry. She is sure she'll recognize it again. Even in those days there was a small shop attached to the house. We pulled up. A couple of sheepish black customers are sitting in front of the shop, basking in the sun. We explain our visit to the woman now occupying the house, and she allows us to retrace our steps. Skippingmate takes snapshots. Ounooi gaily recognizes everything, yet doesn't really. I search my breast for the pang of memory (or remorse) but the heart is blind. Ounooi says I was born on a Saturday, around one at night, toward the end of the dance, somewhere between inebriety and hangover, that a flying saucer flew into a tree, and that the beadle hanged himself from the bell-rope in the steeple with the result that everyone overslept the following morning; in addition I kicked up the most dreadful row it seems, because I was nine months hungry and no one brought me anything to eat; everyone was asleep, see. She also recounts that I had a monstrously large head — not *then* in its figurative sense, not yet — with dark red and purple birthmarks between the eyebrows and that those parts were drawn together in a sullen frown, too, into a knot of wrinkles. It stayed like that for a long time. Grandpa Jan just clicked his tongue pityingly on seeing the double-yolked egghead, with the all-wise comment that something must either be very wrong or very right.

The house we moved into next, opposite the old church which is the church hall nowadays — the Lord demanded a newer shinier church — and where I came to my senses, still looks just as spruce: green pillars, red iron roof, small gate, and flowers. We drive on to Uncle Nick and Aunt Joey's house and nothing has changed there either. Only, Aunt Joey has grown older and grayer, and Nicholas bigger. The house still smells, as always, of ginger and coolness. Outside in the vegetable garden and among the fruit trees the red lumps of earth sparkle and steam. My uncle is the finest gardener in the land — even better than my father and better still than Uncle Koos Kock, and that takes some doing. All kinds of things sprout from his soil — pumpkins and flowers and apricot trees — and everything is plump. They were never rich, but I know of no one else living in such harmony with the earth and the water and the blue sky. We are in the kitchen when Uncle Nick arrives — as I have remembered him all these years: his wonderful blue eyes, his hat which is sometimes pushed to the back of his head or else rests half on his nose, the blade of grass in his mouth, the pants which look as if they're about to slip down, the simple but clean shirt with the short sleeves.

It is peaceful and we sit down to eat. A Bible is lying on a side table and there are framed Bible texts on the walls. Also a color print of the family crest, probably palmed off onto the family years ago by a glib-tongued peddler. I translate for Hopscotch. It's just as I thought, of course — we are of very old aristocratic stock. Related to all the royal houses by derivation. With a rightful claim to various thrones. Aunt Joey dishes up — meat and vegetables and salads. Rice and potatoes, the way it should be. And virtually all from the garden. Delicious. Food for human beings. Uncle Niek pours a semi-sweet wine. We say grace and we eat and we are not anxious and time will not catch up with us for it has always been like this. And even if we do pass on, it doesn't matter. There's a thread running through, a love. During the meal we learn how old and how neglected Uncle Jors and Aunt Hannie have become; how Uncle Jors is just about blind and is swindled out of his small change by butcher and shopkeeper alike because he is continually offering them a handful of notes when it comes to paying. But how fond he still is of the bottle! A Breytenbach! An obstinate old mule. Alcohol and blood combined in the veins. And when Ounooi talks about our visit to the house of my birth, Uncle Niek tells us that she has made a mistake. But what does it matter? Don't all things perish?

After lunch we get into the car to look up the real house. After all this time the present occupants still recognize our family! Where the verandah used to be, there is a store now, selling rolls of material, and knives and matches. Inside we are conducted around the house by an old gentleman with a little panama hat and a walking cane, jacketed, and tied. He suffers from some ailment or other. His eyelids are red and puffy and a shiny liquid oozes out of the pustules on his face. But he is excited and lets us see everything. On the hallway walls, behind glass, are newspaper photographs of Doctor Malan and General Smuts, in color. It feels to me as though I am returning to get something I had forgotten (or thrown away?) The scents of the lush back garden permeate the house. The spirit of a baby looks at me perhaps, mocking and with a masked and inflamed third eye on its forehead. I'm sure that that spirit prefers to remain with the gray old man and the sausage dog keeping up a constant cheeky yapping, and the garden. And how right it would be! We are intruders upon our own youth.

Then we drive to the graveyard, past Grandpa's house, which is still exactly as it always was, brown and isolated. There is even a motionless figure sitting on the same back verandah and maybe even on the same unrelenting brown wooden chair. A figure watching the hills, and the neighboring graveyard, and the bluegums.

In this house my Grandpa died — simply of stubbornness. Jan "Afrikaner" they called him. And apparently my father is referred to as "Rebel." And I hear they're calling me the "Black Peril." We keep up with the times! "Your Grandfather had no book-learning," Uncle Koot told us the other evening in the backyard of Grevilleas. "He learned just enough in order to be confirmed in the Church. But he saw a *long* way . . . a *long* . . . way . . . to the other side of the mountains." It was he who, with a friend, caught and tamed the first ostriches, Uncle Koot told us; in the vicinity of Oudtshoorn they tracked a hen on horseback and watched the nest. And then others got rich on it! And with his last breath he gripped the hand of one of his sons — and Grandpa Jan's grip was strong and feared in this area — and his grip was powerful, and he said: "Please live in love and peace with one another."

Uncle Koot wanted me to write down the story of the Breytenbachs for a change, instead of all this nonsense. And he wanted me to never look down on my people, no matter how bad they were, even if they were lying under the table, because they are *my* people. And now we stand beside the grave where the two old people have been put away, with Uncle Niek, Grandpa's youngest. A simple granite stone. Grandma Anna was my Grandpa's second wife. His first died when she was bitten by a snake which was hiding in a pile of wood. The graveyard is teeming with ants. Huge ball-biters crawl out of holes and slits everywhere along the grave-tombs and climb up our legs. These ants are fat, with huge pinchers. I'm obliged to piggyback my wife to a safer place away from the rest of us. Uncle Nick arranges the flowers on the grave. There is black moss on the tombstone. I scratch a bit of moss off and take a pebble and wrap it in a scrap of paper. It is quiet. The tree tops stir slightly but we don't hear the wind. Just see that it is blue. The sun lies everywhere. As though it is shining here especially. An eternity. This graveyard is not a place of concealment. It is laid bare to the bone. Rest and peace. Where there had been a handful of graves belonging to brown people, the Municipality has since planted a grass-green lawn over the remains, with a couple of benches to rest on and from where you can see the koppies with their twinkling ironstone reflections. The footprints of the sun. We look also at two fresh and as yet unoccupied graves. Comfortably large they look, and the sides have been plastered with cement, as is the bottom in fact. Waterproof. One doesn't want the dead to drown. The ants swarm over our ankles.

Back. Uncle Niek and I go and talk among the fruit trees. Uncle Niek has become a prominent man in the village. Worked at the Divisional Council for years. Then on the church council. And now he has been elected to the town council. He wasn't going to run at first. But he allowed himself to be talked into attempting to counteract the total takeover of every living soul by the Broederbond. My heart expands an inch with joy on hearing that my modest uncle has the courage to stand up to that dark sect. And in his gentle way Uncle Nick in turn tries to bring me around to other ways of thinking. He talks about the history of the Afrikaner, about his struggle for independence. His blue eyes search the horizon. On the hill opposite his house whitewashed stones proclaim: 1838–1938. The Centenary.* He speaks also of justice. And that one ought to understand and respect another man's point of view. Around us all the shrubs and the trees he has planted are in flower. I would almost believe that they incline toward him to listen.

Then we climb through the fence between his garden and the tomato field next-door, and we pick a basketful of red tomatoes.

*Of the *Great Trek*.

Under the green leaves they hang from their tendrils which are supported by galvanized wire. The muddy soil clings to our shoes. The land has probably been watered a few hours ago. The smell is one of fresh soil and tomatoes.

It's time to go. With Uncle Niek's permission I fill a small empty bottle I have brought for that purpose with the red soil from his garden. For me, beginning and end lies in this earth. We have to start saying goodbye. We are given a big paper bag filled with fruit and vegetables. And on top of that jars of apricot jam and dried figs and raisins. I kiss Uncle Niek and Aunt Joey. Uncle Niek says: "And tell your Pa to send his old used banknotes my way."

When we drive off a fine cloud of dust rises behind us like a column of smoke. Nicolene remains standing in the sun and the dust and with one hand in the air for a long time. The hills are vertical and silent. In a moment they will be shrouded in purple shadows, but it will be as though the shadows emerge from the hills themselves, because the sun never sets over Bonnievale.

N.B.: And after all that, a few days after the above, Yippie discovered that all those photographs she had so lovingly taken, have been lost. The spool seems to have jammed. Yet thus the images we wish to retain are tucked away more intimately still.

a handful of earth sweet and red
to clutch a world
in lands remote from here

a handful of earth, mute
yet bringing a touch of blue from the hills
of trees offering shade against the sun
of a sky filled with blue sun
and of ripening fruit

a handful of earth where men have trodden
where migrant birds still linger
and a dog in the night
chases a pitch-black train into the night

230

mingle my ashes with these sweet-smelling herbs
and scatter them about to capture death,
with this earth I am back in the South
back in the earth the excursion is completed

(and onward on a bicycle)

Stranger,
        when you linger here for a heartbeat
with a cold eye
on a wind-cleansed whisper-morning/when the trees are shaking
and the sun falls a blue bird in the sky —
then listen carefully:

I had no voice
I was simply a vocal chord as old as breath
derived from the people and attached to the heart
beaming as centrally as the grave,
and what I had to say was only to give
to those who had tuned me in

listen carefully
with your ear in the ground
to the running of the revolution
aimed at making the earth round/listen
to the sun singing in every ear
in honor of peasant and laborer,
listen carefully to the wind trembling —
the earth reeks of justice

listen carefully
and then go your own way
no one can suppress death
and inside you something of us lives on

March 22

(Yesterday was Sharpeville Day.)* Political landmarks are gradually shifting in this country. The event of the deepest significance, which will ultimately have far-reaching consequences, was the growing strikes over the last months. The *black* proletariat, the working class are becoming aware of their class-nature, of the nature of their exploitation, of their potential power. And this awareness is finding increasing expression on a national level. (The *white* workers, the bribed, the noble laborers will eventually be affected by this, too.) These striking and agitating workers are the bearers of the hope for change in South Africa; they are the people of the future and not those Government-appointed yapping lap-dogs, the chiefs in the reserves.

(be alert as a hare!
don't mull over things
call a spade a spade
and start digging for the right word!)

In Wellington and environs it is time for the grape harvest. Trucks heavily laden with loads of ripe grapes rattle through the back streets of the village en route to the wine press and distillery. At night I sleep like a hole in the ground.

but first you are captured by nightfall
and wind coming from the trees
tearing branches and fruit to pieces
in its haste to get out
into the pitch-blue sky: clouds fleeing
into the mountain

beneath the Hawekwa Mountains the farmers are pressing wine
farmers pressing night and day:
workers calling out to be silent in pure sound,
grapes purple and yellow
and pale forming a mound in a vat

*21st March, 1960, the day on which a confrontation took place between the South African Police and a crowd of black people demonstrating about the pass laws at Sharpeville in the Transvaal, during which there were a number of fatal casualties.

the must is the shadow that lurked in the grape,
the moon, after all, is a vat
the stars intoxicated — clouds
making music in the mountains . . .

tomorrow it will be hot
and white with the dust of the sun o
tomorrow's cool wine will be refreshment
the wind a dry flame on the mountainous mountains
sniffing the trees like breath

the maggot in the Afrikaner

ancient heart, the two of us
have come a long way together,
turned back together to face this land,
so why go on gnawing and gnawing at me?

master, I gnaw at your very guts,
I am the maggot you've got to feed,
I'll devour your eyes as well,
and bathe in your blood

but why, heart, why?
I gave you mountain and ocean
and sun and dream and the sinuous smell of the sea,
I give you whatever you desire

sire, too much you're giving me,
I am yours: and
the gnawing throb you can hear,
the rhythm of death, is death

I throb for you

233

From March 23rd

like when you are weary
and lie down on your back
beneath the tall tree
your weapons in the dust

watching the gathering dust
gathering the birds in the tree
until the stars in swarms
perch on the branches

watching the yellow moon
lying on her back, her hair
like rays around her
drowning in the night

until blinded by tears
and the morning sun you do not see
the birds fly up
to devour the corpse

so lies your death:
waiting within you:
a reverberating silence:
a miracle

    I was late for our appointment. When I arrived in Somerset West in the afternoon, the others were already waiting, and quite impatient. Canned food and articles of clothing were strewn over the floor, and my friends were packing their rucksacks in such a way as to ensure that the weight would be equally distributed among the bearers.

    But my delayed arrival had not been intentional. A start to the preparations for the trip into the mountains had been made some days ago — yet, now that our sojourn in paradise was nearly at an end, now that time was racing at a terrifying speed toward the point of departure, there was suddenly so much still to be done, there were suddenly so many people we would still like to see. And the throat tightened. There was a premonition of autumn in the air.

I bought myself a sun hat in the city, a blue one. Before noon on the 23rd Pa and Mouche took me to the station. What had to accompany me up the mountain was in my briefcase: 2 tins of canned peas, corned beef, coffee, condensed milk, a pocketknife, matches, sugar, eating utensils, sleeping pills, torch, pull-over sweater, dried soup, clean underpants, pipe, a small tin of English tobacco, my tennis ball, an extra stem for my pipe, and paper. The highway to the Cape passes farms, and close to the city, passes also through new townships and residential areas. The railway, however, runs along the back of the décor, as it were, and between Paarl and the Cape there are so many semi-decayed locations, cardboard shacks and tin shanties, one strung to the other. Puke. Tattered children play on garbage dumps. Unemployed youths, dressed in defiant cheap clothes, stand or lean against iron hovels.

At Cape Town station I was met by Adam and his wife and Jakes and his spouse. (Jakes like a dark African mask, laconic, inscrutable.) And in Adam's car they took me out to Somerset West. My waiting friends poured somber red wine, there was a sluggish light over the ocean, and we were ready to leave.

Always, even from the very beginning, as far back as I can remember, the Cedarberg Mountains have been a place of refuge; but more than that, a place of magic, a prehistoric place, where there are no complications and little pain, where it is possible to touch the edge of the earth, virgin, undefiled, unknown, yet devoid of all peril; mountains without questions where the moon is born from a gorge and extinguished in the sea.

Always, even from the very beginning, as far back as I can remember, the Cedarberg Mountains have been a place of refuge; but more than that, a place of magic, a prehistoric place, where there are no complications and little pain, where it is possible to touch the edge of the earth, virgin, undefiled, unknown, yet devoid of all peril; mountains without questions where the moon is born from a gorge and extinguished in the sea.

I had been there several times before, many years ago — and then always for two or three days at a time, high up in the golden light and in the spacious desert-tent of stars at night. There, shortly

235

before my departure at that time. I learned my first few French words from Jan Rabie, and I remember the color of the clumps of grass and the way they bent down, it was on a slight elevation and there was a wind low over the ground. *"Je m'en fiche, je m'en fous, merde."* And on occasion, on the way back, we stopped near Blaauwbergstrand among the Port Jacksons, and Kees de Jong, the one-eyed Hollander, ran into the sea with all his clothes on. The old crowd of then have almost all gone now, have been beaten and scattered — for this land devours its young like a tigress demented with pain. Kenny — he vanished into the mist of exile; Kees — he too is abroad and holding his heart with both hands; Wilhelm — Wilhelm has not been well for some time now; Marius — the Boers have been keeping him in jail, in the clink, behind bars for years . . . . Friends, if this installment be of any value, and if it please you, I humbly dedicate it to you.

We would go to the mountains to breathe, to walk the soot and the nightmares out of our bodies, to find, without it being spoken, a point of silence again. People are living up on the Mountain, mostly the Jouberts, Uncle Frederik and his brothers, descendants of the Huguenots who have seldom if ever traveled further than their dwelling-cave and the forestry station or the few mission villages. Buchu farmers and mountain guides. Daantjie is the one who is increasingly looking after them. The Cedarberg Mountains are purgatory. As Daantjie says, if you want to see what a fellow's worth, if you want to know what there is to him, you take him to the Cedarberg Mountains for a couple of days. And he states that he plans to send his son to the Jouberts for a few years, as soon as he is old enough, so that the goats may kick him and he may become fully *human*. It's true, you may travel through the gorges and sleep out in the open under the wind and listen to the ghosts of the brown people, to the anthems of the spirits; you may taste eternity there alongside a complete stranger and although you may not remember the name of that friend, and although you may never see him again, you will be conscious for ever after of *knowing* him.

One day when I am free and no longer exist, I want to go and live in a fold of that dead world with my wife, May is her name, her name is Morning Glory. We will build a *dojo*, a meditation hall with white walls and an endless host of stars will pass by above our heads, and in the morning we will dance with our mouths open and our breasts turned to the exploding sun, dance slowly like herons writing manifests in the dust, and in the evenings we will turn our eyes and our foreheads to where the sun takes its fire-gown off and we will dance, slowly and on one leg like herons at bedtime, and there will be a fountain, and boulders in the garden, and I will plant a fig tree and wait until it grows tall and green to sit under that tree for the awakening, and at nightfall we will keep company outside in the dark until we are no longer able to distinguish visitor from rock or shrub, and we will grow older and not die, just smell nicer and nicer, and opposite the marsh beyond the hill where the pretty red flower grows, there will be a small shop where we shall be able to buy the newspaper now and then, and a bottle of whisky.

We left in two cars. Jan, that is Jan Biltong who doesn't want to grow any older, only wilder and more cantankerous, and Jim (Swami), old mournful Jim, and myself were in one car with a couple of knapsacks and cartons of wine in the trunk. In the other car were Daantjie, Nici, Barend of Porterville, and Barry, with the rest of the luggage and the other wine. Revel would be following on his own early the next morning before first light.

The road to the Cedarberg Mountains runs through the Swartland, wheat territory, a landscape of gradual undulations, a region where the language becomes guttural and exuberant and moist, a drowsy-scape, charged with sadness, where the mice dart among the clods, playing tricks with the weather.

Now that I have all my characters more or less lined up in the cars, I suppose I should do something with them. There isn't much to be done with them because I started them off too late and then it grew dark meanwhile, so that the reader won't get to see much on the way. It will be better, then, if they just talk.

But one doesn't go to the Mountain to talk. They did try, I'll give them that. As a matter of fact, Swami and the communist picked up the kind of conversation which can't really be exhausted, because talking cannot truly embrace those things, just the opposite; it would be like attempting to scale a mountain in a rowboat, if you know what I mean; and hopefully that conversation of theirs will continue for many years yet.

By urgent request Biltong succeeded in disengaging one of the

237

bottles from the contents of the trunk so that the inner man might be fortified. That, I am inclined to think, was more or less exactly what the conversation had begun to touch upon: the inner man, or at least the non-existence of the ego (but the presence of the observation point) and furthermore about the nature of experience. It often strikes me in South Africa how deeply and how passionately one may fall into a conversation with people you like, like dogs desperately and stubbornly holding each other by the throat. Maybe it must be blamed on the shared abyssal feeling.

On either side of the beams from the car lights, the night was an abyss. Malmesbury, Moorreesburg, bypassing Piketberg and via Citrusdal. After a while one car after the other disappeared into the bundu. And suddenly, out of nowhere, out of damnation virtually, in the pitchdark, a ghostly gray-white donkey beneath a tree and a little further on another and another. And, shielding his eyes from the devouring lamps of the vehicles, ahead, out of the night, suddenly uncle Frikkie too, with his shy voice and his humble hat and his soft shoes. That was the spot where the cars were to be left. By the alien light of the stars one could detect the bulky outline of the first mountain slope on the far side of the stream. We got out and stretched our legs. We unloaded. We wandered a short distance into the darkness, into the fragrant and rustling (and talkative) veld to urinate with legs wide. Such is tranquility. Here ends the world. Here begins the world.

Uncle Freek had had a good fire going for some time. We made coffee and food. Grass and other greenery was made into soft beds. That night we slept close to the earth. Everyone found himself a place to sit or lie down. Uncle Frik squatted next to the fire. The donkeys stood just outside the circle of light. Groping, one turned in upon oneself, one began to smell and listen and see, started fitting one's small body into these unchanging surroundings. Frogs croaked where the noisy mountain stream flowed and formed small pools. A little further up across the river there was evidently a yard and some of the dogs barked now and then. But they were all sounds which wouldn't keep you awake. In the veld you sleep with your ears open.

We killed some of the bottles. Bit by bit we got rid of the city-talk. I became embroiled in a nasty argument with Daantjie. He stated that he only publishes books written by friends, that his concern is with friendship, not with the work, not with the money but the mare. I felt bad because I wanted him to publish my work on merit — and how would he know how good my books are if he doesn't even read them? The fire smoked on. Bull found himself a place to settle down for the night, a little away from the rest of us, near the rippling water. Biltong busied himself with his buckles and bits of rope. He attended to his knapsack and accessories like a scout who is going to be sent on a mission into hostile territory tomorrow. Tomorrow became a long day's walking, but the weather was fine and clear.

We slept. The fire smoked.

During the night I attempted the ideal journey. It was the journey of the disciple of Emmaus, or some such:

"The best way to travel, of course, is to pick your moment of departure carefully, to ensure that you set out in exactly the right way and that your sights are set on an ideal point of arrival. Then make the point of your narrative, and *voilà!*

"It is best of all, therefore, to leave very early in the morning from a small village with white flat-roofed houses. You rise very early on the allotted morning, well before the sun is properly hatched, and you walk to the tinkling fountain in the village square. While you are walking you adjust your trousers and your suspenders so that they do not chafe or pinch in any spot. See how the cottages rest, locked in their slumbers. Occasionally, through the windows, you hear the light snoring of shopkeepers and peasants attempting to take the last turns, slipping all the while, before groping, with creaking jaws and bloody disobedient fingers, for their boots under their beds. On the hill facing us the first cock crows in the widow Hoewa's yard — sharp already like his mistress, and you know that the area's feathered folk are about to start prodding and pestering the sun, one by one, are about to quarrel about the sun, first the red one near the green roof in the valley, then Gak's two gamecocks of which he is so proud, and in between a rooster or two, probably, behind the barracks where they're kept for the pot (which means a new bird nearly every day and actually it pretends to scream only from longing and loneliness), and so on across the hills and vales with their homesteads and their share-croppers' cottages and back again, until even the old blind rooster

239

under the fig tree in Nina's backyard (your house borders on hers, doesn't it?) will start growling and chewing and then playing his gullet, in all his glory. That's when you know that the light is touching Groenkop. How many mornings have you lain dreaming thus, following the sun in all its walks across valleys and seas, the roosters cutting the blue canopy with the shears of their voices? But today is the day that old Blindrooster's sobs will be a farewell and when the sun takes the village, they will search for you in vain.

"Below near the fountain you thrust your whole head under the mouth of the carved lion, hair and all, letting the water run down your back in cool trickles. Then you cup your hands and drink the fresh liquid with greedy gulps (it's your way of crowing back to front!). Now you wipe the remaining drops from your mustache and eyebrows with the back of your hand and when you turn around to walk back, you see Uncle Philip wearing his little black hat sauntering toward you, doggedly following his old sheepdog and his fist-led walking stick. You had forgotten just how early the old chap's gout drives him to the veld, and now you simply pretend not to be able to get him clearly within your sights and walk hurriedly home up the cobbled street, his sparrow-brown eyes focused on your spine.

"The screen door opens with creaking hinges. The coffee water which you had balanced on the small gas stove before going out, is boiling like snake-eyes, and when you have made sure that your equipment and accessories are lying in the suitcase as they should be, you place yourself next to the kitchen table with eyes narrowed (because today you will be obliged to peer across plains and winding roads against the run from the very beginning) and drink the coffee from the blue mug which your great-grandfather bequeathed to you at one time, which also serves to dip your rusk into and can even be used for shaving if necessary.

"You tie a red handkerchief around your neck because you seem more of a traveler that way, seize your little case and walk out onto the verandah and through the dawn-glimmering garden. In passing you pick up your straw hat from the wooden table beneath the arbor where you had left it lying yesterday and tap it against your leg — in case of dampness and spiders.

"Godalmighty! This village won't see me again. Now it's the

bundu and me!

"You turn left up the cobbled street until you get to the main street and you are able to turn left again, now you climb the uphill (the village fountain is on your right). The cafés are still closed and won't be opening for a while yet — you know them: all like Stiflos, talk about sea voyages, islands, lakes, fords, mountain passes and egrets, but which of them has ever been farther than Blomomdraai? And that's only as far as the in-laws'! The tables under the trees are deserted and weary. The old men will come to prop them up much later with bitter coffee, schnapps, and cards, when the sun will already be flaunting herself a hand's breadth above the widow Hoewa's poplars. How easily their tongues will wag today about your adventures!

"Where the village surrenders, Janief's mongrel jumps up against the rotten old garden gate with a thundering racket and then kicks up even more of a row for the distance your shoes clip-clop on the road, raging along the entire length of the whitewashed ring-wall. You've suspected for some time that this dog is mad. Now you would like to shake the dust of the village from your soles, but the ground is still sucking up the dew, and the only things falling across your tracks are small worms of half-caked mud.

"In former years Janief's farmhouse was almost one kilometer from the village. Now it has merged with the village, but once you start strolling through his orchards bordering the road on both sides, you know that you're finally leaving the village.

"The silence of the morning is cracked by the grating of soldiers' boots marching rhythmically toward a bend in the road. It's last night's patrol returning with much grumbling, but full of smiles and jokes all the same, full of their victory which gladdens your heart too, for as long as everyone can win, no one is killed, and you raise your hat with a flourish to greet the triumphant troops.

"Nina's rooster — as blind as the figs above the comb on his head — will start grunting any moment now, and if one turns around one will see how the first rays of the sun begin to define the dark. The smoke of small morning fires spirals upward in a few places, and from here the bleating of a bell-goat can be heard below the village, followed by faint jingling, a dog barking, and some more bleating. Someone is taking his sheep to the veld; Gareb, perhaps, who won the new vacuum cleaner last week in the raffle, and everyone was whispering about how strange it was for so god-fearing a man to . . . Wonder if the thing would work in the sheep pen?

"Now my village is no longer empty and my footsteps lose their hollowness. A slimy kind of twilight lingers in Janief's pear orchard on the right — spittle-fine threads are just beginning to gleam from leaf to leaf. Tall, fat pear trees. Those make enough on the market to feed and clothe you, your aging wife and all three of your buxom marriageable first-class cow-milking daughters. Particularly if you know the art of penny-pinching, like old Janief, the old miser. He *knows* about palm grease. But I'm digressing.

"Further along the road one passes a gathering of young almond trees. I'm very fond of almond trees because they're always in blossom. It will be a pity, actually, when they start bearing one day. Just look at these blossoms, as Van Gogh would have liked to dream them.

"Beyond the almonds I first sit down. At the thought of the imminent sun. If I want to make a journey, I must make sure that all my necessary things and stuff are in the suitcase. I reassure myself about that first and then adjust my shoelaces a little. It won't be any good if my feet were to cramp up. And so on, up and legging it, hat over brows, whistling of cuckoos and wood pigeons deep in the ear — Blomomdraai is a hell of a long way, actually!

"Now I won't bore you with all my adventures. Later, far across the other side of the hill, I help myself to some of Jop Gris' yellow radiant oranges next to the road, drink from his creek and then wait, dozing, beneath one of his trees for the cool shade of late afternoon. A straw hat is the only thing that doesn't smother me when I place it over my nose, eyes, and mouth.

"Refreshed, I strike out on the road again when, twenty paces or so ahead of me, I see another traveler get up from beneath his tree and brush the dust from his long, gleaming white robe. He must have been waiting under that tree for a long time, and for me, if you don't mind, for as I approach he says loudly and clearly (so that my ears ring): 'Hi, Pumpkin Breytenbach! I am an angel with a message for you concerning your journey.'

"The sun is hot and I can see how wearily the wings on his shoulder blades quiver. We walk back, chatting as we go, to Jop

Gris' refreshing orange orchard, and each of us picks a few golden ones to suck and to sweeten the words. The fellow in shiny armor tells me many things which I don't want to repeat now owing to lack of space. From time to time I want to protest, but a messenger from heaven doesn't allow himself to be messed with.

"And so we shake hands and each continues on his way, I to find a place to sleep for the night en route to my suggested destination, and he to the nearest airfield more than likely. I am quite a long way from my point of arrival, admittedly, but already the shadows are beginning to scrub at line and form of rock and cloud, and from here it is downhill.

"Dusk comes romping heavily and limping into the street (if cripples can romp, of course), and up above, the fleece clouds are Monet's, as I pace the last rise before the village above Janief's dusty orchard on the left; old Green Mountain starts trembling under the onslaught of the dark, and lower down past the little tables outside the restaurants where the old men are sitting, leaning on their hands, motionless and mute after the day's talking in the evening coolness, from here one hears the sad victory songs of the soldiers in their barracks; then right down the cobbled street and through your front gate, behind the wall, Nina's rooster clucks blindly and also scratches himself a place to rest for the night; up onto the verandah and I smell the delicious evening meal my wife is preparing; one doesn't get far on Jop Gris' oranges; and I fling my hat under the arbor and go inside to kiss my wife behind the ears, so blissfully happy to be home again. And prepared for tomorrow."

We struck camp early on the morning of the 24th, Saturday. The sun wasn't up yet and it was cold enough first thing in the day, especially at the stream where we had to wash and get water for our coffee. There was a low mistiness in the valley.

Fox arrived while it was still dark. One by one the climbers brought their knapsacks into readiness for the long hike of the day. The heavy stuff, and the wine, were packed into grain bags and tied to the donkeys' backs with straps.

Few words were exchanged.

Bull started out first. Then Biltong and me. Through the stream at the rocky ford and then over a slight plateau to where the first incline begins, to where the uneven footpath starts twisting upward between rocks and forest. On our left, higher up along the river, the farmstead where the dogs were heard barking last night came into view. Already there were signs of life in the yard. The cocks had started crowing early and now one heard chickens squawking and cackling and sometimes the shrill calls of a child which travel a long way through the pure mountain air. People were moving between house and barn. Biltong and I climbed to where we could look back on last night's camp where the smoke from our little fire still rose, coiling above the last of the mistiness. Then our comrades came down to the water one by one, and out again on the opposite side to the foot of the first steep rise. Barely a hundred feet farther up among the cliffs a baboon called — judging by his voice, according to Biltong, it had to be an old male. We left the path, each to squat behind his own bush.

Everything was fresh. Everything sparkled. We were acutely conscious of every separate smell and sound. Distances were deceptive; if you called out to the people you saw climbing upward not far below you, they appeared not to hear. At first it was also difficult to find your own walking rhythm again. With something like surprise, amazement even, you rediscovered your muscles — the flabby ones as well as the ones you could still count on. Rhythm is a matter of breathing — the body is a pump. It takes a while to gain control over the rhythm, so that whatever the body does becomes automatic and you forget about it. With Zazen, or meditation (though meditation is really a big word for what is little more than sitting crosslegged) it is exactly the same; though you sit quietly and without moving, it requires a conscious effort to let the breath come and go, come and go more deeply and smoothly — the solution of extremes!

Another word used for Zen is *do* which means "way," "road," or "route." Thus, in Japan, reference is not made to Buddhism, but to *Butsudo* — the way of Buddha, and a *dojo* is not only a meditation hall, but literally a place where one exercises for the way.

They say that there are people in Tibet, high in the roof of the world, who can walk terribly fast, and that those people start their training by being locked up for a few years in a small room. I have never really been locked up — excepting the confines of the word —

244

and so, if I ever found myself on the way one day, I probably couldn't move along very quickly.

In the meantime it turned out to be an uphill struggle. Now and then we stopped to inspect and admire a flower, a woody protea, perhaps, or a gnarled tree growing out of a crevice, or a rock formation. After a while we had to move out of the way to allow Uncle Frederik and his pack-donkeys to pass. When the sun caught us at last, we had already reached the caves of Welbedacht. We turned off to go and look at the caves and then walked on again. It was less steep now — we were on a kind of elevation. Grass grew there and streams were fairly plentiful. In a pool beneath an open cave — the water clear and icy — we had a swim. That is to say, we lay down in water so cold it took your breath away. That is really to say that we would have liked to go on lying in the water if Swami hadn't kicked up so much mud.

It was quiet, and yet there was wind. The clouds sailed through the sky with small ripping sounds. The moaning sounds of clouds skimming through the heavens. Clouds scouring through space with small sad sounds. An old Chinese poem suddenly flashed through my mind:

Snow-white in the sky the one-eyed moon
Propped up on tree-beams of light . . .

Across a ridge we came down into another valley, deeper in the mountains. Gorges on both sides, but no vegetation to speak of. Prehistoric fissures in the earth's crust. The rock faces were red. Canyons alternating with peaks of stacked rocks. No sign of life. It was as though one were facing a deserted battlefield.

"On the fields opening up before me, many flags are fluttering. There are craters and crevices. Broken lances are lying there, blownup horses, and silver-gray birds picking at the uniforms of soldiers, or the blinkers on the shining eyes of the horses."

"I think I have experienced death. I think I am now no longer afraid of death. (Now I only have to *earn* it honestly.) Now I even think I won't die anymore. Because I have felt it in the flesh; I have accepted it. That doesn't mean that I was ever dead. But I'm no longer what I used to be. It's another "I." And besides, I know death because I have killed. (It's not clear.)"

"And when the birds of death come for us. And when we shall be seed for the white birds of death. And when the birds of death come for us, we must be light and free like water, light as drawings of bone so that we may travel right into the target. The heart is the wing-beat of the bird."

"We must not become bullets. Bullets are small and determined and dark. Bullets are indigestible. We must retain our humanity."

"I squandered and murdered. The touch of my hands has alienated that which I have touched, has caused it to degenerate. I have embraced feelings and allowed them to slip from my hands. I became a monster. When I poke my head out of the small window, the saliva is suspended from my chin in glistening threads, like the drivel from the mouth of the eland running far across the plains of the Kalahari, and I laugh. The flies are the troops of my brain. I build stalagmites out of the water in my mouth. The dog has the head of a horse."

"I am thin, and the stems from the heart are thinner still. If they had had no shadows, one might have been able to say: 'They do not exist.' But luckily the heart is the fruit of shadows. Luckily the heart is where the shadows hide."

"I unearthed the words from the dark inner haunts, dusted them down, held them against the light and then used them again for the last time. (Alas, I could no longer hear what they themselves wanted to say.) To use a word, is to reject it. Therefore, words are landmarks planted on graves."

We sat down in the shade of a big tree in the gorge below where we had found water again, and prepared breakfast. The heat and the first weariness were beginning to tell on us. The water was clear but shallow and there was little of it.

From there the trail slowly climbed again, following a ridge of the mountain. There, far from the polluting hand of civilization, we found the first of the cedar trees. There are only three places in the world, it seems, where cedar trees grow — in Malawi, in Lebanon, and here. Cedar trees are even more gnarled and gray than the oldest olive trees. With ease they bridge the gap between life and death:

246

when they emerge from the ground, they seem old, and when they are fully-grown, it's hard to believe that they contain any moisture at all. Like fossilized gray breaths, fire and ashes at once, they stand on the slopes. But just take a small log — the wood is light and less gray on the inside — and smell it or throw a chunk of it onto the fire: the delicious cedar fragrance, a preservative balm, is everywhere.

The warmer it grew, the fewer our words became. Only Daantjie told strings of jokes. His mouth was constantly bubbling with wisecracks. He told jokes the way Uncle Martin farts, blandly and spontaneously.

We crossed a slab of rock and started descending — occasionally leaping and breaking. Below us lay a valley which was partially cultivated. There were a few cottages and a threshing-floor, though we saw no people. Under the dusty trees where some grass grew, Uncle Freek and his donkeys were waiting for us, long since unsaddled and rested. Uncle Frederik is well into his seventies, apparently, but he goes so fast, he is so tough (and on top of that he has to drive the pack-animals on, too), that not one of us would be able to keep up. We took our shoes and boots off and stripped our socks from our feet. It seems that there is no drinking water around there, but we found the odd muddy seepage-puddle at least, in which to bathe our feet. I'd had it. One really tries not to eat too much, afraid of the thirst which is always just behind the throat.

Had lunch. Put on shoes and socks again. Fox rubbed soap onto his feet and in between his toes and then put on two pairs of socks. It helps to prevent chafing and blisters, he said. You can see that he was a soldier in the desert in his time. Grain sacks loaded onto the patient donkeys again, I helped to keep them still. Donkeys say nothing, but look as if they'd like to drop an ironical remark or two. Jan Biltong alleges that that which cannot be said in words is sacred . . .? Then presumably donkeys are sacred.

"a poem:
the ceiling of concealing . . ."

Then we tried to find a shortcut through the veld. From there, there is a kind of wagon trail to Eselsbank. That was where we wanted to spend the night. The heat from the veld and from the sky had become

247

a kind of buzzing in the ears. The head was a sun. Nici said nothing, merely smiled. Her face was shiny and red, but her tread was stronger than any of ours. Swami had picked up a long walking stick. He was a pilgrim with a staff and took the lead, perhaps because he is so lean and sinewy. A small donkey-cart full of mountain people passed us from the front. We heard their voices coming toward us far across the veld. In the mountains the spirits wander about in broad daylight. Behind us lay the red walls of the mountains.

My new Italian shoes were clearly never designed for this kind of expedition. The soles were too smooth and the uppers too thin and too soft. I felt the stones with my feet.

In the late afternoon when the fireball was already beginning to touch the mountain peaks — scorching smoke on the horizon — we arrived at Eselsbank. We walked through the village, or better, we passed the cottages, for it's not a true village yet, in single file. Hurriedly, like donkeys smelling water. Almost sobbing with fatigue.

On the far side of the houses, close by the stream, in a natural clearing, but sheltered by large boulders, we took off our packs. And then made a bee-line for the water and plunged, naked, into the pool, into the tingling ice-cold water. The scratches we had acquired en route, the bruises and scrapes were now on fire. Lord, what a wonderful swim! We bellowed and roared and returned to the camp on tender bare feet.

The sun touched the wide mountain ranges around us, the cedar trees and the red cliffs, the wide basin in which we found ourselves and the sparse cottages and the squealing children and the dogs barking in the dust and the tall rustling poplars beside the stream — all that.

A finger of eternity?

In *Journey to Ixtlan* Castaneda describes how he is sitting with his old master on a mountain peak at the close of a day. Don Juan has told him that he is a warrior and that his whole life — when he will have come to realize that his life is a quest for personal power and when he will have come face to face with his first worthy opponent — that his whole life will be a dance. The posture, the attitude of a warrior is the portrayal of his life, and on the day he dies Death will see him dancing, then he will be able to hold Death captive for a moment in the spell of his dance, his dance which is the mirror of his life's stored power.

"Will I too dance to my death, don Juan?"

"Certainly. You are hunting personal power even though you don't live like a warrior yet. Today the sun gave you an omen. Your best production in your life's work will be done towards the end of the day. Obviously you don't like the youthful brilliancy of early light. Journeying in the morning doesn't appeal to you. But your cup of tea is the dying sun, old yellowish, and mellow. You don't like the heat, you like the glow.

"And thus you will dance to your death here, on this hilltop, at the end of the day. And in your last dance you will tell of your struggle, of the battles you have won and of those you have lost; you will tell of your joys and bewilderments upon encountering personal power. Your dance will tell about the secrets and about the marvels you have stored. And your death will sit here and watch you.

"The dying sun will glow on you without burning, as it has done today. The wind will be soft and mellow and your hilltop will tremble. As you reach the end of your dance you will look at the sun, for you will never see it again in walking or in *dreaming,* and then your death will point to the south. To the vastness."

a.
(then he dances the dry dance of death
raising the clouds of dust —
broad gestures specks of dust
caught in perspiration
in the shaggy fleece around the wrists —
indicating absence with the hands
and caressing the contours of what is not there —
a landscape oscillating
and revolving on its own:
turn, o landscape, turn!
turn yourself to a standstill
so that other ranges may rise here
and seas lie down at their feet
and people may squat behind the bushes in the sun

[drunk? Saturday?]

so he dances his dry dance
his perspiration spashing in the dust)

b.
to dance as one should
you must be blind
and groping

with as your audience
your entire spent life
as echo and mocking moon

but before you begin to dance
blindly, cast a measure of your blood
into the dust

and model in mud
notes
for your song

behold the music: behold
the music: violins clouds flutes
tumblebirds

tuned trees and violence
gurgling holes tumults symbols
and base crowbar-arrows

and a drum round and red
dangling from a string around
the sun

listen to the throbbing beats burning, dustbag
listen to the pain gnawing at the string
listen

and then, blind man, dance . . .)

It was dusk. Swami went and bought a bottle of fresh goat milk at one of the houses, with the promise of another bottle for tomorrow morning. Bull, well rested and not the least bit tired after the day's hike, carefully shared out bottle tops of whisky. Bliss! We pick Hottentot bedding and other shrubs to serve as mattresses for our sleeping bags. In the vast bedroom of the night, beneath stars of the canopy, each of us found himself just the right spot to lie down. We collected some wood for the fire. It grew dark.

After the meal two visitors made their appearance, one with a guitar. Two Viljoen brothers, farmers from the local village and elders of the church. Religious men. The village and its surroundings, the fields and pastures, belong to the Mission community, but the local people all have a say in the community. Nevertheless, it does happen that they are forced at times to work for neighboring white farmers. So they know about the white man, they know his tricks, they know how hard and fierce he can be, how much he demands and how little he pays, because you see, he isn't really human, is he? he cannot experience and accept *others* as *human beings*.

The Viljoen brothers, elders, didn't just say all that matter-of-factly; it emerged much later and more by hint and suggestion. When the wine started giving freedom to the tongues. For the wine was flowing. Wine and God have always gone hand in hand.

There was much joking and teasing and storytelling and singing. Uncle Frik told us about Hans Moller once more. About how they were picking buchu in a deep gorge — that would be Duiwelsgat — and his, that is Hans', wife was also there, though heavily pregnant. And how she went into labor by evening and then died in childbirth, and the child stillborn too. And that it was too late to carry the corpse out of the gorge, and how the other people left, because the gorge is the favorite haunt of baboons, and where there are baboons, leopards aren't far away. But Hans could not bring himself to leave the mortal remains of his loved one to the beasts of the veld like that. And how Hans was the master fiddler of the area. So he placed his wife's corpse across his knees and took out his fiddle and right through the night he played while the predators sat around him with gleaming eyes, listening. Then, with the youthful light of the new day, the young day, the fresh one, he carried her from the gorge, unscathed, and down the mountain, away from the place of death where the medicine smells so sweetly.

In turn, the Viljoen brothers tell a story about Dirk Ligter. Of how Dirk Ligter never let himself be booked by the cops, because he would run very fast and very far, dancing and prancing out of reach of the fastest horse, unless he felt like giving himself up for some reason. He was the best sheep thief of the area — and that takes some doing! He could conjure. He would change himself into something else to dodge the police. Once, when the police were looking for him in a clearing in the veld, he changed himself into an anthill, and one of the men even climbed on top of him to get a better view of the veld. Saw nothing, of course, and then just had a quick pee against the same anthill. Another time, when he was locked up in a cell, he escaped by simply blowing on the lock of the door, and the door swung open of its own accord.

Each of us acquired his own particular manner of talking. It was interesting to see how different people reacted to the "stranger" while we sat around the same fire. Bull and Barry and Fox didn't say very much, just listened. Nici was asleep already. Biltong was more or less sullenly in search of a former collective and lost primeval past. Swami tried to steer the conversation in the direction of the social, the political even, with much gentle love and comradeship. Daantjie automatically reverted to the fatherly and rough-hewn white-man-brown-man relationship.

The tongues weren't simply becoming freer. Other tongues, too, were employed in praise and warning. The Viljoen brothers, elders, put all their effort into converting Jan Biltong. Right there, that very night, around the fire. Before it is too late. Because the day of judgment, God help us, is at hand. As luck would have it, there was just the spot for a christening in the river nearby. The Lord was commanding them at that very moment to help this sinner. Biltong protested, and what they weren't aware of, of course, was that he has always been a good Christian anyway, even though he may be angry at times at what mankind gets up to.

Uncle Freek let rip with a hymn — as a child he used to sing second part with his late mother in church — taking the second part though there was no longer a first, harmonizing with the dark and holding his hat on his head with a long forearm while looking deeply into the smoke.

The stars unfurled their wings and started floating. We all lay on our backs with our eyes turned to the stars.

(And sometimes you wake up at night, the whole world sleeping darkly, sad about the terrifying desolation and loneliness of the moon. Then you're happy for the moon to rest lightly a while on the place where you sleep, on your breast and stomach and forehead and in your eyes. Before continuing its journey. You can only comfort, not redeem.)

Just because

a.
in Eselsbank a man was born
with countless fingers and ears full of corn —
why so fingers
and for what such ears
to stand on tiptoe
when the night is loud and high
and pick the leaking stars
before they cry

b.
in Eselsbank a shyster was born
with counting fingers and ears forlorn —
he hears from where the weeping comes
and bruises the stars to do his sums
and at Christmas it's the fate of his kin
to heed the frogs and angels who sing
and to see how the mountains rock and roll

c.
in Eselsbank our Savior was born
with telltale fingers and ears all torn,
when he hiccups the very mountains take fright,
he motions, he points, he fashions in light —
the familiar dog comes to tug at his coat,
the chickens with consternation are smote,
uncle Frik has deigned to tie his tie —

253

"Lord, Lord, give us
a sign!"

d.
in Eselsbank our Land was born
with handsful of fingers and ears unshorn —
"Lord God, why shall I not smite
then man who is white? he who devours
and steals what comes to his hand
to steal? he who all love
has renounced and now like
a chained dog with his fear
like a white thing in the mouth
crouches cursing?
he who has murdered, Lord God!
he who has played god, Lord God!
little white god, Lord God! pisspotgod, Lord God!
Lord God, Hottentot god, where is thy sign
and where my target?"

e.
I say unto you, from the heart of the country
he will come to you, one of your
own people, for black and brown and
yellow as comes forth from the earth
are also your own people when they
have walked under the same stars
and stumbled under the same shame
— it's same-size shame: the shame of
those who torture and soothe and the shame
of those unable to vomit in time —
of those who had to catch your shit in small buckets
and take it home
and in joy like the joy of prayer
rub it under the swollen spots below the heart
as a comfort against poverty

f.
I say unto you, from the heart of the country
he will come to you, one of you,
strung on blood
        he will be of your making
and where he goes a way will be paved
and women will drop their stitches
and fire will emerge barking from the barrels of guns
houses will grow black
fig trees will wither
he will command armies
he will avenge injustice
and settle old scores
for all those years of existing without a decent living wage
when you laborers had to sleep on cement,
content with porridge

g.
some of you will of course — it's in man's nature —
lie down on your stomachs like bloated worms
and polish your ancient worn-out dentures
offering them on saucers left over from the Sunday set
rimmed with small red roses, a gift of penance,
anything, "anything, master Kaffir, no
matter what, anything but death, oh, my own
mashter Kaffir"
        he will be wearing a gorgeous smile
and a halo and a Sten and he will
not harm the sparrows of the veld
neither will he rip the choppers
from the locusts

March 24

"and I must live on
propped up on my own death
like a cripple on his crutch," or something along those lines, said the
poet.

We are up quite early, all somewhat stiff as a result of yesterday's hardship, and the morning light was like fresh milk being
poured out over the earth. My task today is to get all these dear good
people down from the mountain in complete safety by means of the
word. It shouldn't prove too difficult; for the road is rocky but not
steep and, almost without exception, the members of the company
are firm-legged. Most people walk without any help.

We do not discover the real Eselsbank, consisting of more
houses than we had expected, until we reach the other side of the
river. The village is built hard up against the vertical face of the first
cliff, and the large scattered boulders occasionally serve as corner-
posts for pens or stables. With its low houses and its single broad
main-street the hamlet bears some resemblance to a cowboy town
from a Western.

From here our trail takes us to Wupperthal. Uncle Freek already
well ahead with the pack-donkeys which today are carrying a
considerably lighter load of wine. The Cedarberg Mountains are
ancient mountains, one gentle incline and slope after another, but
not very steep, really, except for the canyon walls. Only the valleys,
and presumably parts of the gorges too, have sufficient water and
greenery to start a farm.

By the time the sun eventually touches our necks and shoulders,
we have already begun our descent, keeping close to a brook which
forms small pools here and there. And we make full use of every
decent pool. We lose sight of Uncle Frederik and his donkeys, since
they are taking a different route higher up along a faint mountain
trail. But the long, distant notes of his conversation with his donkeys
travel down to us.

And then what was bound to happen sooner or later, finally
happens — the slippery soles of my shoes lose their grip on one of the
round rocks, washed to a smooth shape by the endless flow of the

256

water which probably cascades down the mountain during heavy storms, and I take a dive. When I pick myself up again, there is a deep gash across my right shin, so that the slashed red flesh exposes something whitish underneath. "How could he hope to find a firm footing on our tough African soil with those European shoes of his?" asks Jan Biltong sardonically.

The blood flows freely and the wound throbs, but the cool mountain water and the good sun build a first scab over the raw spot, and I struggle on rather bravely.

We decide to press on to Wupperthal. After noon, with the sun at its hottest, we reach the last rise above the Mission Station. Water, folks, water flows past the village in a gleaming course. And small, almost shy little monuments to man's presence in this vastness: cottages, a church, patches of cultivated earth. It had been agreed beforehand that my wife, Whiff (Maypicture is her name, her name Mayflower), and my brother-in-law, Clucky Spare Wheel, would meet me here, but I don't see their van yet.

We're in such a hurry to get to the village and the shade that we don't even bother to remove our shoes before wading through the shallow ford in the river. Today is Sunday and it's long past lunchtime, and the entire village seems to be dozing and waiting for the heat to pass; the people lie dozing in their rooms inside, entrenched behind verandahs and small flower gardens. There are trails of bougainvillea and we see peonies growing, silky, Chinese, and ranunculus . . . .

We stop beneath a few sparse trees in front of the local café-restaurant, hungry and thirsty and hot, and wait for the proprietor to open up. And when he finally shows up, we descend upon his cold drinks and his candy like locusts — I thought I would never get enough to drink again.

We're still eating and drinking (though it's more like guzzling and gulping) when Ostrich-donkey's van pulls up in front of the cafe, with my wife perched pertly beside him.

Swami and Bull want to drive back with us to civilization — they have to return to work tomorrow, Monday— and the others will spend the night near the village and climb and walk back to the spot where we left our vehicles, taking a different route. Now we're only waiting for Uncle Freek and the donkeys bearing all our knapsacks.

But there's no sign of him!

Meanwhile we take a look at the village. The whitewashed houses with their thatched roofs and verandahs and pergolas are all neatly lined up in three rows. In earlier times the name of the place was Rietmond. In 1830 it was bought by a Missionary Society for 3000 rixdollars and rechristened Wupperthal. The farmers of the village have their fields in the fertile alluvial soil along the Tra-Tra River beyond the settlement. Virtually all the farmhouses a little further on still have good threshing-floors. The trail we followed goes to Eselsbank via Kerskop, while the gravel road for cars runs back to Clanwilliam via Kouberg. Wupperthal is the provincial capital, so to speak, of this region and the names of the settlements (other than Eselsbank) are Heuningvlei, Heiveld, Witwater, Kleinvlei, Menskraal, Suurrug, Langkloof, Martinsrus, Nuweplaas . . . . "The highlight of life in Wupperthal," I read in the leaflet given to me by the vicar later that afternoon, "is the time of Advent and Christmas, when all the children come home. Then there is singing on Singkop and a spirit of gaiety prevails in the village." On New Year's Eve every house kills a goat so that the New Year may be celebrated with togetherness and plenty.

The village industry, however, is shoemaking, a craft the people were taught by Louis Leipoldt's grandfather, Gottlieb, who came from Germany to be a missionary here. And Wupperthal's rough hide shoes are rightly renowned far and wide across the country. The shopkeeper, an amiable German, opens up for us, and we buy ourselves some of these strong shoes with their thick soles made out of rubber tires.

We have tea with the vicar and his wife and then walk on to take a look at the simple and peaceful church with its cool walls and then on to the churchyard where Gottlieb Leipoldt and his wife, too, are buried in small white graves. The graves resemble petrified little mounds of bones.

Among the graves I pick up a sheet of paper, weathered and discolored by wind and rain. It contains FUNERAL HYMNS.

Moving testimonies.

"Abide with me; fast falls the eventide:
the darkness deepens; Lord, with me abide;

when other helpers fail, and comforts flee,
Help of the helpless. O abide with me.

Hold Thou thy cross before my closing eyes. . . ."

And in the next hymn:

"Angelic songs are swelling . . .

Rest comes at length;
though life be long and dreary,
the day must dawn
and the darksome night be past;
faith's journey ends
in welcomes to the weary,
and heaven, the heart's true
home, will come at last."

The cicadas are singing for the dead as they sing for the living. We walk up the gentle slope behind the graveyard to a marvelous, large, clear pool between rocky ledges in the river. We swim and try to drown each other.

Eventually, back in the village, we become increasingly concerned about Uncle Frikkie and his donkeys of whom there is still no sign.

And now Wifewoman tells me, she hasn't said anything about it all day because she didn't want the others to see how unhappy we were — she didn't want to embarrass them with our grief — that Oubaas had a heart attack yesterday afternoon at five and was rushed to the hospital in Paarl. She tells me this as we walk on a thick carpet of dry pine needles beneath old, tall, groaning trees, and with her back to the others and tears pouring down her cheeks. Luckily the worst is over, but the doctors aren't sure yet how badly the heart has been damaged. He will have to remain in hospital, very quietly.

I won't try to gloss over with words what I felt then. My father was and still is a giant to me, a proud man, a tree. He stands tall like a tree, and like a tree he knows how temporary and transient everything is, and he accepts it, and he remains strong. And at once I

259

think: "It is my fault." I knew, I saw how hard our visit was for him. Not the visit itself, of course, because he was so happy to see us, but the unpleasantness surrounding it. I recall how a short time ago, after some whorenalist or other had churned out the umpteenth bit of filth about us, he had suggested that we invite the fellow to Wellington for an "interview." And how we would be waiting for him in Pa's office and would lock the door behind him, and Pa would take his horse whip down from the wall and we would give the fellow the thrashing of his life. He feels all that happens to us, every tension, personally, but his gaze simply becomes quieter; not once did he complain about it. And I began to realize how trying it must be for him and for Ounooi, must *have been,* all those years, with what petty-mindedness some neighbors in the village and elsewhere act toward them, for the sole reason that he is my father.

Now we're in a hurry to get back. Toktokkie next to me here bravely tries to smile, but she is silent and tense. A new darkness opens up beneath me. Uncle Frederick appears at last. We meet him with the van. Uncle Freek is drenched in sweat. On a narrow ledge, you see, halfway up a cliff, the donkeys had refused to cart their load another inch, and he had been compelled to make a detour right around that-a-way. We pile the sacks into the van and say goodbye to Uncle Frederik and our friends. How many of them will I see again? We drop off the sacks beneath the pine trees and then drive up the mountain, back.

Around us night begins to fall. The golden light of dying, of mellowness, of peace, of eternity. The shadows blue. The whole mountain like solid fire, fixed for a moment. Elsewhere, already the murmuring darkness. Fantastic rock formations on both sides of the road. On a hill, in the twilight, we pass Louis Leipoldt's grave. "A handful of grit from the Hantam. . . ."*

Dear old Spare Tire, trying to talk, gesticulate, and drive, all at the same time as usual, nearly overturns the van. We fill up at a gas station and I take a turn at the wheel. Already the end is at hand. Everything we see now, and everything we don't see is branded by our departure. We dart off into the void, away from our loved ones, faster and faster.

*A translation of the first line of a poem by an early Afrikaans poet, C. Louis Leipoldt (1880-1947): "n Handvol gruis uit die Hantam . . ."

And all stored images, all that bears a name but cannot be said in words because it comprises smells, because it lies deeper than one's very body — everything now opens up and washes back. It's no blueprint of a dream, it's no longer a desire, it's nothing but a splintering, and a release maybe, of all that has been locked up in and behind the mirrors — and the years, the stars, the trees are mirrors. We drive over the narrow rattling old bridge across the Berg River between Wellington and Paarl. We flash past the dark wine presses and past the small building near the station — the Station School — where Basjan and I went to school, and to Sunday school also. We had no hair yet in those days, and the name of the teacher — one teacher only for all the classes — was Sarie. She was habitually blinking her eyes nervously. If you were lucky, you and a friend were ordered, even before lessons had ended, to get the heavy bucket of soup from the fat old lady, the kind old brown lady who prepared it for the children and who lived on the far side of the station bridge. It was this very bridge. The soup bucket was heavy, but oh, the heavenly smell of that soup! Did we attend this village school because we were too poor for the big school, or because it was closest to home? Frikkie and Freddie and Alwyn — "Pig" — Theart were also here with us. Fierce and quarrelsome. And Noël (we said "Noely" because we didn't know any better) who was destined to become a fly-half one day, and ungodly Deon Louw, and Reinier-with-the-breath, and Hettie and Hilda. Below us are the marshes near Nora Bok's father's distillery which had such a pungent smell, Nora with the cuddly bum which I never dared to touch because she was Hansie's girl, and Hansie was bigger and stronger than I. The marshes and the river where I was Tarzan. And Brother Whale who had been smoking from an early age and so had to be content with a policeman's job, as had Andries Kriel who spent years waiting in standard six for the time when he would be old enough to leave school, and poor clumsy old Jan Malan who couldn't even get beyond standard four — but that was later, in the big school, the boys' school. Yeagh! Those enormous spoons of cod liver oil we were forced to swallow each morning. And the wonderful maps and posters on the wall — remember that huge drawing of "the ox"? Oh, my clogged memory. Even then there was a longing for the farm. Wagter, wagging his tail at home, trailing after my sister — and then a snake almost bit her one day near the hens' nests. The snake rose in front of her, spreading its hood, arched, hissing. And at Christmas time we little ones were the angels at the manger, with stars and wings. Cloete was Joseph, a long cotton wool beard. Sun. The donkey we bought at the pound. . . .

The house is silent. In the back of the van Swami, tired to death, has fallen asleep.

The last few days pass. Barney Bull comes specially from the Cape to bring us a small bowl of marsh lilies.* We relish them. It's like old times. It's a taste belonging to a bygone era. Adam calls on us, inquires after Pa, eats with us. We discuss poetry. (Braga is the name of the god of poetry.) (Braggard.) I sit on my father's chair in the office and look at the armchair in which Grandpa used to sit. We drive to Paarl every day to visit Pa in the hospital. Pa is much grayer when he takes off his glasses. Ounooi, dear wonderful brave Ounooi, putters around, keeps herself busy, tries to laugh, struggles against the heat, tries to look after Oubaas' affairs, talks to the doctors, brings clean underwear to the hospital, sees to it that everything is within easy reach, packs and unpacks his clothes into and out of the wardrobe, smooths the blankets with her hand, and if we hadn't been there to stop her, she would have been taking him food as well. Basjan flies to the Cape from Durban. I pick him up at Cloete's in the city, and on the way back I crash Oubaas' lovely car. Jerry's — Jerry who played for Boland — garage tows the car in. I drive back in the hot and shaking truck with a friendly mechanic covered with oil stains. Now Uncle Okkie has to take us to the hospital. In his shorts. At nightfall the sprinklers spray the lawns. A smell of dust and then of fresh and damp earth. The newspapers phone and casually inquire whether they may take photographs of the sad parting in the hospital — although the time hasn't actually arrived yet, we could simply

---

*Afrikaans *waterblommetjies:* "little water flowers," loosely applied to several species preferring a damp habitat or growing in water, esp. to *Aponogeton distachyos,* now being commercially cultivated in some dams. The heads and flowers, freshly picked and boiled, make a traditional Cape dish which may, in taste and appearance, be compared to spinach, and which is known as *waterblommetjiebredie* (-ragout or -stew).

"pretend" to be saying goodbye, couldn't we? Imagine those lovely heartrending pictures. My people, the white people, the dead.

And suddenly departure is upon us. We are in the hospital with Oubaas. We don't know what we are saying. Yolie is crying in the corridor. Oubaas calls for her, and when she comes he takes her hand. Wonderful man, wonderful man — as long as I live, he will walk this earth. When we're outside I hear him weeping like a child. I want to kneel at his side. If only I could comfort him. His broad chest. His strong arms so much out of place in this white bed. His gray tears.

one nurse comes to take your pulse
you had no wish to be ill
but the other nurse has nice legs
through the windows the dregs of blue mountains
sediment in the bottom of the bottle of the sky
and nearer still the tops of trees covered in pale dust
when we climb into the earth
the blue mountains will endure
and the tree tops continue to lure the pale dust

when I say goodbye you weep
I have never seen you weep before
I lay my hands upon your gray head
but I cannot pronounce a blessing for I cannot pray
and gray tears trickle down your cheeks
your sleeves are damp
will we ever meet again?
the sea is filled with pearls the night with stars

The night is filled with stars. A last time we eat in Grevilleas, in the old kitchen. Somehow we managed to pack our stuff during the past days. Our room, with all the pretty things Ounooi had placed in it, the shells, the photographs and the flowers, to make our stay a happy one, that room is empty now. High through the night roars an airplane. And outside on the back verandah Mietjie gets a fright because she doesn't like airplanes, and suddenly, out of the blue, and for the very first time, she starts talking about politics. All the

263

pent-up emotions of so many years. About how terrible this government is.

Then the moment splinters. We are outside in the yard beside the van. A little light from the back door spills across the brown earth. One moment Ounooi is still laughing, still trying to keep to the gestures of looking after the loading of our luggage into the vehicle. But then she is my mother in my arms and her whole body trembles and I feel how her words scorch my breast, and her glasses are misty, and then she disappears into the house and the house is dark at once.

Through the gate, past Okkie's palm tree, past the church tower, past the graveyard, past Newtown and Huguenot and Paarl and Klapmuts and Kraaifontein.

Ah quanto a dir qual era è cosa dura
esta selva selvaggia e aspra e forte
Che nel pensier rinova la paura!
Tant' e amara che poco è pui morte;

To be in that night is to be swept along devoid of strength by a dark floodwater. There is wind outside and it starts raining. Cloete takes us to the airport, also Basjan who has to catch a plane back to Durban. Daantjie is at the airport too — freshly shaven and teeth chattering, and after a while Adam as well. An odious photographer and an even more odious reporter try like hyenas to capture the last emotional kick. Goodbye Baby, goodbye Quintin, goodbye brother Cloete . . . . And we're in the plane.

The earth falls away from under our feet, the land is large and tranquil, the clouds are made of silver.

a wind has come to blow the stars away
I have no heart, no, nothing but an ache
where the heart should be

I dreamt I was sleeping
I dreamt I was sleeping

and then the city was ablaze with light
and dead as a city ablaze with light would be
after the final destruction

the day grew yellow rose up
through palm fronds and eye

the light lay gleaming on the wings of the bird

then the clouds caught fire

"fasten seat-belts"

Friday, March 30th it was. We spent it in Johannesburg with John
and Elsa. I composed a brief note for the guardians of authority and
order and security and justice, the *potpourri,* a pyogenic pirouette of a
prattling pyromaniac. "Conclusion: my partita, my paramnesia (or
paragenesis?) (or parsing? or portion?) in Parnassian language: I want
to note down and offer everything as precisely as possible upon a
paten so that Colonel Huntingdon may perceive in clarity and may
look in post-penumbral light at this matter which smacks of
paranoia. Every apple has its maggot, every Paradise its parvenu
Special Branchers, every orgy its porgy, every party its paroxysm,
every program its pasquinade, every promenade its pass-control,
every parasite sees his piss-hole. The fact that we were able to embark
upon this journey may be attributed to your faithful servants — we
wrote it in unison! I presume they are impressed with my pee-warm
epistle — which, I give my parole as promissor, I swear it with my
paw upon this PARADISE, is the truth, the pulpy truth and
Nothing but the Truth. And devoid of any paradigm of pitiless
pungency
        Peccavi, but I have paid my debt. You think perhaps that I was
nothing but a petty paraphrast (or a palooka) in your Paradise, that I
— suffering from paramnesia, paragnosis, paresthesis, and pap-fix-
ation — (that I) with my potted Latin tried to create a parallel

265

between Purgatory and Saint Albinoka, that I wanted, for my own pleasure and devoid of piety, to create a parament (to be able to parade like a parried *Agapornis* or a plenipotentiary) (and then not with a pen but with a penis!) (and I practically a pedant with pediculosis)? That as a pundit I insisted per se upon making pariahs out of you? That I tried to particularize? That I am a pike or a partisan? That I, petite of posture (piffling picador in pajamas, a pauper to boot) wanted to pee on your Parliament with my pizzle? (While each and every one of you is a perfect Perseus, a paragon, a diamond passing a hundred carats?) Then please pardon me for my petty crimes and peccadilloes — for such an inference and conclusion would be a paralogy; far removed from my unique persiflage! I, puny paladine, now depart from your heavenly pastures pari passu with my Parisienne, Penthesileia Pandora, back to Paris (post other peregrinations). And you are left a priori with two possibilities: either the plane, my perilous palanquin, plunges—pardi!—to our pullulating planet, and I am stuck without a parachute, exploding in a puff, or I am punished with paragraphitis, like a penguin without his pants.) So I take up my staff of pilgrimage, my panga and my package and part from my pals and podestas. Apace I, pawnee Panus Perineum, take my pass along as precious pusaka, to avoid pickles with the police or other prancing poulterers — for where they're concerned I mind my P's and Q's: they pelt below the belt! My perks are post factum. (And already the pasometer is punctured, therefore: end of paragraph, page, pen, and pencil.) (Till the next passage in a parsec or two!)

It started raining again in the evening. Friends took us to the airport. There was a finality about everything now. The press had already installed itself in the departures lounge. What did they want? A final shout? A resumé? My nerves were shattered.

And then, at the very last minute, just as we were about to board the aircraft, having long since passed through customs and immigration control, in the very last embarkation hall where only passengers are permitted, a heavy hand seized my elbow and an icy voice wanted to know why I had never contacted them, then? It was the colonel, and the captain whose name sounds like Lamort, and another man called "Colleague." It would have given them such pleasure, you see, to have entertained me today in a suite in the

Holiday Inn or somewhere like that. For we have so much to talk about. And how about having a chat right now? They could quite easily delay the flight, if necessary . . . . Fortunately the communist's wife had already reached the exit near the aircraft. Would they make a scene right there? I honestly believe that they had no idea what decision to make just then. (Or had they really come to see me off in all sincerity — considering what close friends we are?) A bearded blond photographer dived from behind a pillar and took a picture of us together. "Oh!" said the colonel as though he were surprised. (But I was grateful to him for his amateurish attempt at concealment.) So why the photograph? Surely they had plenty of shots of my mug already? Or was it to have a record of all of us together? One knows how fastidious these hard-working state-paid officials are when it comes to their files. What would this photograph be called upon to prove one day? Who would be confronted and intimidated with it? Or was it to be hung on a wall along with the other trophies — in the way that hunters also collect the horns and skins? Colleague, the dog, grimaced and put his hands in the pockets of his fatigues.

Then we were through the door and out of the country.

for ninety days I lingered here
in my land,
I looked on darkness a great deal,
I saw little
but heard
        sometimes
among stains of shade and moon-trail and scrubby shrubs in the garden
the chattering clicks of a tongue in dry mouth
and footsteps beyond blurred hills
or shouts barely audible above the hissing of the waves

my ancestors speak to me,
in the water-furrow lies a dove with broken wings,
District Six has gone blind,
military vehicles gleam in garages,
in prison-cells it is neither night nor early day,
and all are servants holed up in a lasting dusk

my ancestors speak to me:
as far back as the breath can recount
the remains of my people lie in the lap of this earth:
dusty semen
I have an investment
                    here
a humble token of confidence in the world without end
of the dead

ninety nights from north to south and back again
to an eternity,
accompanied all the way by familiar voices of the dark,
jokes and complaints, curses and comfort,
                              now
I stand on the runway,
it has rained
and drops are squirming sparkling like worms on the tarmac,
the stars are suspended above oh wreaths of immortelles,
and behind the glass three grimacing
security police are waving
clods in hands
        goodbye

I shall take off in this blackened aircraft,
provisionally free
and deprived finally of all genealogy and memory and security,
in search of the frontiers of the night

APPENDIXES

NOTES ON PERSONS AND PLACES

A. PERSONS

I. Fully named or named by surname (other names in brackets):

Ben Barka, Mehdi: (1920-1965?) Prominent left-wing politician and Opposition leader until 1963 in Morocco. Exiled from Paris 1965.

Boonzaaier, Gregoire: (1908-) South African artist.

Bosman, (Herman Charles): (Herman Malan, *pseud.*) (1905-1951) Author of short stories, novels, verse in English; socio-humorist; journalist.

Brink, André: (1935-) *Avant-garde* Afrikaans novelist, playwright, critic, and lifelong friend of Breytenbach. (Also referred to in text as *Andreas, Andries.*)

Brown, Mr. Abe: Secretary of Buren Publishers.

Buthelezi, Gatsha: Chief Minister of KwaZulu, the homeland (*see* Glossary) of the Zulu in Zululand and Natal. One of the most respected and staunchest opponents of the present regime and its policies, and reviver of *Inkatha* (first founded in 1928 by Zulu King Dinizulu as a cultural and social organization) which is termed a Zulu National Liberation Movement, and is seen as a means for black South Africans, significantly not just Zulus, to aim for a single South African State with equality for all.

Cabral, Amilcar: (1926-1973) Founder M.P.L.A. (Angola), 1956, and P.A.I.G.C. [Guinea (Bissau) and Cape Verde], 1963. Assassinated Guinea (Bissau), 1973.

Haron, Imam Abdullah: Prominent Muslim preacher from Cape Town, one of the first political detainees to die under suspicious circumstances while being detained (1969).

Hiemstra, General (R.C.): Former head of the Defense Force.

Higgs, Cecil: (1906-) South African artist.

Joubert, Elsa: (1922-) Afrikaans novelist.

Koks: One of the Griqua (*see* Glossary) "dynasties" whose head, Adam

Kok II, settled his people in what became treaty states linked to the Cape Government and situated on the north bank of the Orange River in the 1830's.

Krige, Uys: (1910-) Afrikaans poet and playwright who also wrote in English and translated extensively from Spanish and French.

Krüger, Paul: President of the Zuid-Afrikaansche Republiek, (now the Transvaal Province), one of the two Boer Republics, from 1883-1902, i.e. at the time of the Anglo-Boer War (*see* Glossary).

Leipoldt, C. Louis: (1880-1947) Afrikaans poet and playwright. Also wrote in English. Physician and writer of books on traditional Cape cooking.

Leipoldt, Gottlieb: Grandfather of C. Louis Leipoldt (q.v.).

Leon, Sonny: Former leader of (Colored) Labour Party. Strongly opposed to Government policy.

Ligter, Dirk: Born ca. 1880 at Clanwilliam. Stock-thief of mixed descent and singularly engaging temperament. Became legendary villain-turned-hero figure, particularly because of the way he could outrun a horse — fully dressed — in the blistering Karoo sun.

Louw, Boy: Former outstanding Rugby Springbok (*see* Glossary Springbok).

Lumumba, (Patrice): (1925-1961) President National Congolese Movement and first prime minister of Congo (now Zaïre). Killed at Lubumbashi.

Luthuli, (Albert, Chief): Teacher, Tribal Head, President-General of the African National Congress, winner of the Nobel Peace Prize, 1961. Died 1967.

Malan, Doctor (D.F.): First Nationalist South African Prime Minister, 1948-1954.

Marais, Eugène: (1871-1936) Afrikaans poet and naturalist. Also wrote in English.

Mondhlane, (Dr. Eduardo): (1920-1969) Established FRELIMO in Moçambique. Assassinated at Dar es Salaam.

Nakasa, Nat: (1937-1965) Black writer. Committed suicide in New York. Work banned.

Nkosi, West: Black Soweto saxophone player.

Pama, C.: (1916-) Publisher, heraldist, editor.

Pienaar, Schalk: Prominent *"verligte"* (enlightened) Afrikaans newspaper editor and journalist. Died recently.

272

Pitman, A.S.K., Mr.: Prominent Senior Defense Council in many controversial political trials.

Pretorius, Paul: Former N.U.S.A.S. president, banned in 1973 after widespread student unrest.

Rabies, Jan Rabie: (1920-) Afrikaans writer, and his wife, frequently referred to as Biltong and Joors.

Saayman, Daantjie (Stoffel): Director of Buren Publishers, also referred to as Daniël Stoffelus Dingo Baas Daantjie, Baas, Daantjie Thunder, Dingo, Mr. Snaayman, Linus, Baas Linus, Baas Daan. His wife: Nici.

Shaka: Also *Chaka* (1787-1828) Powerful Zulu chief and warrior, revered by Zulus as a hero; regarded by most white South Africans as a tyrant: tales of his alleged cruelty abound.

Smuts, General (J.C.): Famous South African Prime Minister, 1919-1924 and 1939-1948.

Sobukwe, Robert: Founder of Pan-Africanist Congress in 1959. Campaign to defy pass laws (*see* Glossary) in 1960 led to riot at Sharpeville (*see* footnote, page 232); jailed for three years and detained for an additional six years on annual decision of Parliament.

Stander, Siegfried: (nicknamed Siegie) Writer in English.

Susan, Hendrik: Popular Afrikaans singer and accordion player and member of a *boereorkes* (*see* Glossary) in 'forties and 'fifties.

Themba Can: (1924-1969) Black writer. Drank himself to death in Swaziland. Work banned in South Africa.

Trichardt, Louis: (1783-1838) One of the leaders of the Great Trek, 1830's (*see* Glossary Trek).

Tutuola, Amos: (1920-) Nigerian novelist.

Van Heerden, Ernst: (1916-) Afrikaans poet and academic teacher at the University of the Witwatersrand.

Van Zyl, Kobus: Afrikaans writer.

Wepener, Louw: (1812-1865) Boer hero: died heroically in battle against Moshweshwe and (Southern) Sotho in 1865.

II. Named in part or disguised (other names supplied in brackets):

Adam (Small): (1936-) Brown Afrikaans poet and playwright.

Alta (Brink): Wife of André Brink (*see* I). *See also* Danie.

Ampie (Coetzee): Afrikaans academic and critic. *See also* Stella.

Biltong see I. *Rabies*

Danie (Brink): Son of André Brink (*see* I) and Alta (Brink) (q.v.).

Diffuse, Lord: Word-play. Sir de Villiers Graaff, former leader of the Opposition.

Djords, King see footnote, page 108

Elsa (Miles): Wife of John Miles (q.v.).

Fanie (Olivier): Afrikaans poet: (1949-).

Jack (Cope): (1913-) Writer and poet in English.

John (Miles): Avant-garde Afrikaans writer. *See also* Elsa.

Joors see I. *Rabies*

Lewis (Nkosi): (1935-) Black playwright, critic, editor. Exit permit. Resident in London.

Nici see I. *Saayman, Daantjie*

Pooh: Winnie Mandela, wife of Nelson Mandela (*see* Thingamebob). Detained for 17 months; acquitted, but placed under house arrest two weeks later in 1970. Author has obviously arrived at this name via the famous A.A. Milne character, *Winnie the Pooh.*

Richard (Rive): (1931-) Brown writer, poet and critic (English).

Roargrumble: Also Rumblegrumble. Abraham de Vries. Afrikaans writer.

Rumblegrumble see *Roargrumble*

Stella (Coetzee): Wife of Ampie (Coetzee) (q.v.).

Thingamebob: Nelson Mandela. Former leader of African National Congress; founder of *Umkonto we Sizwe* (Spear of the Nation); sentenced to life imprisonment in 1964 at Rivonia sabotage trial; detained since on Robben Island.

Zeke (Ezekiel Mphahlele): (1919-) Black novelist, essayist, critic, journalist. Now returned from exile and holding chair of African Studies at University of Witwatersrand.

III. Breyten Breytenbach's immediate family:

Father: called Oubaas throughout.

Mother: called Ounooi throughout. Maiden name: Cloete

Brothers:

Jan: Also Blikkies.

Cloete: Also Cloete Stinkie. *Children:* Anna and Koos (Sebastiaan):

274

Called Basjan throughout; also Bearman the Boxer, the Bear.

Sister:

Rachel: Also Baby, Puddles, Pinkydoll, Raggy.

Husband:

Quintin, also Cockadoodle, Cocky, Clucks, Ostrich-ass, Spare Wheel.

Wife:

(Ngo Thi Hoang Lien) Yolande: Also called Moes Sgaalp, Sgapal, Gapsel, Maspel Thi Mymsol, Mymlons, Tokkiemym, Jobba, Yb, Jolie, Yolie, J-Y, Captain Crow, Honeybox, Lambkin, Little Missie, Boesman, Chortle, Jopie, Jaaplamb, Gamso, Nosmas, Wife, Sweet-tongue, Honey-tongue, Heavenly Body, Flame Lily, Skippingmoon, Skippingmate, Yippie, Mouche, May, Mayflower, Wifewoman, Morning Glory, Moonchild, Toktokkie.

B. PLACES

Bloemfontein: Capital of the Orange Free State, and the seat of South Africa's Appeal Court.

Boland: Southern part of the Western Cape Province and principal wine and wheat-growing area of South Africa. Scenically, one of the most beautiful. First white colonists settled in this fertile region in the 17th and 18th centuries.

Border: Region of the Eastern Cape Province on border with Transkei, now no longer clearly distinguishable from Ciskei (*see* homelands).

Botswana see *Neighboring States*

Cape see *Provinces of South Africa*

Cape Peninsula: Peninsula extending into the Atlantic Ocean on the southwestern coast of South Africa. The mountains which form the backbone of the Peninsula slope steeply down to the sea, and the many sheltered bays and coves provide the holiday resorts for which the Cape is famous. At its northern point are Table Bay and Cape Town which is situated on the slopes of Table Mountain. The southern tip of the Peninsula is Cape Point, and just west of this is the Cape of Good Hope itself. On the eastern side of the Peninsula is False Bay with Muizenberg, St. James, Kalk Bay,

Fish Hoek, and Simonstown, which has been a naval headquarters since 1741. On the other side of the Peninsula are Kommetjie, Hout Bay, Llandudno, Camps Bay, Clifton and Sea Point, all regarded as part of "Greater Cape Town."

Cape Town: Capital of South Africa's largest province. Parliament sits here.

Drakensberg: The great African Escarpment sweeps from north to south through the Eastern Transvaal, from the Soutpansberg in Northern Transvaal to the massive buttresses of the Transvaal Drakensberg Mountain Range and then southeastward in a great semi-circle along the Lesotho border with Natal, where it becomes the Natal Drakensberg.

Durban: Largest city in Natal and South Africa's largest seaport.

Eastern Province: Eastern part of Cape Province. Fertile farming country and the area in which the British immigrants settled in 1820, having landed at Algoa Bay, now Port Elizabeth.

Garden Route: Spectacular stretch of country along the southern Cape coast between Cape Town (Western Cape) and Port 'Elizabeth (Eastern Cape). The country varies a great deal: at the western end are the downs and wheatlands around Swellemdam and Riversdale, merging near Mossel Bay with the "Garden" itself — a web of coastal lagoons, lakes and indigenous forests — which lies between the mountains and the sea and extends in the east almost to Humansdorp.

Gondwanaland: Name given to a super-continent of which South Africa was once a part. Existed for 300 million years from the Silurian to the Cretaceous period, then fractured into the widely separate parts of S. America, Africa, India, Australia, Antarctica, etc., during what is known as the "Continental Drift."

Hell: Properly *The Hell:* Also *Gamkaskloof.* A valley north of Oudtshoorn in the Swartberg Mountains. (*see also* footnote on page 123)

homelands: South Africa is divided into provinces (q.v.) and homelands (*see also* Glossary). Of the latter, three have become "independent," viz. Transkei, Bophuthatswana, and Venda. The others are: Gazankulu, Lebowa, KwaZulu, Qwaqua, Ciskei, Southern Ndebele, and Swazi.

Johannesburg: Also known colloq. as *Joey's, Joh'burg, the Golden City, iGoldie, Joni.* Center of the Witwatersrand goldfields, biggest city in Transvaal and South Africa, financial capital and hub of commerce and industry.

Kalahari: Desert stretching from Northern Cape well into Botswana.

Kango/Cango Caves: In the Great Swartberg Mountains north of Oudtshoorn. Contain some of the finest stalactite formations in the world.

Kar(r)oo: Also *Great Karoo:* lies between the mountains of the escarpment to the north and the parallel ranges of the Swartberg and Langeberg Mountains to the south. Dry, hot, and semi-desert, but has a charm and fascination of its own. Scenery is characteristic: scrub-covered veld broken abruptly by flat-topped koppies, whose kloofs are overgrown with thorn trees, aloes, and succulents. (See also *Little Karoo*)

Kimberley: Town in Northern Cape near border with Orange Free State, which became world-famous for its diamond mines.

Kinshasa: Capital of Zaïre in Central Africa.

Kruger National Park see footnote, page 193

Lesotho see *Neighboring States*

Little Kar(r)oo: lies inland between the Langeberg and the Swartberg Mountains — the first of many steps by which the interior rises from the sea to the plateaux beyond the great escarpment. Karoo scenery is in striking contrast to the verdure of the coastal belt and the lush, fertile Boland region: thorn-trees, karoo-bush and succulents are much in evidence, the kloofs are rocky and overgrown with euphorbia and aloes, and the rivers are for most of the year no more than chains of muddy water holes, transformed after heavy summer rains into rushing, destructive torrents. The Little Karoo gradually merges with the Great Karoo (q.v.) in the Eastern Province (q.v.) and Border (q.v.) regions of the Cape Province.

Louveld: Sub-tropical area of the Northern and Eastern Transvaal where malaria is endemic. Climate of intense heat and damp is generally considered unhealthy.

Namakwaland/Namaqualand: Barren, desolate country, ranging from thorn-bush and scrub inland, to windswept dunes fringing the Atlantic. Stretches from Boland (q.v.) in the south to southern

277

border of South West Africa Namibia. Rain falls mainly in June/ July, transforming country within a few weeks by covering desert hillsides and valleys with a carpet of wild flowers.

Nambia see *Neighboring States:* South West Africa Namibia.

Natal see *Provinces of South Africa*

Neighboring States: To the north: South West·Africa Namibia (South African Mandate), Botswana (formerly Bechuanaland) and Zimbabwe-Rhodesia. To the east: Moçambique. States entirely enclosed by South Africa: Lesotho (formerly Basutoland) and Swaziland. Botswana, Lesotho, and Swaziland are former High Commission Territories or Protectorates.

Orange Free State see *Provinces of South Africa*

Peninsula see *Cape Peninsula*

Pretoria: Large city in Transvaal near Johannesburg (q.v.) South Africa's administrative capital and headquarters of the public service, the defense force, and the diplomatic corps.

Provinces of South Africa: South Africa is divided up into a number of homelands (q.v.) and provinces: 1) Cape. Largest province. Stretches from Atlantic in the west to Botswana and Southwest Africa-Namibia in the north, the Indian Ocean in the south, and the borders of the Transvaal, the Orange Free State, Lesotho, and Natal in the east. Capital Cape Town. Divided into following regions: Western Cape, including Cape Peninsula (q.v.) Southwestern Cape (rugged mountain ranges; broad, fertile valleys watered by many rivers; coast characterized by rocky promontories and sheltered bays; Mediterranean-type climate with cold, wet winters and dry summers), Boland (q.v.) Swartland (wheat-growing area, north of Cape Town) and Little Namaqualand, stretching to border with Southwest Africa Namibia; Southern Cape, including Garden Route (q.v.), Eastern Province (q.v.), and the Wild Coast and its hinterland [now largely part of Transkei (q.v.) and Ciskei (*see* homelands)]; Cape Midlands, Great Karoo (q.v.), and Northern Cape. 2) Natal. Bordered by Indian Ocean in south and winter. Summer rainfall area. Capital Bloemfontein. 4) Transvaal, Swaziland, and Moçambique in north. Capital Pietermaritzburg. Smallest province. Climate sub-tropical on south and north coast, in KwaZulu and Natal Midlands; cold in Drakensberg (q.v.) to

278

north. 3) Orange Free State. Stretches from Cape in west and south, to Transvaal in north, Natal and Lesotho in east. Most of this province is high-veld with flat-topped koppies and grassy, scrub-covered plains. Eastern border mountainous. Climate temperate: warm and sunny in summer, cool and bracing in winter. Summer rainful area. Capital Bloemfontein. 4) Transvaal. Bordered by the Cape and Botswana to the west, Zimbabwe-Rhodesia to the north, Mocambique and Swaziland to the east, and Natal and the Orange Free State to the south. Divided into following regions: Southern Transvaal Highveld [mostly rolling grassland, broken by hilly ridges such as Witwatersrand (q.v.), and very cold in winter; gold mines are here and capital, Pretoria], Great Escarpment (from north to south through Eastern Transvaal, i.e. from Soutpansberg Mountains near Zimbabwe-Rhodesian border to Transvaal Drakensburg), Lowveld (q.v.), and Northern and Western Transvaal Bushveld. The Cape and Natal are predominantly English-speaking, Transvaal and the Orange Free State predominantly Afrikaans.

Robben Island see footnote on page 79

Swaziland see *Neighboring States*

Transkei: The territories between East London on the Border (q.v.) and the Natal Border are the Ciskei, Transkei (now "independent"), Tembuland, Pondoland, and Griqualand East. Transkei is the homeland of the Xhosa peoples who belong to the South Nguni group who are said to have left the Lake Victoria area centuries ago, moved south, reached the Kei River (Border) by 1700, and settled in Transkei to which Author refers as Xhosaland). The area stretches roughly from the Kei River on the eastern border of the Cape Province (east of East London) to Natal in the east and to Lesotho in the north. It is a country of vivid green downs, windswept hillsides studded with clusters of huts, encircled by flowering hedges or aloes, wild, rugged country toward the Drakensberg, cleft by many gorges, and thickly covered with indigenous bush, and some of the most beautiful coastal scenery in South Africa along the Wild Coast.

Transvaal see *Provinces of South Africa*

Umtata: Capital of Transkei (q.v.).

Witwatersrand: ("White water ridge") Hilly ridge in the Southern Transvaal Highveld, and location of South Africa's famous goldfields and its biggest city, Johannesburg (q.v.).

Zimbabwe see *Neighboring States:* Zimbabwe-Rhodesia.

GLOSSARY

aloe, *n. pl.* -s. Generic name both for a large number of species of African aloe and for certain other superficially similar genera e.g. *Agave,* the "American ~." Plants have erect spikes and flowers and bitter juice sometimes used for medicinal purposes.

Anglo-Boer War, *n.* The South African War of 1899-1902 between the British and the *Boers* (q.v.) also known as *Boer War, Second Transvaal War of Independence,* and *South African War.*

assegai, *n. pl.* -s. Spear, either short, for stabbing, as introduced by Shaka (see *Notes on Persons and Places*) for the *Zulu* (q.v.) armies, or long, for throwing, usually with an iron blade: used from earliest times by Africans both in hunting and war.

baas, *n.p.* -s. Master, Sir: mode of address usually by non-Whites (see *non-Europeans*) to the master or employer, often with definite article in the third person, occasionally *my* ~ for emphasis or when making a request. Also mode of reference to the master, usually with definite article. cf. Jamaican English *backra* when used as equivalent of boss, master, and Anglo-Indian *sahib.* (Afrikaans from Dutch *baas* master, captain)

Bantu, *pl. n.* usually capitalized, literally People: official designation of black South Africans by Government. The term is disliked by Afrikan people partly on political and partly on linguistic grounds; especially erroneous forms ~ *s* and a ~ . (from **Bantu** *pl. prefix aba+ntu stem* signifying person. *Singular form um(u)ntu* one person) Also *attrib.* and in combinations: ~ *stan* (see *homeland).*

biltong, *n.* Sun-dried strips of boneless meat cut usually from the haunch of buck or beef: *game* ~ . cf. U.S. *jerky/charqui,* (dried meat, usually beef.

bluegum, *n. pl.* -s. Also Australian. Used loosely of any of several species of *Eucalyptus.*

bobotie, *n.* A traditional Cape dish of curried minced meat, sometimes including dried apricots and/or almonds, covered

281

with a savory custard preparation. cf. U.S. *bobotee,* Canadian *rubaboo.*

boer *n. pl.* -s, -e. 1. An Afrikaner, often in a political sense. 2. *historical* often in combination *Dutch* -: an early Dutch inhabitant of the Cape. 3. A farmer. 4. A fighter on the Republican side in the *Anglo-* ~ *War* (q.v.) *Note:* as a prefix it occurs in numerous combinations, in the forms *Boer, boer-* or *boere-.* The first of these has a national or political significance, the two latter forms have numerous and not easily separable meanings such as "Afrikaaner style," "homemade," "folk," "country style," "of or pertaining to farming folk," "rustic," "indigenous," etc. (Afrikaans from Dutch *boer* agriculturist, farmer)

boeremusiek, *n.* Rhythmic country-style dance music played usually by a *boereorkes* (q.v.) cf. U.S. blue-grass. (Afrikaans *boere* country, folk + *musiek* music)

boereorkes, *n.* A band, consisting usually of a concertina or piano accordion, mouth organ, fiddle and/or guitar, sometimes a piano, playing boeremusiek (q.v.), usually for dancing. (Afrikaans *boere* country people('s) + *orkes* orchestra, band)

Boer War see *Anglo-Boer War*

borehole, *n. pl.* -s. In South Africa a well drilled to tap underground water source, usually operated by means of a windmill-type pump.

bowls, *n.* A popular South African game played with ~ , i.e. wooden balls made slightly out of spherical shape or weighted on one side to make it run a curved course, on grass. Players are dressed all in white.

Broederbond, *n. prop.* A largely secret Afrikaans organization with limited membership, also known as the *Bond.* It is a very influential organization, being composed of Afrikaners holding key positions in all walks of life. (Afrikaans from Dutch *broeder* brother + *bond* league, fellowship)

buchu, *n.* Any of several species of *Rutaceae,* the leaves of which have been used medicinally for stomach complaints since the seventeenth century, also used cosmetically mixed with sheep's fat by the *Hottentots* (q.v.) for anointing their bodies: the name being extended to a number of other species. (from Hottentot *buku,* plant name)

bundu, *n.* Wild, open country remote from civilization and cities. cf. U.S. *boondocks,* Canadian *the sticks.* (probably from Shona *bundo* grasslands)

Bushman, *n. pl.* -men. A primeval indigenous race of nomadic hunters of Southern Africa now largely living in the Kalahari desert (see *Notes on Persons and Places*) See also *Khoi-Khoin.* (Dutch *Boschjesman,* Afrikaans *Boesman*)

Cape Colored see *Colored*

chinkerinchee, *n. pl.* -s. Also *chincherinchee* and colloq. *"chink,"* various species of white flowered *Ornithogalum,* especially *O. thyrsoides,* poisonous to livestock, which instinctively avoid them. Picked in the bud, these are exported overseas in the Northern winter where they last several weeks in water.

clay-ox, *n. pl.* -en. Child's plaything: an ox modeled in clay, used by South African children from the early days. (from Afrikaans *klei* clay + *os* ox)

clay-stick, *n. pl.* -s. A "clay twig" used in a game of the same name played by children, the missile being a ball of mud or clay propelled by flicking it off a springy twig. (from Afrikaans *kleilat:* from Dutch *klei* clay + *lat* twig)

Colored, *n. pl.* -s. and adj./modifier. 1. A South African of mixed descent, speaking either Afrikaans or English as his mother tongue. Also combination *Cape* ~ those resident in the Cape Peninsula (see *Notes on Persons and Places*) or surrounding area. 2. A racial group in terms of the Population Registration Act, i.e. the official registration of an individual as a member of one or other race group defined by the Act. 3. *modifier.* Of or pertaining to those of mixed descent: see (1) *Colored.* 4. *modifier.* Of or pertaining to possessions, etc., of the ~ people, e.g. ~ *township* (q.v.) See also *Malay, Griqua.*

donga, *n. pl.* -s. A usually dry, eroded waterway running only in times of heavy rain. Usually a feature of soil erosion. (From Nguni *-donga* washed out ravine, gully)

dorp, *n. pl.* -s. Country town or village, sometimes colloq. in a derogatory sense signifying a backward or unprogressive place. Also found as *suffix in numerous place names, e.g. Bredasdorp.* cf. U.S. *place name suffixes -town, -ton, -ville.*

eland, *n. pl. unmarked.* Elk. (Afrikaans from Dutch *eland,* from

German *Elentier* elk, moose) *Taurotragus oryx,* the largest of the African antelopes believed to have been called by the Hottentots (q.v.) *kanna.*

Fanagalo, Fanakalo, *n. prop.* A pidgin language, a mixture of Zulu (q.v.), Afrikaans, and English, used and sometimes taught to facilitate communication between different ethnic and racial groups, especially in the mines: formerly called *mine kaffir.* cf. Canadian *Chinook Jargon,* simplified trade language used between Indians and Whites. (Nguni *fana* be like + *ka possessive* 'of' + *lo* this)

flyhalf, *n.pl.* -ves. (Rugby football) The player who plays the game in close association with the scrumhalf (q.v.), usually determining the line of attack adopted by the team and initiating it. See also *football.*

fontein, *n. pl.* -s. Spring, fountain, natural water source. Also as *suffix* found in numerous place names e.g. Bloemfontein. (Afrikaans from Dutch *fontein* spring, fountain)

football, *n.* Usually refers to *rugby* football, South Africa's "national game." Played by two opposing teams of fifteen players each, with a large elliptical inflated ball. See also *flyhalf, scrimmage, scrumhalf, touch-line.*

frangipani, frangipane, *n. pl.* -s. Red jasmine; any of several varieties of tropical American flowering shrubs, with white or red flowers.

gnu, *n. pl. unmarked.* Also *wildebeest:* any of several large ungainly South African antelopes of the Connochaetes with ox-like head and other characteristics, but with a mane and tail not unlike a horse. (From Bushman *nqu*)

gôrê, gora, gorra, *n. pl.* -s. Shallow hole, usually in a river bed, in which seepage water collects. (probably from Bushman)

Griqua, *n. pl.* -s. A member of a people of mixed descent, Hottentot (q.v.), White, and Bushmen (see *Bushman*) who settled in what was formerly Griqualand in the Cape Province near the Natal border (see *Notes on Persons and Places*). See also *Colored.*

Group Areas Act, *n. prop.* Act 41 of 1950 which provided for the establishment in each urban area of a separate *Group area* for each race group, and prohibited occupation or ownership by members of any other racial group. See also *separate development.*

guarri, guarriboom, guarribos, *n.* Any of several species of *Euclea* especially *E. undulata,* or of the allied genus *Royena,* a shrub of up to 2.5m in height much browsed upon by livestock, having succulent, slightly astringent fruit. Also makes excellent firewood.

homeland, *n. pl.* -s. One of those areas set aside under the policy of separate development (q.v.) for a particular African people or "nation," being developed with financial support from Government, each with its own Chief Minister (see *Notes on Persons and Places: Gatsha Buthelezi*). Also known as *Bantustans* (see *Bantu*).

hop-dance, *n. pl.* -s. Also *vastrap,* meaning "firm tread" (Afrikaans from Dutch *vasttrappen* to stamp, tread down): a fast dance danced to boeremusiek (q.v.) often by country people. Also a dance or "hop" in the country.

Hottentot, *n.pl.* -s. 1. An indigenous people of South Africa at the time of the original white settlement (1652). 2. no *pl.* The Khoisan (q.v.) language spoken by the -s. 3. *prefix n.* numerous plant and other names e.g. *Hottentot god* praying mantis, *hotnots fig Carpobrotus (mesembryanthemum) edulis.* Note: hotnot, *n. pl.* -s. An offensive mode of address or reference to a colored person (Afrikaans *hotnot* Hottentot). cf. U.S. *coon.* See also *Khoi Khoin, Colored.*

Hottentot bedding, Hottentotbedding, *n.* Also "hotnot-skooigoed" (Afrikaans equivalent): any one of several related herbaceous shrubs with soft gray and aromatic branches used as a mattress by people camping in the veld (q.v.); *Helichrysum spp.*

impala, *n. pl. either unmarked or* -s. One of the larger and most common of the South African antelopes *AEpyceros melampus,* bright russet-colored with a white belly, curved black stripe on the haunch, the male with slender ringed horns.

influx control, *n. phr.* Government control of entry by black Africans into urban areas without workseekers' or other permits.

karee, karree, *n.* Also *kiri:* honey beer, a type of mead made in South Africa from the earliest times; also a drink prepared from prickly pear syrup. In combination ~ *moer (kirimoer):* the powdered root of any of several plants especially *Trichodiadema stellatum* used as the ferment in making ~ (Afrikaans from Hottentot *karib*) kareemoer see *karee*

Khaki, khaki *n. pl.* -(e)s. Boer (q.v.) name for a British soldier during the Anglo-Boer War (q.v.) on account of the khaki-colored uniforms (Hindi *khaki* dust-colored from Persian *khak* dust).

Khoi-Khoin, *n. prop.* Also *Khoekoen:* the self-styled name of the Hottentots (q.v.). (Hottentot *khoii* a man + *khoin* the men); *deriv. Eng. adj.* form. *Khoisan* of or pertaining to the Hottentot and Bushman (q.v.) races or their languages.

Khoisan see *Khoi-Khoin*

kloof, *n. pl.* -s. A deep ravine or valley, usually wooded; gorge between mountains. cf. Canadian *draw, gulch* gully or ravine (Afrikaans from Dutch *kloof* ravine, gorge *cognate with* cleft). Also found in South African place names as *prefix* or as *suffix* e.g. Kloofnek, Langkloof.

knobkerrie, knobkierie, *n. pl.* -s. Also *knob/knopstick* (rare): a fighting club or stick with a knobbed head. cf. Canadian *casse-tête* war club. (Afrikaans *knop* knob + Afrikaans from Hottentot *kirri/keeri* stick)

kombi, *n. pl.* -s. (Originally *n. prop.*) Also *kombimotor* (rare): station wagon (from German make of car *Volkswagen Kombi*).

koppie, *n. pl.* -s. A hillock, flat topped or pointed, a common feature of the South African veld (q.v.). Also in descriptive combinations e.g. ironkoppie, fortresskoppie. (Afrikaans *kop* hill, peak + *dimin. suffix* -(p)ie; from Dutch *kopje* head)

kraal, *n. pl.* -s. 1. An enclosure, pen, or fold for farm animals. cf. U.S. *corral,* Jamaican English *crawl.* (Afrikaans from old Dutch *koraal* from Portuguese *curral/corral* fold, pen) 2. A village or settlement occupied by an indigenous tribe, formerly Hottentot or African, now usually African. cf. Canadian *rancherie,* an Indian village. 3. A cluster of huts occupied by one (African) family or "clan."

kukumakranka, *n. pl.* -s. Any of the species of *Gethyllis:* usually signifying their fragrant club-shaped fruit which are dried for scenting rooms or cupboards, eaten, or infused as ~ *brandy.* (Hottentot name. Afrikaans form *koekoemakranka*)

lapa, *adv./modifier colloq.* "Here," or *demon.* "this" as in Fanagalo (q.v.) *lapa side/lapaside* (Nguni *lapa* here, this side). Note·

Author uses *lapasait* in Afrikaans, which I have translated with *lapasite*.

lapasite see *lapa*

location, *n. pl.* -s. Also *township*. A segregated area on the outskirts of a town, city or village, set aside for non-European (q.v.), i.e. Colored (q.v.) or African, etc., occupation which whites require a permit to enter, e.g. Langa, Soweto (see *Notes on Persons and Places*). (From Latin *locatus,* from *locare* to place) See also *separate development*.

Malay, *n. pl.* -s. usually *Cape* $\sim$: Muslims (Mohammedans) of Asian descent, living largely in the Cape (see *Notes on Persons and Places*), now officially classified as Colored (q.v.) Descendants of slaves brought from Java and other formerly Dutch colonies.

morgen, *n. pl. unmarked.* A Dutch land measure used in South Africa until the adoption of the metric system. A $\sim$, roughly regarded as the amount of land which could be plowed in a morning (Dutch *morgen* morning), is just under a hectare, and just over two acres. 1 morgen = 0.856 ha.

non-European, *n. prop. pl.* -s. also *modifier.* A member of any racial group which is not *European* i.e. a white-skinned person descended from the Caucasian races, so called in South Africa without regard for any actual ties with Europe: now largely replaced by *non-White,* any person of color whether of African, Asian or mixed ancestry. See also *Colored.* Note: Both *non-European* and *non-White* are terms resented by many people of color.

oubaas, *n.* and *n. prop.* Old master (Afrikaans from Dutch *oud* old + *baas* boss, master). Mode of address or reference, often affectionate, to the master, if he is an elderly man, or occasionally to the father of the master or mistress of a household.

ounooi, *n.* and *n. prop.* Old mistress (Afrikaans from Dutch *oud* old + Afrikaans *nooi* probably from Malay *nyonyah/njonjah* related to Portuguese *dona* from Latin *domina* mistress): a mode of address or reference, often affectionate, to the mistress, if she is an elderly woman, or occasionally to the mother of the master or mistress of the household.

pass, *n. pl.* -es. Also *passbook* now known as *reference book* and in African English "book-pass," *domboek* (Afrikaans *dom* stupid +

boek book) and *dompas(s)*, an identity document carried by all black Africans with details of employment and other personal data. Frequently in combination ∼ *law*.

protea, *n. pl.* -s. Any of several of the genera and species of the Proteaceae especially of the showy flowered varieties including *P. cynaroides* the giant or king — ; *P. mellifera*, also called *sugarbush; P. arborea (grandiflora)*. The protea is the national flower (shrub) of South Africa. (from Greek god *Proteus*)

putu, *n.* Traditional African preparation of mealie meal i.e. finely ground, granular corn meal, white or yellow, the staple food of much of the South African population (cf. U.S. *hominy grits*), cooked until it forms dry crumbs and eaten by African with meat and gravy etc. It is also a popular breakfast food among white people, served instead of cereal, or it may be served with barbecued meat. (Nguni *uphutu* crumb porridge, anything crumbly e.g. earth)

rand 1. ridge, reef (Afrikaans from Dutch *rand* ridge). Also *-rand- n. prefix and suffix* found in place names e.g. Randfontein, Witwatersrand (see *Notes on Persons and Places*). 2. *n. pl. unmarked* or -s. The unit of South African currency consisting of 100 cents. [from *Rand, the, n. prop.:* the gold mining area of the Transvaal, also known as the *Reef,* of which Johannesburg is the chief city (see *Notes on Persons and Places*). (*abbr.* Witwatersrand)]

rhebuck, rhebok, *n. pl. unmarked.* Either of two species of small South African antelope, also *ribbok,* with curved horns *Redunca fulvorufula,* or the *vaal*/grey ∼ *Pelea capreolus* with straight horns.

rixdollar, *n. pl.* -s *historical.* The monetary unit at the Cape (see *Notes on Persons and Places*), first issued by the Dutch East India Company.

rondavel, *n. pl.* -s. Also *rondawel* (Afrikaans form): a circular house, usually of one room with a conical thatched roof, resembling an African hut in shape, the latter therefore usually being referred to by this term.

San man see *Bushman*

scrimmage, scrummage, *n. & v.t. & t.* 1. (Rugby football; usually *scru- ;* also *abbr. scrum*) tight mass of all the forwards with ball on ground in middle. See also *football.*

scrum see *scrimmage*

scrumhalf, scrum half, *n. pl.* -ves. Rugby football. The halfback who puts the ball into the scrum (see *scrimmage*). See also *football*.

sea-ear, *n. pl.* -s. Also *Venus-ear shell, ormer,* (U.S.) *abalone:* one of largest South African shellfish, used of several edible species of *Haliotis* especially *H. midae.*

Second Transvaal War of Independence see *Anglo-Boer War*

separate development, *n.* The policy of "grand" *apartheid* particularly in the development of the African *homelands* (q.v.) or *Bantustans* (see *homelands*) in which social, geographical, and political separation is envisaged as well as a measure of self-rule. This policy has been pursued since 1948 when the National Party came to power. Its goal is the eventual creation of national states for South Africa's tribes through a staged process bringing more autonomy at each step. See also *Group Areas Act, homeland, location.*

South African War see *Anglo-Boer War*

springbok, springbuck, *n. pl. unmarked,* -s. 1. *Antidorcas marsupialis,* an antelope peculiar to South Africa; a swift gazelle well known for its habit of jumping considerable distances, whether escaping from pursuers or engaging in display: also formerly known as *pronkbok* (Afrikaans *pronk* prance). As a national emblem it is seen on aircraft, airlines uniforms, sports blazers (see 2.) etc. (Afrikaans from Dutch *springen* to jump + *bok* buck). 2. *n. pl.* -s, and *n. modifier.* A South African sportsman or woman representing the country in international matches or contests, freq. in *abbr. Bok(s);* as modifier: ~ blazer, ~ captain, etc. (from — as national emblem) 3. *n. prop.* The commercial channel of Radio South Africa (as above).

stock, *n.* and *n. modifier.* Livestock, farm animals occasionally extended to game. (*abbr.* livestock or *translation* of Afrikaans *vee* cattle). Note: *stock-feeding* is a colloq. term referring to the supplementary feeding of stock in times of drought when natural grazing and pasturage is insufficient.

stock-feeding see *stock*

strandloper, *n.pl.* -s. 1. A member of a prehistoric (middle to later Stone Age) coastal race of South Africa who inhabited the Cape coast up to the time of the arrival of the white man, possibly forerunners of both the Bushman (q.v.) and Hottentot (q.v.). (Afrikaans from Dutch *strand* beach + *loop* go + *agent. suffix* -er)

289

2. A bushman race living on the coast near South West Africa (Namibia); also *sandlopers*. (prob. from [1]) See also *Khoi-Khoin*.

threshing-floor, thrashing-floor, *n. pl.* -s. Area on which grain was threshed or thrashed i.e. beaten out or separated (from corn etc.).

touch-line, *n.* (Rugby football) One of the side limits or goal-lines of the field. See also *football*.

township see *location*

transport rider, *n. pl.* -s. Formerly a carrier of goods by oxwagon, also known as *transport driver* (translit. Afrikaans *transportryer* transport rider; *ry* convey, cart).

trek 1. *vb. usually intrns. occasionally trns.* To make a difficult and arduous overland journey, to travel, to migrate (Afrikaans *trek* to journey, travel, migrate from Dutch *trekken* to migrate) 2. *n.pl.* -s. a) *historical.* A journey by ox wagon especially an organized migration of people overland as in the *Great Trek* (see *Voortrekker*) b) Any journey or migration.

veld 1. *n.* The South African countryside, landscape etc. cf. U.S. & Canadian *prairie* (Afrikaans from Dutch *veld,* cognate with field, used as general equivalent of "country") 2. *n.* and *n. modifier.* Grazing land, or the grazing, indigenous or planted, supported by it 3. *n.* Region, country: found in South African place names usually of districts e.g. Lowveld.

Voortrekker, *n. pl.* -s. A Boer pioneer usually a member of the *Great Trek* (see *trek*) from the Cape Colony to the Transvaal (see *Notes on Persons and Places*) in 1834 and 1837, of those dissatisfied with British rule and with the abolition of slavery (Afrikaans from Dutch *voor* advance, cognate with fore + *trekken* to travel, migrate, march + *agent. suffix -er*).

water bailiff, *n. pl.* -s. Also *water fiscal.* The official in control of the water furrows, i.e. the man-made water courses usually for irrigation purposes, urban or agricultural.

Xhosa, *n. pl.* ama-, -s, also *modifier.* 1. The African people of Transkei (see *Notes on Persons and Places*) and the Ciskei (*do*) formerly, now obsolete, known as *Kaffirs:* consisting of the AmaXhosa, AmaPondo and AmaTembu 2. no *pl.* The language of the Xhosa people, related to Zulu (q.v.) and to Swazi with

which it combines to form the Nguni group of languages.
3. A member of the ~ people.

Zulu, *n. pl.* -s, ama-. 1. The African people or nation concentrated in Zululand and Natal (see *Notes on Persons and Places*) 2. The language of the ~ people which with Xhosa (q.v.) and Swazi makes up the Nguni group of Bantu (q.v.) languages.